Walking Wild Shores
Portraits of the Natural World

WALKING WILD SHORES

Portraits of the Natural World

Kevin Winker

Two Harbors Press
212 3rd Avenue North, Suite 290
Minneapolis, MN 55401
612.455.2293
www.TwoHarborsPress.com

ISBN-13: 978-1-62652-062-2
LCCN: 2013904227

Distributed by Itasca Books

Cover Design by Alan Pranke
Typeset by Steve Porter

Printed in the United States of America

Contents

Preface

ON A HOT, SUNNY DAY at the edge of remnant forest near Huimanguillo, Tabasco, in southern Mexico, a printed email message arrived and was slapped down on the rough-sawn timber table beside me. The well-traveled email had taken quite a journey, from Fairbanks, Alaska, to Front Royal, Virginia, and from there it had been forwarded to Mexico City, and then to Villahermosa, Tabasco, where it had been printed out and then hand-carried to this remote location where I was leading a group to survey birds near the border with Chiapas. I had a Yellow-bellied Flycatcher in my hand, which was fitting. We'd timed our survey to include the migratory bird species that overwintered here before they began migrating to their northern breeding grounds. This small bird would soon be returning to the boreal forests of the far north, and it carried none of the fat it would need for this long journey; so our timing was good. The email was a message inviting me to migrate north to the boreal forest, too, for a job interview at the University of Alaska Fairbanks.

My mind leapt to memories of a summer several years past, spent in western Alaska surveying bird and mammal populations on tundra and seacoast. We'd counted cliff-nesting seabirds, walrus, and harbor seals in the company of a wide variety of landbirds and other wildlife. On many of our coastal trips in the small skiff we were checked out by seemingly fearless Steller's sea lions. On these occasions, large, adult sea lions reared up out of the water a good two to three feet and gave us a careful look over. At distances of only ten or fifteen feet, this could cause heart stoppage, and we made sure all our limbs were inside the boat. One day from the cliff top overlooking the tip of the cape, I counted fifty-two gray whales in a ten-minute period, blowing and breathing close in to shore as they migrated farther north into the Bering and Chukchi seas. And I remembered flushing a fledgling Savannah Sparrow in dune grass and watching as it flew weakly downwind when suddenly a Parasitic Jaeger swooped in from behind me to snatch the little songbird up in midair with its bill. It would be good to go north again.

The interview itself was like visiting friends I hadn't met before. I came away from that first visit to Fairbanks eager for the opportunity to return and to delve into Alaska biology, especially its birds. Most Alaska birds are migratory, coming to the state from six continents to breed each summer: Antarctica, Australia, Africa, Asia, South America, and from elsewhere in North America. The opportunity to get to know these birds better did come, and a little over a year later I was out on the Seward Peninsula in western Alaska with Dr. Robert W. Dickerman, surveying the bird community there. One morning as we drove up a decent gravel road called the Nome-Taylor Highway in a light rain and fog, with the wipers flapping back and forth, I saw a large pair of antlers in the road ahead—finally, a look at a reindeer, which had thus far been an elusive animal. I slowed down and then stopped as a magnificent bull walked across the road in front of us.

As we watched it go slowly across, Bob said, "What on earth is that animal doing out here all alone?"

As he said this, my eyes were slowly moving to the right, and by the time he'd completed his rhetorical question I had finally noticed the forest of antlers encompassing our entire right flank. A herd of more than a thousand animals was bedded down not fifty yards from us, and over two thousand eyes were calmly watching our intrusion into their country. If these animals could have laughed at our keen powers of observation, we would have been deafened. When we had finished laughing at ourselves and had admired the herd a little longer, we continued on with our observations and adventures.

As a field biologist and trained observer working at the confluence of two of the world's largest avian migration systems, I am fortunate to have opportunities that are uncommon, even among my colleagues. My wife Rose Meier and I came to Alaska in 1997 from the Smithsonian Institution, and the events in this book begin in that year.

Long ago I made myself get better at taking notes, especially at the end of field days. When I found myself often having to repeat field experiences to interested people, I began to write out summaries that could be sent to family and friends. Unusual things are interesting to many, and being a field biologist can often put you in some unusual situations. This is a collection of some of those stories from an Alaska base. The chapters were written contemporaneously, so some of the details are now part of history. The dates of each chapter's events are given in the Afterword. All of the species in the text that have been determined have their scientific names provided in the Appendix.

An important driving force behind much of the book is the study of nature from the perspective of a museum biologist. It is a wonderful time to be a biologist. We are privileged to be able to continue in the best traditions of natural history research and biological exploration, observing and making records of the natural world, and then being able to apply new technologies in areas such as genomics, computation, and molecular analyses to explore new scientific frontiers. This book concentrates on the natural world and our human interactions with it, rather than on the scientific pursuits. For those interested, more details on the science can be found in the Afterword. What follows are some of the experiences that can happen along the way.

Kevin Winker

Fairbanks, Alaska

January 2013

1
Deadhorse, Ho!

I HAD BEEN INTO THE OFFICE every single day since 12 January, and Rose had been pretty tolerant about it. But the semester and associated business, like committee meetings, were over, and now that it was June it was time to escape. The contrast between now and mid-January could hardly be greater: then, short days and -20° F with great skiing; now, very long days, temperatures in the seventies, and forest green, with Hammond's Flycatchers and Townsend's Warblers singing in the backyard. It was a good time to get away from the office.

Rose and I set off on Saturday morning with some supplies, hoping for the best and knowing it would be an interesting trip. We were headed all the way to Deadhorse, where the haul road (Dalton Highway) ends to the public just shy of the Arctic Ocean (Beaufort Sea). The road was built in 1974 to support pipeline construction and the Prudhoe Bay oilfields, and it was closed to the public north of Coldfoot (halfway to Deadhorse) until 1994. The haul road, or Dalton Highway, is a little over 400 miles of rough gravel road beginning in the White Mountains, passing through the Brooks Range, and extending out onto the North Slope tundra to Prudhoe Bay. It transects what is probably the most remote road-accessible wilderness in North America. Gas can be obtained (for a relatively high price) at three points on the road: the Yukon River[1] (about sixty miles south of the Arctic Circle), Coldfoot (sixty miles north of the Arctic Circle), and

---

1. Unfortunately, this station has since closed, leaving just two places to refuel on this long road.

Deadhorse (about 300 miles north of the Arctic Circle). The last station (credit card operated, with some interesting weather-required features) is the northernmost gas station in the US.

Figure 1.1. Rose Meier in camp on the Koyukuk River, Brooks Range, Alaska.

We moseyed up past the Arctic Circle and Coldfoot (halfway to Deadhorse from Fairbanks) on Saturday and pitched camp on a tributary to the Koyukuk River. The tent was soon up, and we were cooking dinner. That's when Rose noticed several Dall sheep feeding on the precipice across the river from us. We were impressed. As we had bratwursts cooked over an open flame on sourdough buns with horseradish mustard and an Oregon stout, we considered ourselves to be in a sort of epicurean wilderness. As we hit the sleeping bags, the sun was still high in the sky; the sheep were still nibbling on lichens, and I noticed that we had a flat tire. It was the first one in 102,000 miles on this vehicle! And what a place for it.

On Sunday morning we put on the fake spare and limped back in to Coldfoot, hoping for what we found: not one but two very cheerful tire repairmen just waiting for us to appear. Very lucky, we headed north again just half an hour later, overjoyed that the haul road doesn't recognize days of the week.

Figure 1.2. Atigun Pass, Brooks Range, Alaska.

Atigun Pass in the Brooks Range was just a name until we went there. It's the highest road-transected pass in the state, at 4,739 feet (1,444 meters). It was a major challenge in the construction of the pipeline. In its snow-clad ruggedness, it was really awe-inspiring to behold. And it was closed due to an avalanche. But, again, the road is the supply line to the oil camps on the North Slope, so road crews don't pay attention to what day of the week it is. The state folks were out clearing the mass of fallen snow. We were through as soon as the last scoops gave enough room. So were several eighteen-wheelers, the supply link to Big Oil and Deadhorse. Just on the other side, a female Dall sheep and last year's lamb hopped down to the roadside to eat the mineral-laden dirt, and I was able to get frame-filling shots with a 200 mm lens backed off to about 150 mm.

Figure 1.3. Dall sheep (Ovus dalli) *eating mineral-laden earth in Atigun Pass, Brooks Range, Alaska.*

The sheer distance opening out north of the Brooks Range is visually staggering. If not for the occasional caribou and infrequent muskox, the only occupants would be the arctic ground squirrels and seasonally breeding birds. Long-tailed Jaegers, Lapland Longspurs, and Savannah Sparrows seemed the most ubiquitous. We kept zooming north, bent on reaching Deadhorse by evening. Near the pipeline Pump Station No. 3, we ran across a grizzly bear poking along, feeding on roots and searching for other hapless prey along the Sagavanirktok River. After a few more pictures, we were off into the coastal fog, which extended at least sixty miles inland.

It was cold now, and windy, but with most of the smaller tundra potholes free of ice and little snow remaining. And the densities of waterfowl went way up: Greater White-fronted Geese, Snow Geese, Northern Pintails, Mallards, and a few Tundra Swans watched us zipping by. There were also occasional Short-eared Owls and Rough-legged Hawks. And we saw a Snowy Owl carrying a drake Mallard it had apparently just killed. But Deadhorse was the halfway point of a long drive. It was about 7:00 p.m. We needed gas and a serious driving boost to get somewhere back south again—hopefully back out of the fog and into the sun to camp for the night and have some of the long road knocked off for the return trip on Monday.

Deadhorse was remarkable for its otherworldliness: oversized steel boxes and equipment, mud, and concrete in a cold, windy, foggy setting. Different business clusters of big, ugly, large steel boxes loomed up out of the fog and were passed quickly by as we searched for the no-attendant gas station. Aside from a small group of Stilt Sandpipers and a whirling Red-necked Phalarope on a small pond among the looming structures, the "town" seemed deserted. We stopped at the steel box General Store and stepped from a deserted winter fogland into a surreal, surprisingly normal-looking

Figure 1.4. Musk ox (Ovibos moschatus), *North Slope, Alaska.*

store — complete with people and rock music. But no bathroom. With a five-dollar six-pack of Coke, we headed south again, agreed upon a goal of getting out of the cold, windy 20° F and back into the midnight sun.

The fog had moved inland, so we had quite a haul before finding a decent camp in the sun at about 10:30 p.m. on the bank of the Sagavanirktok River. The ice was still going out, and we drifted off as midnight approached (in full sunlight) to a somewhat crunchy-sounding current.

We had only gone about a mile the next morning when we spied three muskox about 100 yards off the road. We changed into boots that would allow us to walk across the wet tundra, and slowly walked out to the calmly grazing animals while taking pictures. To our surprise, they let us come to within twenty feet. As we approached, I learned what the strange new bird songs were as a male Smith's Longspur sang and scampered within a few feet of me while it foraged. This hour was one of those lifetime High Moments.

There were a lot more stops as we continued south. The bear was still along the road. Caribou were migrating through Atigun Pass. And sheep still sprinkled the steep mountain slopes of the Brooks Range. They're amazingly sure-footed creatures. And all of the snowshoe hares made the correct calculations in their dashing about and missed our tires.

Back at Coldfoot, we got needed gas, had a late lunch, and launched again for Fairbanks. But just forty miles south of there, we had another flat while going 55 mph on the rough gravel road. This one ate the tire before we caught it, but with the previous tire's practice, we had the bad one off and the fake one on very quickly. With such a poor backup we limped along much more carefully, poking along at 30 mph or less headed for the Yukon, and hoping against hope that the fake spare would last and that the small Yukon station might have a replacement tire.

Seventy miles later we were greatly relieved when both hopes were borne out, and at about 6:30 p.m. we headed out, going fast again on an expensive new tire. Things went well until we stopped at about 7:30 to help out what turned out to be the only woman trucker on the haul road route. She was on her way back from hauling a load of explosives up to Deadhorse.

We'd been passing each other all day. She was having fuel delivery problems to the engine, and we shuttled fuel from tanks, blew on lines, etc., for about three whole hours with the added help of another trucker who stopped and lent a hand. We left him towing her at 10:30; but half an hour later, she whistled by us like a bat out of hell, headed for Fairbanks. Apparently, pull-starting it had finally paid off. Although I wanted to, I never asked her if a pierced tragus was painful[2].

We pulled in at home at about 1:00 a.m., pretty tired from a very memorable trip. It was still light out—it's too close to the solstice to get dark anymore. You have to drive a long way to have the chance of seeing the North Slope wilderness. It was a 1,070 mile round trip for us, and it is no longer surprising to me to learn that people who have lived up here for many years have never made the journey. The moral of our trip is to go, because the vast open spaces alone will make for a memorable trip, but take four days and two spare tires. You don't want to be tire shopping from the meager rack on the Yukon River.

---

2. The tragus is the small, pointed projection in the front of the ear canal. This part of the ear made its lasting impression on me when I learned to measure them when preparing bat specimens.

2

Oh, Sweet Canada,
Canada, Canada.

WENT TO CANADA, EH? But we know what that's aboot. Nice people who sound almost like those of us from the United States until they finish a sentence or hit an "ou." These are almost the only clues that you're in a foreign country, except for money that has birds and the queen of England on it. The Canadian economy wasn't racing along like that in the US at the time, so the exchange rate was favorable; but gasoline was more expensive.

It is surprising how many avian subspecies limits occur at the US–Canada border. In the case of southeast Alaska, many of them are probably true, because there is a complex biogeographical history in this region, especially among the islands. But in the case of the Yukon-Alaska border, there are no real environmental or geographic boundaries, and the supposed population limits are probably in almost all cases false. These sorts of problems often crop up at international boundaries, because these political limits affect the movements of the scientists who study these things. It was the complexities among the *Catharus* thrushes that first brought my attention to the region of southeast Alaska and western British Columbia. Since coming to Alaska, however, more of the species involved in the problem became interesting—surely in part because the biological puzzle is now part of my own state of residence.

The islands of western Canada and southeast Alaska are producing large quantities of old-growth timber as their forests are harvested by many different companies. In both countries, the logging of the island old-growth forests is causing a fair amount of social turmoil. In the US, we saw a major political battle fought over the possible listing under the Endangered Species Act of two endemic populations in the region: the subspecies of timber wolf (*Canis lupus ligoni*) and Northern Goshawk (*Accipiter gentilis laingi*) found in southeast Alaska. Neither population was listed. And the battle between logging interests and environmentalists continues. Among all of the forest birds are many other species besides the goshawk that are endemic to the region. The US Forest Service is concerned about how its management of these old-growth forests is going to affect the many populations in the region. And it does have management plans, island by island, that are supposed to protect each population. The problem is that, among many of these populations, we don't know which are unique and which are the same old "vanilla flavor" found everywhere else. It seemed like a good idea to begin looking across a number of species in the region to see which are really unique.

So I began typing my way onto the scene, writing requests for permits to collect birds in British Columbia.[3] This process began over a year ago; but, perhaps because of the strife between Alaska and Canada over salmon (a major battle that had long been going), we never received a permit until too late in the season to do anything about it. But that was last year's tale. This year, despite more problems, I did get a permit from the Canadian federal system. It was a sorry permit compared with what I'd requested, and it had been changed substantially from last year's (without any justification). But it was good enough to start the comparative work necessary. At least this year I didn't have three of us twiddling our thumbs waiting to go—it

---

3. Collecting some bird specimens for museum research collections remains an important way to develop biological knowledge. More on this can be found in the Afterword.

was just me; and my schedule was very flexible.

The main goal of the trip was to get samples from the Queen Charlotte Islands (or Haida Gwaii), an isolated group of islands off the western coast of British Columbia and southeast of the islands of southeast Alaska. There are many endemic forms of birds there, and it will be very interesting to see which are shared between Alaska and the Charlottes. This entire offshore region is viewed as probably having been a glacial refugium during the last ice age: an area free of ice with real wooded habitats where isolated plant and animal populations held out until the glaciers retreated again. It is thought that many of these populations became unique during the long period of glaciation and isolation.

It's a long drive to Prince Rupert, BC, from Fairbanks—nearly thirty hours. At least that's what it took us last year in total driving time when we made a short trip there while hanging out in Hyder, Alaska, waiting for a permit. It's this kind of drive that makes it clear just how massive Alaska really is. In the old days, back in Minnesota, driving this long took me well down into Tamaulipas, Mexico. Here it just takes me outside of the southeast corner of the state. I was alone on this trip, because it seemed useful for last year's companions to take advantage of other opportunities. Bob Dickerman had the chance to go to the island of Sulawesi in Indonesia. Dan Gibson had gone out to represent the University of Alaska Museum when a coveted space opened up on the USFWS research vessel *Tiglax* on a cruise in the western Aleutians. As Dan and I looked at our big wall map before we went our separate ways, I remarked that at the apexes of our simultaneous journeys, the distance separating us would be equivalent to my being on the peninsula of Florida and his being somewhere in southern California. Alaska is damned big. Between Dan and me, our collections overlapped in only two species. We don't know what Bob found.

OH, SWEET CANADA, CANADA, CANADA.

The route from Fairbanks to Prince Rupert goes through some wild and lonely places in Alaska, Yukon, and British Columbia. The Alcan and Cassiar highways (two-lane, sometimes unpaved roads) go through some spectacular scenery. They're also the kind of roads that keep you alert, so you aren't likely to fall asleep. On this run, the scenery alone kept me awake. Fortunately, there were few of what Dan calls "spaceships"—a cynical nickname for the massive mobile homes that seem to multiply in the lower latitudes and migrate north in herds during spring and summer. They are so incongruous and impersonal that, as Dan says, on the very rare occasions when you see one stopped and the door opens and a living being actually steps down to earth, you just want to say, "Welcome to our planet." On two-lane roads, these craft make driving anything else a real trial.

I spent two days in Hyder, increasing our sample sizes of some mainland birds before matching up with the ferry schedule out of Prince Rupert and getting a ride out to the Charlottes. The sea was smooth, and the seven-hour trip was idyllic. As my first views of the Queen Charlotte Islands sunk in, an impression formed that was not to leave: Beautiful islands with a bad haircut.

The clearcut logging of old-growth forest that is conducted here is what we call butt ugly. One source of the social turmoil associated with the logging must be the blasted, moonscape-quality landscape left behind. Nothing is left standing, and a lot of wood remains. It seems to me that it would be a major public relations gain to selectively log the commercially useful timber and leave behind something resembling woodlands. As it is, these clearcuts are the last places you'd want to spend any time, and they're everywhere. And the quantity and quality of wood left behind is mind boggling—not just all the high-quality firewood you could ever hope to use, but enough to support small-scale commercial operations making roofing shakes, for example, with abandoned old-growth cedar. Each night it was little effort to have a fragrant campfire of this delightfully scented wood.

Figure 2.1. Hermit Thrush (Catharus guttatus), *Haida Gwaii, British Columbia, Canada.*

I hit Graham Island on a Sunday evening and headed straight for the network of logging roads north of Queen Charlotte City. I found a good camping spot on one of the older logging roads in the heart of young second-growth spruce-hemlock-cedar-alder forest that was growing back in a clearcut. Surrounded by *Catharus* thrush song (two species), I collected a few birds before setting up camp and calling it a night—still quite light out at 11:00 p.m.

Before leaving Fairbanks, I'd sent my specially built cooler down to Anchorage for 100 pounds of dry ice for this trip. Fairbanks was the largest town on my route, and you can't even buy quality dry ice there. For backup, I had ten liters of liquid nitrogen. By the time I reached the ferry in Prince Rupert on the way over, it was clear that the ice wasn't going to last as long as I thought it would. My guess (later verified) was that the cooler had been roughly handled on its return from Anchorage, and that the bottom seal had been broken. There was nothing I could do about it now but go fast.

And so I did, collecting more birds in four full field days (and a couple of hours of two others) than I'd ever done before. Working most of the daylight hours, searching out individuals of target species, was both exhausting and successful. I found that clearcutting was doing wonders for the populations of some of the birds I was after. *Catharus* thrushes, for example, have probably never been more common there. But, because they're crepuscular (active at low light), I had to hunt them in the twilight hours, meaning very long days and short nights. During the middle of the day, I could pursue other target species.

On Tuesday morning, I didn't expect to be shooting Dusky Grouse at 5:00 a.m. in my underwear, but in this business, I've come to be prepared for the unexpected. The deep booming of a displaying male had awakened me from much-needed sleep, and he was clearly very close. This was one species I really wanted to get, but I didn't hold out much hope for obtaining any. In southeast Alaska, they boom from high, inaccessible places. This one was plainly visible with my tent door zipped down just six inches. I watched the beautiful display as he filled his yellow throat air sacs and boomed again a few times before I loaded one of my gamebird shells and gave off a single boom myself. (I sleep with my shotgun in bear country.) It was a sad moment; like other human hunters, I feel a great respect for and affinity with my prey, and taking the life of such an impressive creature is a negative experience only rendered positive, on the balance, by the gains one can achieve with the specimen.[4] But it was quick, and he didn't feel a thing.

---

4. Elliott Coues, one of the founders of ornithology in North America, put it well when he wrote that collecting birds should ". . . be tempered with mercy; your humanity will be continually shocked with the havoc you work, and should never permit you to take life wantonly. Never shoot a bird you do not fully intend to preserve, or to utilize in some proper way." (Field Ornithology, 1874, 30).

This was good, because I would not have enjoyed running barefoot through the very spiny Sitka spruce, in my underwear, chasing a wounded grouse.

There is a very large endemic black bear (*Ursus americanus carlottae*) on the Charlottes, and a small introduced deer—the Sitka deer (a subspecies of mule deer). The deer were abundant and a serious problem for regenerating forest undergrowth. To me they looked smaller than the tiny Florida key deer (a subspecies of white-tailed deer). In driving from site to site, I frequently found spotted fawns less than a foot tall out on the logging roads. As I drove slowly along, they ran with tiny little bounds in front of me until finding a convenient spot to get off of the road. On dry days their hooves kicked up little spurts of dust with every bound. It occurred to me that an excellent means of deer control might be developed if someone could find a way to sell these miniature fawns for Easter.

My dry ice ran out on Thursday night, and on Friday morning I began using my liquid nitrogen backup to keep the birds frozen. It wound up taking almost all day Friday to get an export permit, but a couple of friendly conservation officers did the job for me at 8:30 p.m. This gave me just enough time to go over to see the fun at Skidegate Days (pronounced "skid-eh-gat"), an important seasonal gathering and celebration for people on the island. I was just in time to see the Haida canoe races. Earlier in the day, while waiting for a permit, I'd had the chance to visit the museum of the Haida Indians in Skidegate. Their art is superb (and expensive also, when it is for sale). Their huge single-log canoes were housed in a log house next to the museum, and that evening I was able to watch them race these beautiful craft on the sea before I had to get on the ferry. The Haida remain a major cultural force on the Queen Charlotte Islands, and it is in their tongue that the islands bear the name Haida Gwaii. On a future visit with a better bird freezing plan, I hope to learn more about them.

Figure 2.2. Haida canoe at sea, Skidegate, Graham Island, British Columbia, Canada.

The overnight ferry trip provided a little sleep (damned dogs were barking in the hold all night) before I had to drive like a maniac back from Prince Rupert. I stopped for six hours of sleep along the way and was able to condense about thirty hours of driving into just over twenty-five hours. Although I poured liquid nitrogen on the birds every eight to ten hours after Thursday night, there was a little thawing on top by the time I made it back on Sunday afternoon. But upon preparation, I found them all to be in excellent condition.

It took a total of seven permits to pull off this trip. Far, far more time was spent on them than in the field. I needed a federal permit from Canada to collect most of the birds, a provincial permit from British Columbia to collect samples of the species that they controlled, a federal salvage permit to pick up any roadkills found, an export permit from British Columbia to take the birds out of the province and country, a permit to carry and use a firearm in Canada, a US Fish and Wildlife Service import/export permit, and a US Department of Agriculture animal health permit to allow me to bring specimens back into the US. Collectively, getting all of these permits took years. Once I had them all, everything went smoothly. But I can see now why one would rather just draw subspecies and population limits at the international boundary.

3

Mountains, Ghost Towns, Rivers, and Fish

THE UNIVERSITY OF ALASKA gives two days off for the Fourth of July, which provided us with a four-day weekend this year.[5] We had in mind a trip down to the Copper River to try our hands at dip netting, but we wanted to avoid the bulk of the weekenders with similar ideas, so we worked on Friday and took off Tuesday instead. To further offset our netting from the bulk of the weekend crowd, we also planned a trip to McCarthy and Kennicott, two small towns in the middle of Wrangell–St. Elias National Park and just sixty miles from the town of Chitina (pronounced "chit'na"), the heart of the Copper River dip-net fishery.

On Saturday we drove the six hours from Fairbanks to Chitina, and then continued on along the sixty-mile gravel road to McCarthy. "Poor" is the word to describe this road. *The Milepost* (the road guide to Alaska and western Canada) said that one could average 20 mph along it, but that was an exaggeration for our vehicle. After two hours we'd gone just halfway, and there we camped for the night. We hadn't been down to Wrangell–St. Elias before. The scenery as one approaches is spectacular: commanding, snowcapped peaks are spread majestically across the landscape. Once on the dirt road to McCarthy, however, the scenery is largely gone—unless one appreciates enough washboard (road) for everyone on the planet to do laundry, with space left over for any latecomers. But the weather was perfect: that dry, mid-seventies, just-enough-clouds-to-look-interesting

---

5. While I am on a nine-month faculty contract with summers "off," Rose has a grant-funded staff position with less time off.

weather that makes summer in the interior very enjoyable. There weren't enough insects to be bothersome as we set up camp in the woods by a clear, fast mountain stream.

On Sunday morning we hit the road again—it was another beautiful day—and after two hours of washboard road, I was hoping that what lay at the far end was worth a visit. It was. The road ends where the bridge over the Kennicott River is washed out. This is about half a mile from the town of McCarthy. The old hand-pulled cable tram was replaced last year with a foot bridge, making the crossing over the rushing glacial river simple, if less entertaining. We rented bicycles on the near side and rode across, because the abandoned mining town of Kennicott is four-and-a-half miles beyond McCarthy.

We pedaled leisurely along an uphill trail through the woods to the ghost town of Kennicott, popping out just below it on the valley wall, with a broad view of the great masses of gravel till representing the base of the Kennicott Glacier. Gravel is not a particularly attractive material, but in this quantity and in these massive piles that make you feel very small, it is pretty spectacular. In case anyone had any doubts, this view represents a close-up look of a valley full of silent testimony to the massive power of a glacier. We didn't take the trail up the additional mile or more to overlook pure glacial ice, but that ice formed an important part of the mountain scenery up the valley.

Kennicott was established in the very early 1900s as a copper-mining town. It was shut down when the ore played out and the mine was closed in 1938, and its red buildings with white trim stand there slowly fading and falling apart for visiting tourists with cameras. Enough tourists come each season that there is a lodge and restaurant there. When the weather is as perfect as it was the day we were there, it's a great spot from which to appreciate the park. After inspecting the town and looking around on our bikes for a while, we had a Coke in the lodge and read some of the old Kennicott Mining Co. bills tacked to the walls. I remember one from the 1920s billing the company for, among other things, 600-plus pounds of beef at fourteen cents a pound.

Figure 3.1. The ghost town of Kennicott, Wrangell Mountains, Alaska.

As afternoon wore on, we rode the easy downhill ride back to McCarthy and went through the small museum there. They have a lot of good photographs of Kennicott in its living years and some good short written history of the area. McCarthy was a mining town, too, but it looks like the tourist industry has prevented its demise. It was interesting to learn that the founder of McCarthy had died in 1961; someone had described it for interested readers as his having pasted away. I'd never seen that given as a cause of death before, and as we walked away, Rose remarked that it must have taken a lot of glue.

Clouds were rolling in from the south as we took our bikes back and began the slow return drive to Chitina. Our driving on this trip was mostly in a radio-free region, so just before we left I'd grabbed a few books on tape left over from the DC-area commuting days. On the way down we listened to excerpts from the *Iliad* and had had a refresher in Greek gods, egos, and the childish tantrums of grown men as we followed the adventures of Achilles, Agamemnon, and the Achaean princes in the siege against Troy to recover Helen. Helen's fate wasn't resolved by the end, but Achilles did triumph over Hector, son of Priam, in a legendary battle. As we beat our way back down the long road to Chitina, we listened to the *Voyage of the Argo*. Jason and his Argonauts were doing their best to get the Golden Fleece, and the lovely young witch, Medea, had just been smitten by one of those love arrows (for Jason) from Eros (at Hera's request to Aphrodite, mother of Eros) when we pulled into a cold, windy, rainy campground on the shores of the Copper River. As we put up the tent and tried to cook on the camp stove, discussions revolved around campers and other paraphernalia that we didn't have that would make this kind of weather a lot more tolerable. But we turned in, hoping for a change in the weather and thinking about fish.

Dip netting is a type of fishing that we'd never heard of before coming to Alaska. It's what they call a "personal use" fishery that allows state residents to fish for salmon in quantity. The limit per household is thirty fish per year. The fishery is conducted in this case in a river too turbid to enable any typical sportfishing. The water is so silt laden that you can't see into it at all. It's like watching dirty, gray-brown skim milk roar by. The current is ferocious, and trees and chunks of former trees were constantly whipping by at rapid speeds. This is the kind of river that kills people, although in this case it's probably because they're crazy enough to cling to the cliffs of the Chitina area, hanging over the rushing water with a big net in their hands, hoping for a fish to swim in. We were sure looking forward to trying it.

It's hard to sleep when it doesn't really get dark out, and it's raining, and the tent wall is slapping you in the head all night in a strong wind. But I'd had some practice in this during field work in the Bering Sea, and so I didn't feel too tired when we finally quit trying to sleep at about 4:00 a.m. the next morning and got up to face a dismal-looking day. Rose, on the other hand, was unaccustomed to such sleep deprivation and arose a little more reluctantly. Wearing all of our clothes and heavy rain gear, and remarking that this was pretty cold weather for the sixth of July, we sized up what looked like a pretty miserable day for fishing. It had rained too much to try to go down the old railbed trail along the riverbank cliffs in our two-wheel drive vehicle—but that was the preferred way to go to get salmon, because it gets you (for free) down into areas where the river is channeled tightly through a canyon.

The only alternative is to pay a charter vessel to take you out to some rock somewhere and drop you off for the day, or part of a day. This was our only choice. They were a good group of guys who were brutally honest about what to expect: the salmon had been running great last week but were really down this week; we'd be very lucky to get our limit in a day. Well, we were there, and we had to try it, so we elected to try part of the day at least. We plunked down our hundred bucks, waited until the boat was ready, and zoomed up the raging, murky river to a windy little spot at the base of a set of cliffs and bluffs. The guide (Mike) called it the "Honey Hole," and he pointed out the currents and the rock wall and told us exactly where to place our net. We disembarked, wedged in, tied off, and got that net in the water. And we waited.

The spot where we had been dropped was a place where the roaring river seemed to graze some underwater rock formation that caused an upward boiling and fast *upstream* current just at the river's edge. This upstream current was too strong to allow one to just hold the net there, but by wedging the handle against a projecting rock on the cliff, one could, if one was sufficiently motivated to be a contortionist, hold the net steady there for long periods of time. Neither of us is a regularly practicing contortionist, so we were glad to be able to trade off at the net and have a chance to relax and stretch the many muscles involved in staying on the rock and keeping the net in place. The spot was seriously uncomfortable and more than a little dangerous. The net handler wore the life jacket and was tied off to the only tree in the neighborhood (a wizened spruce). There were two things to concentrate on: the net, and activity there; and keeping yourself on the rock in the most stable and comfortable position possible. Almost all muscles were occupied, although it wasn't until twenty-four hours later and all the stiffness set in that we learned the complete extent of the effort involved.

Before coming on this trip, we'd had to buy a few things to make it possible. A dip net ($40) is essential. We had one between the two of us, because we weren't sure whether this strange type of fishing warranted an investment in each of us having a net.[6] And of course licenses and permits are necessary ($40). A life jacket, miscellaneous ropes, and a 120-quart cooler are also required ($100), as is a big freezer ($500, our first major appliance). You can bet we were hoping to get our limit! But after the first half hour, it was clear that the fish were running slowly. When I finally felt one hit and pulled it in, I calculated that if we considered this one to be a $780 fish, an expenditure of a little over $100 per pound, then any more that we caught would be free. When we'd left Fairbanks, red salmon filets were selling for $7 a pound. That didn't seem to be such a bad deal as we continued to wait on a cold and windy cliff for more fish to swim into the

---

6. We were naive and made a rookie mistake in having just one net. Others customize their nets and even bring spares. We had some real beginners' luck and were apparently the only ones to limit out that afternoon.

invisible net.

But pretty soon the sun came out, and Rose took over at the net and caught a couple more fish. Things were looking up. The weather was improving, and the scenery was great. The wind continued, but the guide had told us that the natives in the area had a saying: If the wind stops, it means God is mad. And the moving air turned out to be welcome when the day continued to heat up.

We were switching off again, and I was putting on the life jacket with the rope hanging there loose when Rose said she felt a bump. I said, "Pull it in," but noticed that the net wasn't moving.

So I said it again; and Rose said, "I can't!"

I reached over and tried myself. Wow—it was almost immobile. We jerked it off of the bracing rock and let the current help us bring it up. It was a good thing we were both there and well braced, for when it finally did come up there was a beautiful 20–25 pound king salmon and a 7-pound red salmon in there at the same time. Quite a heavy, vigorously flopping load! We dragged it up onto a flat spot, and I was finally able to use an oosik[7] for its second intended purpose in clubbing the king into submission. I let Rose with the magic hands stay on that net for a while after that.

The fish picked up to become regular after our first two hours there. When the guide came to check on us, we had seventeen and wanted to stay out longer. He added another guy to our rock to fish just upstream a few feet. This young Coast Guard guy from Valdez had caught only one fish all day in another spot, and he was happy to have this change of luck. His longer-handled net was able to fish another good spot, and he picked up fish that we didn't have a chance of catching, including another king salmon. By 5:30 a.m. Rose and I had limited out and had been throwing

---

7. An oosik is the baculum of a bull walrus; it is about two feet long, thick and strong, and it makes a great fish club. A baculum is a penis bone, a bone that male humans lack.

Figure 3.2. Rose Meier shows off her salmon at O'Brien Creek, Chitina, Copper River, Alaska.

small ones back to fill out our remaining few. We'd both had a great deal of fun catching fish, wrestling them into submission, and getting them onto stringers. Before the guide came back to pick us up, we were able to gut half of the catch and enjoy watching the Coast Guard guy rapidly pick up his catch to nearly twenty fish.

Back at the campground and charter headquarters we gutted the rest of the fish and rinsed them all in the fast, clear water of O'Brien Creek, which runs through the place. Flocks of Herring and Mew gulls made short work of the guts. As I gutted, Rose stacked the fish into our big cooler layered with the six bags of ice that we'd brought along. There was just enough space. We were exhausted from such an incredible day, but the wind was up again and rain was threatening. So at 8:00 p.m. we hit the road, finishing up Jason's adventures with the fleece somewhere in the middle of the night with rain falling, the sun shining, and a double rainbow off to the east. We pulled into home at about 2:00 a.m., slept the sleep of the dead, then got up and cleaned fish for the rest of the day. That night we had a side-by-side, taste-test comparison of broiled red and king salmon. The only difference we could pick up was one of consistency (king has coarser muscle fibers). The next day we tried something I hadn't been willing to risk before at the price of salmon: we grilled one of the small ones whole. It was indescribably delicious. Now we're salmon addicts and can't wait until next year.

4

To Nome for Feathered Royalty

OUT IN WESTERN ALASKA, one finds the world's most
extensive overlap of New World and Old World birds. Individuals of both
avifaunas migrate great distances to spend the summers reproducing in
the same habitats as their distant relatives from across the Pacific. When
autumn migration comes around, they part ways, each heading to wintering
grounds that are very far apart. During the winter months, these same birds
can be found everywhere from South America and Middle America to
Southeast Asia, Antarctica, the South Pacific, and even Africa. These are
breeding bird communities composed of real travelers.

This unique assemblage of birds draws a fair number of people each
year who come to western Alaska to see North American birds that don't
get much farther onto our continent. Species with exotic names like the
Northern Wheatear (whose scientific name *Oenanthe oenanthe* is one of
poetic allure), Bluethroat, Bristle-thighed Curlew, Bar-tailed Godwit, Arctic
Warbler, and Eastern Yellow Wagtail draw birdwatchers and researchers
hoping to see them and perhaps learn a little about them, too. And the
Seward Peninsula is in the thick of it all. Thinking of seeing and sampling
these mixed avian communities had been on my mind since before coming
to Alaska. In late July I finally had the chance to go. Accompanying me was
Dr. Robert W. Dickerman. Bob is a professional ornithologist who, since
retiring some years ago, has been better able to pursue his lifelong career.
He ranks as one of the world's greatest volunteers in ornithology, and brings

Figure 4.1. Robert W. Dickerman with a Rock Ptarmigan (Lagopus muta), *near Nome, Seward Peninsula, Alaska.*

to projects of this type incomparable experience. I suspect that Bob has collected and prepared more bird specimens than anyone else alive.

And this is what our trip is about. We have two goals, both of which are simultaneously met when we have a dead bird in our hands. This is the stuff that can give us a bad name with many bird enthusiasts, who often don't understand scientific ornithology—especially when one of the tools of that science is a shotgun. The goals of birdwatchers are often satisfied when they see a bird and can make a mark next to it on their list. Ours are more complex. We're preserving "all but the squeak" for science. Our primary goals on this trip are to make the first extensive tissue collections for genetic studies from this region and to sample the lower intestines of a broad array of birds to see what diseases these travelers are carrying back and forth on their journeys. These communities are widely accepted as strong mixtures of Old World and New World birds, but how extensive the mixing of avian disease might be among them remains completely unknown. These never-before-obtained collections of DNA and diseases were the focus of our trip, but we were also eager to get skin and skeleton specimens for comparative purposes. In fact, when we're finished preparing a specimen, there is very little left over that gets thrown away.

The easiest place from which to launch any expedition on the Seward Peninsula is the town of Nome, which serves as a regional hub for all traffic. It is the isolated road system that extends outward in three directions from Nome that makes it an ideal starting place for our trip. Together, these gravel roads transect nearly all of the habitat types on the southern half of the peninsula. To people unfamiliar with tundra, the landscape may seem to be a comparatively barren, rollingly montane, homogeneous environment. But sun, slope, elevation, and underlying substrate work some profound differences on the tundra, providing a broad variety of tundra habitat types. The birds know the differences well, and species' distributions follow the distributions of tundra types rather tightly.

Going to Nome from Fairbanks can be done by major airline (Alaska Airlines) on a plane with a toilet that goes first to Anchorage. This option, round trip, was $616 and takes something like five or six hours. Or it can be done on a small, local airline (Frontier Flying Service) on a small craft without a toilet that goes straight across. This option was $536 round trip and took a little over two hours. Flying in Alaska is usually expensive. Going to Nome is no exception. Being toilet-trained, impatient, and frugal, we flew Frontier. It was great. The flight was in an eighteen-passenger Beechcraft. We had bigger seats, a better view, and a rest stop in Galena. Wear earplugs if you sit near the propellers. The negative for a field trip with a lot of equipment is that you are charged $1.08 per pound of baggage in excess of your allowance of forty pounds per passenger. This was unexpected and added $133 to our flight cost. My eighty-six pound Action Packer (rigid plastic box for those who don't use them) suddenly got real heavy. But we needed everything we'd packed.

Being scientists from the University of Alaska and reasonably socially acceptable people gives us a real leg up with many of the agencies that operate in the state. I've never seen stronger relationships among major players in a geographic region, and everyone benefits. The agencies can look to the University for expertise and information when they need it, and we can "hitchhike" on their infrastructure when it is not a burden. The infrastructural support we've received from various agencies has been stellar. It tends to cost them little or nothing, but to us it makes a huge difference simply because it makes the impossible routine. Need a ride? Well, we're going that way. Need a place to stay? Well, the bunkhouse there has some space. Our kind of research doesn't tend to generate the grant funds required to pay $300 an hour helicopter costs or $4,000 per day research vessel costs. But if they're going that way anyway and have room for one more, welcome aboard. Similarly, accommodations in remote places can be very expensive, particularly over the course of weeks of field work. But if there's space in a place already set up and running, come on in. Often there are a bunch of "cover your ass" papers to sign so that the government (state or federal) can't be sued if you walk into a propeller or have some other accident, but this is a trivial consideration when it opens up such great opportunities to scientific church mice.

This is a long way of saying that we had a vehicle and a place to stay when we arrived in Nome. The people and the agencies involved were fabulous. The vehicle wasn't scheduled for use during our ten-day visit, and there were empty bunks. Interest in what we were doing was strong and genuine. We just kept our manners on their usual high level (!) and maintained our customary wit and charm (!!) to avoid inadvertently tipping ourselves into the "asshole" bin and thereby preventing similar future ventures. Good guests are welcome back.

When we landed at the small airport terminal of Smythe Air (used by Frontier in Nome), we piled our bags outside. I walked the ten to fifteen minutes to where the truck had been left. In a short time we had our junk dropped off at the bunkhouse and were exploring along the Nome-Council Road, carefully inspecting the property distribution map from the Bureau of Land Management (BLM). This is really big country. But land along these road systems changes by township in a complex pattern that shifts through time as federal lands are selected and then turned over to native corporations and the state in response to settlements associated with the Alaska National Interest Lands Conservation Act (ANILCA, 1980). But, with thousands of square miles accessible from the roads, there remains a lot of public land available for us to do our work. Working freely on native corporation lands would require permission from nine separate organizations—something we preferred not to get into for this short trip. So we just kept track of our position on the map and avoided the native lands, working exclusively on state and federal lands. The maps were absolutely necessary, because on the ground we found only one boundary actually marked with a sign.

One of the most striking features of the Nome region is the awesome size of the country. With no trees and large, rolling hills and mountains, vistas and horizons are vast and magnificent. The roads are used so infrequently on weekdays that you can spend all day near a road thirty to eighty miles from Nome and see just a few vehicles. Walk a couple of miles off of the road, and you are completely alone in hundreds of square miles. We spent a lot of our time in high tundra, which was being abandoned as the birds that bred there earlier in the season moved down to lower, moister elevations. At times it was so quiet that just the breeze over the surface, a quiet sound, became comparatively loud. We were in good time for a multitude of midsummer blossoms, though, so even when there were no birds to be seen, there was a lot to keep one entertained.

Each day we were out on the road by dawn, which was around 6:00 a.m. Nome is almost straight west of Fairbanks, so the day began a little later than what we were used to. When you have to get up at dawn in the subarctic, being farther west in the same time zone and on dates a month later than the summer solstice is very welcome. Being farther south can also help. Each day we drove out to where public lands began and chose habitat types to sample, marching over broad expanses of open tundra. High tundra brought us to Surfbirds, Northern Wheatears, Rock Sandpipers, Rock Ptarmigan, and Snow Buntings. Lower tundra had Whimbrels, Bar-tailed Godwits, Arctic Warblers, and *Pluvialis* plovers (all three species breed here: Pacific and American golden-plovers and the Black-bellied Plover). In between we found such species as Willow Ptarmigan, Eastern Yellow Wagtails, and Bluethroats. Each day we worked steadily from 6:00 a.m., or shortly after, until late in the day. We'd finish up cataloguing, weighing, swabbing cloacas for disease screening, and freezing specimens in the Alaska Department of Fish and Game (ADF&G) laboratory at around 8:00 p.m., then go to dinner.

The first few days were some of those rare field days of perfect weather: temperatures in the seventies, with sun and a light breeze. Sunburn on the tundra. On one of these incredible days we decided to climb up to high tundra on the Nome-Taylor Highway (Kougarok Road). It must have been nearly 80° F, and it was hot in the full sun on the leeward side of a massive sub-mountain. Climbing its steep slope in full field gear was a real effort. Bob and I went different ways on the way up, each taking a different route to the top to cover more of the terrain in search of birds. I rolled up my pants and carried on, taking a long, roundabout way to the top, hearing a Golden-crowned Sparrow sing a last song of the season in the low scrub below dry tundra. Around the south side of the climb I had a few handfuls of snow to cool off in the hot sun.

Nearing the top, I watched two *Pluvialis* plovers in the distance chase a passing Bald Eagle on the shoulders of a snowcapped peak. The top of this particular sub-mountain was a long, rather flat interlude to higher montane country. I strolled around for a while before topping out and looking for Bob. I saw him still below me in the distance, clearly interested in some birds near him. Using my binoculars, I couldn't see the birds, but I could see that Bob was only wearing his underwear. When I caught up with him and the Ruddy Turnstones he was watching, I asked how often he thought one could work on this high tundra—with snow below—in one's underwear. He said he'd be wearing nothing at all if he didn't need a place to keep a couple of extra shotgun shells.

Up on the broad top we found a magical place. A light breeze, the amazing weather, the incredible extent of the country that was visible, and the spectacular view all made it a very memorable long hike. On my roundabout return, I even found a few of the elusive Rock Sandpipers—common at other localities in Alaska, but seemingly uncommon here. The magical interlude on the high tundra began to come to a close shortly thereafter, though. Some three miles or so from the vehicle, I suddenly realized that some massive thunderstorms were brewing over the mountains and reaching out to touch our pocket of nirvana. Bob and I had taken widely different routes down toward the road far below, he aiming to come out a mile or more down the road from where we'd begun and me circling over some country we hadn't covered yet and bringing the vehicle up to meet him. Loud thunder and the first drops of rain arrived with me at the truck, and I drove a little farther on to pick up a guy who wasn't wearing pants.

Our bird work was going well, and we were enjoying a good look at a new region and some birds that were new to us as well. Bluethroats were a surprisingly flighty species. It was difficult to get anywhere near them. The Nome city limits contained a number of Bar-tailed Godwits, hard to find elsewhere, and before our last day it seemed that the only one of these magnificent birds we would ever obtain would be a road-smeared chick that a lot of vehicles had driven over—barely usable for a tissue sample. In fact, we obtained a surprising number of road kills for gravel roads. We missed many more, for several times we encountered Long-tailed Jaegers out keeping the roads clean, carrying off specimens that we ourselves would have had if we'd come by just a few minutes earlier. Overall, the birds were spectacular. Our paths and those of the Bristle-thighed Curlew never crossed, but some spectacular birds always seem to remain aloof, seemingly to entice future visits.

In our many hours of marching across the tundra, we saw what we thought were caribou remains: bones, shed antlers, shed hair, and tracks. We weren't seeing any caribou, though. One of the ADF&G folks set us straight. They weren't caribou—they were reindeer. Caribou had been extirpated from the peninsula since about 1870; but large reindeer herds were maintained both for meat and for the antlers in velvet, which, ground up, are an oriental aphrodisiac (tundra Viagra?). One herder in Nome was reputed to have a herd of 8,000 animals. Apparently, caribou herds were beginning to extend their wanderings farther west, going so far as to cross into reindeer country and take some of their tame brethren along with them when they left on their migrations, much to the consternation of the herdsmen. One morning as we drove up the Nome-Taylor Highway in a light rain and early morning fog with the wipers flapping back and forth, I saw ahead in the road a large pair of antlers that turned out to be our first reindeer. As noted in the Preface, it took us awhile to see the thousand or so others bedded down just to our right, and after we'd had a good look and finished laughing at ourselves, we drove on.

Later that same day, we spied a muskox lying down on a hillside in a patch of fireweed as we returned from the end of the road up on the Kougarok River (By the way, the Nome-Taylor Highway doesn't go to Taylor; it stops at the river, which is probably why it is locally called Kougarok Road.) Thinking back to the muskoxen on the Dalton Highway and how close Rose and I had been able to get to them, I stopped. We got out and walked toward this animal as he calmly watched us. As we approached, he got up and stretched. When we were about eighty feet away and still moving slowly forward, he calmly put his head down into a bush that was about a foot high and modestly gave it a little shake. He gave this display a couple more times until we stopped at about fifty feet. It was a silent and very calmly delivered, "Far enough, boys." Message received. We took a couple of pictures and backed off slowly. By the time we reached the road, he was lying down again, victor of the encounter.

On a different day, a red fox gave us some entertainment. We were headed home along the road and merged with a fellow commuter whose lane was in the ditch on the left—a red fox carrying a big mouthful of arctic ground squirrel and headed pointedly home. He just ignored us until we stopped to look at him. He stopped briefly, looked sideways at us for a moment, and then continued trotting along. We repeated this sequence several times, but each time it was the same. We tired of the game before he did, and we left him far behind trotting determinedly toward some distant family foxhole.

A few days later we were lucky enough to see an arctic fox hunting ptarmigan chicks. Several adult Willow Ptarmigan were giving the animal a serious scolding and boldly rushing it, and eventually the fox gave up and left the annoying, fat little birds, although everyone there knew that there were some succulent little ptarmigan chicks hiding nearby. For all of the territory that we covered in our ten days, the brown bears were almost as elusive as the curlews. We saw a fair amount of fresh sign, but we never saw a bear.

Scattered for many miles along the roads heading out from town are camps and cabins exhibiting what must be some of the most eclectic small-dwelling architecture ever assembled on Earth. Every design fancy and construction material that came to mind or hand lies plopped down wherever someone decided their little home away from home should be. Most are probably related to fishing, hunting, sealing, and berry picking, but others are small country getaways from Nome itself, which, on the coast, is often fogbound and cool in summer, whereas it is clearer and more pleasant in the interior. Drying racks, smokehouses, outhouses, and retired vehicles complete the functional camp. A phenomenon that I'd never noticed before coming to Alaska is very common in the Nome area: when a vehicle stops moving, it becomes a dumpster. Even in town one can pick out of a parking lot all of the vehicles in need of repair by the garbage deposited in them. I suppose the depth might indicate how long they've been out of service.

*Figure 4.2. An abandoned gold dredge, near Nome,
Seward Peninsula, Alaska.*

These parking lots also tend to contain all modes of transportation ready for use at any time: pickups, four-wheelers, bicycles, and snow machines.

Bob summed up the town accurately with the statement that there is nothing endearing about Nome. T-shirts on sale in town for tourists state, "There's no place like Nome." This might be preceded by, "Be it ever so humble." Established a century ago during the gold rush, the riches have been mined and hauled away, and Nome is left behind to make do. It was described to us as a "seven bars and seven churches" town. This was accurate, plus or minus a bar or church or two. If the state and federal governments didn't have such a presence in the area, it's doubtful whether the town would survive at even a quarter of its present size. Tourism is surprisingly strong here, however, at least in summer. The history of the area draws some people, and others come because there is nowhere else in North America where you can find such ready access to such a variety of tundra habitats and bird species. The short-term history of the area is nowhere as evident as in the silent hulks of the old dredges abandoned where their massive scoops ground to a screeching halt years ago when the gold-bearing gravel played out. Visiting these bizarre, formerly floating contraptions makes for an interesting contact with the relatively recent past. Longer-term history can be found in the numerous house pits evident along the road out near Safety Sound, where for centuries natives have gone to their fish camps.

Some commercial mining continues in the area, and recreational miners are a striking feature on the beach at Nome. A number of people live in tents and temporary shelters on the windy beach, panning for gold in the sand and gravel or, for the more adventurous, running floating suction dredges. These motorized rigs are floated a little way off the shore in calmer weather and run by what must be numb divers in dry-suits, out there underwater, controlling the suction hoses taking sand up off of the sea floor and spitting a slurry of sand and water up onto the floating sluice apparatus that separates out the gold flakes using gravity and flowing water. We stopped to watch the proceedings several times. On hot days there

Figure 4.3. Last train to nowhere, Seward Peninsula, Alaska.

would be a line of bikes and a group of kids out swimming. Having had a swim or two in more southerly Bering seas, I could only shake my head at these hardy souls taking serious dips in more northerly waters.

As we sat watching the beach miners before going to the airport for our flight out, I imagined what it would look like from this same place in January and February, with short winter days and sea ice. Bleak. To us, the endearing feature of Nome is its status as an excellent access point to superb tundra and summer bird communities. Next time we'll go earlier and hear some song.[8]

8 We had gone out late (this was the second half of July) to miss the birdwatchers, thus minimizing potential conflict in our rather different goals. To our delight, we didn't miss all of them. One afternoon on Kougarok Road, just after we'd put a lovely Red Knot specimen and our guns into the vehicle, a van stopped to talk with us about the birds we'd seen. The driver introduced himself as David Sonneborn, whom we knew to be a heart surgeon from Anchorage with the top life list for the state (in layman's terms, he'd seen more bird species in Alaska than anyone else). We were not unknown to Dave, either, for when we introduced ourselves, he said, "Bob Dickerman! Where's your gun?" Dave has since been an amazing volunteer for the Department of Ornithology at the museum, and he and his wife Alexandra were founders of the Friends of Ornithology at the university (more on the Friends can be found in the Afterword and Acknowledgments).

5

Go West, Young Man

WHEN THE PROPELLER-DRIVEN AIRPLANE landed
on the surprisingly mountainous Kodiak Island, rain was falling. Bob
Dickerman was there to meet me with a smile and a rental car. We were
scheduled to spend a few days here on Kodiak, collecting specimens before
hitching a ride with the Coast Guard out to Attu Island, far out at the end
of the Aleutian Island chain.

At about the time I arrived in Fairbanks in March 1997, I'd asked
Dan Gibson where in the state he felt we would need to focus immediate
collecting attention: Where was there a closing window of opportunity?
"Attu," Dan said, was Number One. The Coast Guard had a LORAN
station there (LORAN is military shorthand for LOng-Range Aid to
Navigation). This station was scheduled to be shut down at the end of 2000.
Without the Coast Guard there keeping a station open and manned, access
would become very restricted. We were unable to get out in spring because
of competition with the birding tour company, Attour (we didn't want the
friction of working at cross-purposes with birdwatchers), but we were on
our way in the fall.

Kodiak hosts the Coast Guard base from which biweekly logistics
flights are made to Attu. Conveniently, it was also a place from which we
needed bird specimens. So Bob and I had rendezvoused here a few days
early to begin some Kodiak collecting. Kodiak has a history as a glacial
refugium and as a Russian settlement, causing it to be an important locality
for bird sampling. We spent two full days working here to collect specimens

Figure 5.1. Kodiak Island, Alaska.

before packing up to go out to Attu. The Kodiak National Wildlife Refuge was kind enough to let us use their empty bunkhouse, and we set up our center of activity there.

We were able to net some excellent birds nearby, but the real fun came in poking our way south along the winding gravel roads. Scads of pink salmon were coming up every trickle of water to spawn. It was quite a sight. We stopped often and worked the available habitats, picking up important birds like Red Crossbills, Pacific Wrens, and Song Sparrows. One of my favorite habitats here was the old-growth, Sitka-spruce forest.

We got up at 5:15 a.m. on a Wednesday to finish packing and to get to the Coast Guard base at 6:30 for the scheduled 8:00 flight. Unfortunately, I'd picked up a raging sore throat, cold, and fever. I felt crummy all day. And it was a long day. Once we were loaded, we waited quite awhile to learn more about the weather out over Attu and Shemya islands. It seemed good enough to go, so we finally left at 9:30. Flying in a Lockheed C-130 was new to me. It seemed sort of like being strapped into a pickup engine compartment and carried along to who knows where at who can guess what speed. But it was free, and the Coast Guard personnel were very nice. We had good box lunches at about noon, and everyone got to use the "honey pot," which was curtained off behind us in the cargo compartment. We had a seat pallet, but we were strapped in among the cargo going out to Attu. Earplugs were passed out prior to takeoff, and they were needed.

But that day, all our troubles were for nothing. We turned around an hour or so out from Attu; apparently both Shemya and Attu were too socked in to land. So we rode in that sucker for over eight hours doing one big roundabout. When we landed back on the runway on Kodiak, the guy in charge said he was sorry, and that those of us who wanted to try once more were welcome to show up again tomorrow morning.

So we did. Once again, we did the wait, load, wait, board, wait, and zoom. But this time, four-and-a-half hours later we were told to buckle in again; and after about five hours in the air, we were landing. The large airstrip has one very small terminal on it, which we did not see being used. It had a couple of good signs on it, though: "Attu International Airport," and "Pop. 20, 1 dog." The dog's name was Coco, an old St. Bernard.

Attu Island is beautiful, but the southeastern part, where we were, was covered with junk. This was a real hopping place during and after World War II, judging from the amount of garbage everywhere. The Coast Guard station itself is a trim building that is well equipped. We were shown our quarters—just across from the sauna and Jacuzzi room—and after a quick tour of the station, Bob and I unpacked our field gear and hit the nearest beach.

Our first introduction to the birds of the island was incredible. In the

Figure 5.2. Massacre Bay, Attu Island, Aleutian Islands, Alaska. Note old World War II-era docks and debris (chain in foreground).

next couple of hours we collected five shorebirds of five different species, including both tattler species (Wandering and Gray-tailed tattlers) and a Ruff. I didn't know what species the latter was when I shot it just as it flushed, and that's the beauty of working in a remote place like Attu: You can find some very unusual birds. When you see one that you don't know on Attu, there will be few North American specimens. Bob came up as I was stuffing the throat with cotton and asked what I'd gotten, and I replied that I didn't know.

He looked at it and said, "I think it might be a Ruff; I got one in Guatemala in 1968."

Later, with a field guide, we learned that he was right on the identification, and much later I learned that he was right on the Guatemalan date as well. That's a pretty remarkable memory. Prior to this bird, I'd only seen breeding plumage specimens, and those mostly of adult males.

Just as exciting, however, was that we'd seen and gotten acquainted with the gigantic Attu Song Sparrows (*Melospiza melodia maxima*). They are a beach-dwelling animal, and they scuttle around in a seemingly atypical fashion for Song Sparrows. They're twice or more times larger than their lower-forty-eight cousins, and they look strikingly different. But as soon as they call or sing they're unmistakably Song Sparrows. We finished up our first day very happy with the situation.

The next day the weather closed back in; we were glad to be here. I started off the day getting three Gray-tailed Tattlers with two shots— waiting nervously for two to line themselves up, then getting the third as it tried to leave the party. With the low, windy, wet weather, I found the Song Sparrows easy to get with .22 dust[9]. They prefer beachside vegetation with some three-dimensional structure nearby, and they really were numerous where cliffs or bluffs back this up. This makes the available habitat narrow and coastal, but that's how these sedentary birds live out here. (Most other Song Sparrows are migratory, and the species is not known as a beach dweller.)

Reveille is given over the station intercom at 7:00 a.m. Breakfast is from 7:00 to 7:30. "How would you like your eggs?" the cook asked me.

My jaw just dropped. I can't remember what I finally answered, but I can say that the eggs were excellent, and that this was the cushiest field station I've ever worked from. Tents in wet forest came to mind, as did a recently vacated sheep shed in Mexican cloud forest. The accommodations and the fare here on Attu were far superior.

What is decidedly odd, however, is that it doesn't get light here until

---

9. "Dust" is what collectors call 12-shot, the smallest shot size available. Using auxiliary barrel inserts, our side-by-side 12-gauge shotguns can be used to fire .410 and .22 loads as well.

9:00 a.m. Alaska used to have five time zones, but now it only has two: Alaska Standard Time for most of the state, and Hawaii-Aleutian Time for the westernmost part (one hour earlier). Here we're so far west that sunrise takes a long time to arrive in relation to the clock. Bob and I quickly got into the habit of skinning a couple of birds before going out at dawn. (Bob got up at 5:30 a.m. to pull things to thaw and to start drinking coffee.)

Larry Balch, the head of Attour, had been kind enough to let us borrow a couple of Attour bicycles, which were stored over in the old, abandoned LORAN-A building where the Attour visitors stay. We walked over there on our first day and picked up our wheels. There are a lot of WWII-era roads on this part of the island, as well as a network of runways, and bicycles really open up the ability to cover the ground. Bob estimated that he hadn't ridden a bike in about thirty years. We can both vouch for the fact that the old expression about learning to ride a bicycle is true—Bob hadn't forgotten how. Soon enough we were pedaling happily about with our shotguns, looking for birds.

One of the important species for us to get here was the Pacific Wren. Like the Song Sparrows, Pacific Wrens out here are both sedentary and much larger than their mainland relatives. They have another key difference, however: they live in the crags of cliffs. There are no trees here taller than about three feet (scrubby willows); the nearest "classic" Pacific Wren breeding habitat of dense coniferous forest is over a thousand miles away. In the Aleutians they seem to do quite well living on beachside cliffs. But it makes them very difficult to get. In fall they tend to come down from the cliffs to feed in the intertidal zone. With care I was able to find and obtain several as they snuck between the cliffs and the intertidal zone in the tall annual vegetation. They really are large here; one adult male weighed 16 grams, a good 50 percent larger than any of this species I'd seen before.

The pink salmon were running here on Attu also, and after a good rain

Figure 5.3. Banks of spent pink salmon (Onchorhynchus gorbuscha) *thrown up by ocean waves after being washed down Peaceful River, Attu Island, Aleutian Islands, Alaska.*

the Peaceful River rose and flushed a lot of the dead ones out to sea. One of the memorable sights was the grisly windrows of spawned-out salmon that formed at the high-tide line near the mouth of the small river. They were sprinkled artistically with smaller windrows of beautiful pink-orange-red salmon eggs. Common Ravens and Glaucous-winged Gulls could be found at the mouth of the Peaceful River at all hours of the day, gorging on this smorgasbord.

The weather was often Aleutian enough to keep us inside skinning birds. Wind and horizontal rain makes for miserable conditions to work in, so when the weather was bad we tended to work inside until it let up. When it didn't let up, we went out for a few hours at the end of the day on "shorebird patrol" up and down the closest beaches.

Despite the important World War II history of Attu and the fact that hundreds of US soldiers lost their lives in re-taking the island from the Japanese, there is just one small plaque (put up in 1993) to memorialize the fallen US soldiers. There is a striking Japanese monument on Engineer Hill, where the Japanese soldiers made a last ditch effort to fight through to the US supplies and howitzers. When they failed, something on the order of 500 of them committed mass suicide by holding grenades to their chests— death before dishonor. Collecting bird specimens in a place with such a grisly history is a new experience for me. Almost none of our work was in the places where this battle was fought, though. Instead, we worked the beaches and the nearshore areas. The birds really do seem to like to hang out around WWII-era structures and debris, though, and some of our most productive collecting was around fallen buildings and beachside junk.

Figure 5.4. Monument to Japanese soldiers who died in World War II, Attu Island, Aleutian Islands, Alaska.

Attu had a bloody history prior to World War II, too. Geographic place names for prominent features where we worked include "Massacre Bay," "Massacre Valley," and "Murder Point." These place names go back to Russian atrocities perpetrated upon the native Aleuts as the former expanded their fur trade into North America in the late 1700s and early 1800s.

The Attour group stays in the old LORAN station ("A Station"), long since abandoned and falling into disrepair. It now constitutes concrete walls, a leaky roof, and some windows. It's better than camping, but not cushy by any means. In wandering through the old buildings, we were somewhat surprised by the graffiti on the walls. Each season it seemed that someone listed the names of a group of people and beside each name the number of species that the individual had seen in the ABA (American Birding Association) checklist area. This seemed like an arcane personal statistic to record for posterity—a nebulous personal statistic that would matter only to others interested in what the late Allan Phillips called "bird golf." I found myself wondering what I would put beside my name if I were to write it on a distant wall. An institutional affiliation? My place of residence? My pants size? I decided that to me it would be odd even to put my name on the wall, so what would come after it is moot. I left the building being unable to connect with these past visitors, who seemed to be strongly motivated by something that I could see, but not understand. It is great to see this evidence of people becoming fascinated by something that allows them to enjoy this place as much as I do. And I know that if nothing else we share a strong interest in this place, which probably means something special to each of us.

Smeared against the western slopes of one of the mountains near the old station is the wreck of a Coast Guard C-130. The largest piece of it left is the tail section; the rest of it looks to be in smaller pieces. Apparently it's the only Coast Guard C-130 ever to have gone down. It crashed here in about 1982 on a regular logistics ("log") flight. Oral tradition has it that they mistook Casco Cove for the bay in which the station lies, and in poor visibility lined up for the runway one bay too far to the west and a little north. Miraculously, only two people were killed, and the rest of the crew survived. The wreck is a sight to make you take such flights in remote Alaska very seriously. During World War II, more planes were lost in the Aleutians due to weather than from enemy fire. The weather is still something to take very seriously.

Every day, Bob and I worked the country, looking for birds. We got into the routine of it very fast, and we combed and re-combed the same areas again and again looking for arriving migrants. After breakfast, before dawn, when the weather was particularly foul, and in the evenings we sat in our quarters and skinned birds. Our quarters became known among the coasties as the "Death Room," and there were a few comments about the smells that emanated from it. But we had pretty fair odor control going; we didn't think it was bad. We checked our drying skins and skeletons regularly for odor, and we put the really maggot-ridden skeletons that we'd roughed out from birds found on the beaches into the T-building (the room at the base of the LORAN tower) to dry.

In addition to collecting birds, we brought a few snap traps for small mammals. Rats had long ago been introduced on the island, but someone had reported sign of what might be something else more inland than where rats usually hung out. Bob took charge of this aspect of our work; he had been a professional collector for E. Raymond Hall back in the good old days. He had success very quickly, but the traps that had presumably caught animals were gone. He had to stake them out to keep them from being dragged away, whether by large small mammals or by arctic foxes, which had also been introduced onto the island long ago. The staked-out traps began producing rats immediately. One day Bob brought in the biggest rat I've ever seen—a huge female as big as a small cat. Ugh. It made a nice skin, though.

The two weeks sped by unbelievably fast. Altogether too soon, we were packing to leave. On our final day, we had a little time to patrol the beach before the plane was scheduled to arrive, but we didn't find anything worth collecting. A fast, wet storm blew through and dropped some hail (and I thought I heard thunder), and shortly afterward it was announced over the station intercom that the plane was putting in at Shemya and would come over to Attu when the weather cleared. The usual routine is for an Attu pickup, with the plane then going over to Shemya for the night. Bob and I were ready to go; we were eager to sample the shores of Shemya in the afternoon and evening. But it wasn't to be. The plane got socked in on Shemya by the same squall that hit us. So they said they'd come and get us and drop off the logistics supplies in the morning. Bob said, "Well, you know the old saying: F**k." So we partially unpacked and went out to get some more birds and spent the evening and the next morning skinning.

The plane came right over at 9:00 a.m., as promised. While it was on the ground we hopped a ride with a group of the crew going up to see the Japanese monument. Later, back once again in the C-130, the return flight was really neat. They ran part of what they called a "law enforcement" run, going in low and turning and following coastlines for much of the island chain. It was a gorgeous day, and we got a great look at many of the western islands. Several of them had decaying WWII-era military installations on them; this was the main attraction for the flight crew. Bob and I just enjoyed seeing so many islands from the air—each unique in shape and size. When we finally gave up island hopping and went to a higher altitude it got cold inside the cargo hold. On this trip there were only four passengers, and there was not a seat pallet, so we rode in the jump seats: crude, fold-down, single-layer nylon and aluminum pole affairs along the wall. We got up and walked around quite a bit during the flight, so it wasn't so bad.

We made it back to Fairbanks with no further adventures. It had been a wonderful trip—a great introduction to both Kodiak and Attu. And it had also been very productive in the way of bird specimens. It was inevitable that we would be going back to both places again.

6
Wind, Water, and Birds: Cold Bay

SITUATED WAY DOWN ON the Alaska Peninsula, Cold Bay is an out-of-the-way destination for human travelers. Built up into a regionally prominent human settlement during the Aleutian campaign of World War II, Cold Bay remains an important hub for regional transportation and commerce because its long runway can accommodate large aircraft. Still, it's an unlikely destination for humans. Cold Bay was not named inappropriately. It does not have the allure of many other seaside human settlements—no turquoise waters, no tropical warmth, no blazing sun, no quaint seaside village charm. It does have the dubious distinction of being the windiest town on the North American continent. Situated on a very narrow part of the Alaska Peninsula, it lies on the boundary of the cold North Pacific Ocean and the colder Bering Sea. A narrow spit of land does little to slow the howling air movements between these two wild bodies of water, giving Cold Bay one of its main features.

However, the waters of Cold Bay are not simply two notorious seas separated by a little spit of land. All of the aqueous complexities one could hope for in a northern oceanic environment are present: sheltered lagoons, hosting what are perhaps the world's largest eelgrass beds; an extensive mosaic of freshwater lakes and ponds; freshwater creeks and rivers; and an invigorating amount of rain. Given the wind, the rain becomes particularly invigorating when it comes down horizontally at cool and cold temperatures. It would be an understatement to say that Cold Bay is an ideal testing ground for outdoor clothing. But the planet's occupants who are regular travelers to Cold Bay don't go in for clothing. For birds, Cold Bay is an important and very attractive destination.

Cold Bay's eelgrass beds draw in tens of thousands of migratory ducks and geese, who feed on the vegetation while fattening for their migrations onward to destinations as far away as Mexico. And the accumulated dead eelgrass forms a decomposing, muddy ooze that provides nourishment and a home for the invertebrates that tens of thousands of shorebirds happen to enjoy. They, too, come to Cold Bay in fall, to fatten up for migrations into the tropics of both the New World and the Old World. And, together, the wind, water, and birds of Cold Bay constitute remarkable sights to behold.

Reeve Aleutian Airways had a daily scheduled flight to Cold Bay from Anchorage.[10] Considering that Cold Bay had a permanent population of only eighty-one people, it was a surprise to me that the flight was made each day by a Boeing 727. Apparently the air cargo and personnel turnover associated with Cold Bay is quite out of proportion to the town's size. Air travel within Alaska often commands airfares that make travel "Outside" (to the lower forty-eight) look like a bargain. My roundtrip ticket from Fairbanks cost $876. But I was poorly informed here: in September and October Reeve was running a package special for hunters and fishermen that included round trip airfare from Anchorage and three days food and lodging for $550 (airfare alone was usually $750). This was a good deal, and a moderate number of sportsmen were out taking advantage of it. Cold Bay is a superb destination for waterfowl hunting because of the concentrations occurring there in the fall, and the fishing in the streams and rivers is apparently excellent also.

---

10. Alas, Reeve Aleutian Airways has since gone out of business. The company had a distinguished history in Alaska, particularly in the western parts of the state (http://en.wikipedia.org/wiki/Reeve_Aleutian_Airways).

But I was out for different reasons, as usual. As good as it would have been to be out hunting the abundant Cackling Goose and Brant and watching the common Emperor Goose (for which the hunting season was closed), or hunting Mallards, Northern Pintail, or Green-winged Teal and watching the abundant Steller's Eider (for which the season was also closed), I was there for other birds. Migratory birds are real travelers, and as such make excellent disease vectors, carrying their various parasites, microbes, and viruses to and from distant places. And when these birds become concentrated around bodies of water, transmission rates increase as they all arrive to defecate, feed, bathe, and drink in this same water. My goal was to sample some of these birds to learn a little more about the diseases they might be carrying, and also to make the first collections of avian genetic material from this region.

The incredible concentrations of migratory birds that occur here each year have caused much of the area to be preserved as the Izembek National Wildlife Refuge. The refuge includes the extensive eelgrass beds, and, as remote as it is, it represents a jewel in the crown of the national refuge system. The role of the area as a major migratory stopover site is unquestionable, and its status as a refuge allows birds, humans, and associated wildlife to enjoy it in perpetuity. "Associated wildlife" includes such things as four species of salmon, Dolly Varden and Arctic char, caribou, Rock and Willow ptarmigan, and an excellent concentration of brown bears.

Before heading out in a vehicle, I was given a warning about how to park: into the wind. People who don't live in windy places don't give this much thought, but in Cold Bay it is evident that this warning is occasionally forgotten, for one sees doors that are sprung and doors that have been cranked right back and then roughly repaired. Thinking about how my elbow would feel if bent backwards, I was careful to heed the warning.

How windy is it in Cold Bay? The average wind speed in September is 16.4 mph, and the record gust was 95 mph. During this same month the average cloud cover is 91 percent. During my ten-day stay at the end of September, I saw two good blows. The first, for two days, saw sustained winds of about 30–35 mph with gusts into the fifties; the second blow lasted just a single day, but at its peak it had sustained winds of about 50 mph and gusts of perhaps as high as 70 mph. I went out after birds in both, but was not very successful in the second. In that kind of wind, it is a serious effort simply to walk, especially when crossing hummocky Aleutian heath (which on the surface is like tundra, but it lacks permafrost below) or trying to follow a trail in a rough area. Interestingly, you could see every body of water on the tundra from a distance, because the wind was lifting heavy spray directly up off of the surfaces (not just from wavetops) and sending it aloft in dense sheets. Thus, even when it had stopped raining, there was still an amazing amount of water being blown horizontally. It was interesting, however, to observe birds in these winds. The waterbirds seemed to have little difficulty in continuing their tidally related flights. But even when we weren't experiencing high winds, it was still windy. Insects here are not a problem. Nor are trees. Neither can do their thing in these winds.

On my second day I was able to watch a Gyrfalcon out playing near a bluff in windy updrafts with a group of Common Ravens out doing the same. Even they seemed to realize that they were unlikely companions on this aerial playground. Later I saw other Gyrfalcons (and Peregrine Falcons also) out cruising more seriously for avian prey along the beaches. Izembek Lagoon is a remarkable place to spend time marching along beaches. They are the cleanest I've seen yet in Alaska. The barrier islands of the lagoon must capture the great majority of the trash and timber so common on Bering Sea beaches. These barrier islands do not appear to filter out many jellyfish, however, and fresh, four-to-eight inch examples of jewelly jellyfish designs regularly adorned the sand and gravel beaches.

Figure 6.1. Migratory geese pass in front of Frosty Peak, Izembek National Wildlife Refuge, Cold Bay, Alaska Peninsula, Alaska.

Izembek Lagoon is a remote place, and few people walk more than a couple of hundred meters off of the very limited road system. When you set off to walk the area's beaches, chances are excellent that you can walk most of the day and never see another soul. As a consequence, you feel like an intruder into a primeval world. You're certainly outnumbered. When the weather is good, you can see for miles: rolling heath dotted with streams and ponds; extensive bays; the extinct, snowcapped volcano called Frosty Peak; and the extinct oceanic volcano called Amak Island that looms out of the haze and cloud just off the coast. (There's an endemic Song Sparrow population on Amak that I'd sure like to see.[11]) It's all very spectacular. And in this setting, it is absolutely transfixing to walk around a beach corner and flush a few thousand Brant or Cackling Geese and watch them fly around, calling to you and to each other while they decide just what to do about it. This is repeated over and over again on long beach marches, and I found that even with driving rain in my face I stopped to watch these spectacles every time.

On one very long march, I went out to distant Blaine Point to see if I could find flocks of shorebirds roosting there at high tide. I found very few shorebirds on the way out there, and as the weather deteriorated I wondered whether such a long walk was worth it. But out on the tip of the point there was a fairly sheltered spot, and as I came around the corner I was amazed to suddenly come upon a flock of about 2,000 Rock Sandpipers. I'd never seen such a large flock of this species. It's difficult to describe how captivating such a docile, densely packed mass of birds quietly talking to themselves can be. They hardly paid me any attention, letting me approach to within thirty feet of the body of the flock—just fifteen feet away from the closest individuals. I pulled out my camera and walked very slowly past and through them a few times. Their sheer density, gray winter plumage, squeaking voices, and little movements brought teeming rats or mice to mind for an instant, but then a section would depart in rapid, pirouetting flight, whirling and returning to land just a few feet from where they began. These flights were spectacular, twisting and wheeling like smoke, then piling back onto the beach.

It's easy to tell a bear trail from a human trail. With four-legged drive, bears must have better balance than we do. They place their feet directly in a line on each side of the body and so don't trounce the middle of the trail;

---

11. During another season I do eventually make it out to Amak Island and bring home some of these interesting sparrows; see Chapter 16).

this leaves a mohawk strip of untrounced grass between two parallel, bear-foot-wide shuffle tracks. On most beach marches, you'll wind up spending a lot of time on bear trails or walking over their tracks on the beaches, and many of the tracks will be very fresh. I carried the requisite shotgun and bear slugs on the off chance that one might be bold enough to come after me, but I found them to be very polite. After pausing to give it a little thought, the only bear I saw closer than 100 meters decided to swim out to a nearby island rather than share the beach with me. This was a couple of days after I'd had to take off my rubber boots to do a little wading in the bone-numbing Bering Sea, so I thought to myself, *Better you than me.* But the bear seemed to actually be having fun frolicking in the water. It may have been after salmon coming into the lagoon with the incoming tide.

There is surprisingly little structure in the area remaining from World War II, given its buildup in the 1940s. I found one small observation cabin well dug into the tundra overlooking Izembek Lagoon that had withstood the ravages of wind and time. In odd places there are occasional minimal evidences of antipersonnel fencing material sinking into the open tundra. One day I climbed up onto Frosty Peak looking for Rock Ptarmigan and Snow Buntings. I found both of these species in a huge, boulder-strewn amphitheater above an old Army Air Forces station high up on the mountain. Little was left of the installation, which must have been a lonely outpost built for communications. I found the birds I was seeking above these ruins, just below snow line. I had come up onto the mountain because it provided a big block for the howling wind that day. But occasional powerful gusts slipped around the mountainside and made boulder hopping on steep slopes a challenge.

Cold Bay and the larger, nearby community of King Cove were in the national news at this time as battle lines were being drawn around the issue of building a road from King Cove to Cold Bay across national refuge lands. King Cove, an old and important fishing settlement that has the highest per-capita income of any western Alaska native community, wanted road access to the runway in Cold Bay. The most pressing need advanced for such a road was to enable medical evacuations during foul weather, when small planes and boats can't make it from King Cove to Cold Bay. The estimated cost for the desired 27-mile gravel road was thirty million dollars, with an additional half-million each year for maintenance. Opinions raged from Alaska to Washington DC on this issue.

As an outside observer, I would hope that some reasonable heads prevail. There are irregular but legitimate medevac needs in King Cove and in other communities in the area. This road won't solve these needs for the other communities, which seems a real shame given the cost to taxpayers. The Department of the Interior is looking into alternatives; they'd prefer to keep new roads off public conservation lands. Two alternatives being discussed were stationing a medevac helicopter in Cold Bay to service surrounding communities, and developing telemedicine infrastructure and personnel. The latter has great promise for remote communities throughout Alaska. If this amount of money is going to be thrown at the problem, it would be nice to see a solution that benefits all the remote communities in the region.

To waterbirds and any humans enjoying wilderness, birds, and other wildlife, Cold Bay is a good a place to visit. The weather might make you wish you were a duck, but I somehow doubt whether ducks fully appreciate the ambiance—the sight of Frosty Peak as a backdrop to a few thousand flying geese, or Amak Island looming forebodingly out of the cold, gray sea.

7

The Moose That Stole Christmas

WITH ONLY ABOUT FOUR HOURS of sunlight these days, and with day length still decreasing by four minutes each day, Christmas lights mean a lot to some of us here in the great frozen north. Last Sunday it dawned on me that it was dark just about every time I looked out the window. We go to work in the dark; we come home in the dark. Life outside is beautiful, but we just don't see it very often anymore. So I decided it was time to put up some Christmas lights on some trees in the yard so the windows weren't just inky black surfaces. With a flashlight and boots, it was a fairly pleasant task in the fluffy snow, and the small white lights looked great when I finally got two lines plugged in with a new fifty-foot extension cord. It was all very cheery and festive.

Moose are common backyard occupants in the Fairbanks area. They are the bane of gardeners in summer, but we hadn't heard of them being winter pests. We have at least two that spend time in our yard, munching their way through the woods at irregular intervals, usually just leaving their tracks behind to let us know they were there. One of them likes to roam out across our deck, but it doesn't seem to have figured out yet how to eat sunflower seeds from the birdfeeder. It did seem to enjoy the new young tree that Rose planted out in back, and occasionally we see it, a female, smiling and nodding at us as we each go about our business. It's still amazing to me that our deck holds this huge animal.

Last Saturday in at the lab, a couple of the graduate students were passing around a picture of aliens stealing Christmas lights. One of the students had printed it from a web site, and I was a little surprised that anyone had the time to seek out things like this. It's still not entirely clear, but I gather that when they have a little spare time during a molecular procedure, they make up unlikely strings of key words, plug them into a web search engine, then enjoy the sites that pop up. Geez. And we used to just listen to rock and roll and run other procedures.

Well, the picture of those nasty little aliens came right back to me on Monday night when I went out back to plug the lights in—and couldn't find the cord! I could see little drag marks in the snow, but it was late, nearly zero, very dark, and I wasn't wearing boots or a jacket. The unlikely mystery had to wait. Tuesday was skinning night, and some Bluethroats and good music kept me away until late, so it wasn't until Wednesday evening (which was just as dark, with light snow) that I finally had the chance—and the clothing and the boots and the flashlight—to figure things out. Moose tracks. Everywhere. And moose beds. There had been a little moose party in our backyard, and the lights and the cord had been carried away by the partygoers. Half an hour of running a hook across every moose trail I could find in the snow gained me nothing but an appreciation for the cleverness and sheer ruthlessness of the culprits. The spirit of our meager Christmas had been stolen by moose.

What can be done about these large, ungainly creatures? First, everyone should know just how dastardly they are. They seem to strike when it's dark, and now when I look at our inky black windows I imagine them reveling out there, laughing as they look in on our pale, cheerless lives. I don't know. Maybe if we had a Cindy Lou Who doll to put in a lighted window, the culprits would feel guilty and bring back our lights just in the nick of time for us all to sing Yahoo Boring (or whatever it is they sing in Dr. Seuss's

Figure 7.1. Backyard moose (Alces alces), *trying to look completely innocent, Fairbanks, Alaska.*

Whoville) around the tree on Christmas Day. In the meantime I've fluffed up their beds in the backyard, hoping they might drag the damned lights back and I won't be left hunting for them after the snow melts next April. And I might ask around about moose-proof cords and lights for the long, dark nights between now and then.

8

When Mr. F Meets Mr. C, It's Cold in Alaska

IT IS EASY TO IMAGINE that some time long ago on a very cold night in Alaska, two yet-to-become-distinguished physicists met while playing cards in a bar. Their luck was down, and they both quit the game simultaneously after a particularly bad hand. They bellied up to the bar, ordered drinks, and soon wound up in a passionate discussion about the finer points of the measurement of the thermodynamic properties of objects and environments. And, as they stumbled out of a warm, smoky, drunken interior into an intensely starlit and frozen night, they both remarked with admirable expletives how frigging cold it was.

And Mr. F said to Mr. C, "In your vision of a universe in which thermal properties are measured with precision and—hic—accuracy, what friggin' temperature do you suppose *this* would be? Besides just friggin' cold?"

"Well—hic—," said Mr. C, "I dunno; this is so damned cold that it shouldn't be in the normal range of a *real* temperature gradient!"

"I—hic—agree," said Mr. F, "so, if you were the grand master and could make up your own scale, what temperature would it be?"

Mr. C paused and thought, but he was distracted. "I still can't believe I lost forty dollars in that damned poker game!"

"Hey—that's what I lost, too! Forty in the hole! I'm glad the cards aren't that cold every night!" said Mr. F.

"Yes, cold cards—a forty in the hole night!" laughed Mr. C.

And Mr. F's fateful question on this memorable night was never directly answered, for building pressures and the need for relief made it important to get on home. Even yet-to-be distinguished physicists can only do the manly job of averting severe frostbite for so long.

Figure 8.1. A lovely—though short— winter's day, Fairbanks, Alaska.

It was cold here in Fairbanks for the past couple of weeks— down around -40° for days. That is the temperature where the Fahrenheit and Celsius scales meet. And air that dense tends to hang around for a while when it's in the neighborhood. With the proper clothes, this isn't much to get worked up about. It's too cold for skiing, but strolling around out in the crisp air is actually fairly pleasant.

Machinery, on the other hand, ordinarily the Lapdog of Man, takes on a mind of its own. You don't even know your own vehicle. Everything about driving becomes an extraordinary event. Unlocking the door must be done slowly to prevent breaking off the key. Your only hope of starting the engine depends on your having connected to the singlemost important feature of a parking space: an electrical outlet. Every vehicle whose owner expects to be driving away anytime soon is either left running or plugged in. Unless it is started within an hour, a vehicle parked and shut off without a lifegiving socket nearby is scrap metal until the weather changes substantially for the better. And you'd better hope your antifreeze is good to about -60° F, just in case.

Getting the door open can be an accomplishment—the hinges often become so stiff that it seems you'll bend the frame getting the damned thing open far enough to squeeze in. The plugged-in engine starts with no trouble—it's the only thing that works as it's supposed to, and it warms just fine. But hearing the defroster and heater fan in the cab scream in protest at being started at such unholy temperatures is just the first sign that all is not well with other moving parts. Because, unfortunately, you can't get all of the many moving parts outside of the engine to warm up.

Most of the rebelliousness of the formerly trustworthy machine comes from the fundamental changes that occur in lubricants at these temperatures. Plugging in a vehicle keeps the "coolant" and the oil heated, and on some vehicles a small electric blanket keeps the battery temperature up as well. But all the other moving parts are at ambient temperature— making "lubricant" a ridiculous term, because at these temperatures these compounds might be compared with solid, dried rubber cement, or almost-hardened concrete. And these materials are serious about remaining in this inordinately stiff state.

If you haven't experienced it, the comparatively immobile state of familiar vehicular functions is very interesting—at least the first few times. Take my old truck, for example. It worked perfectly for years in the lower forty-eight, and, until now, it has continued to do so. But below -30° F its moving parts have no problem being parts, but every problem with movement. It takes both human and engine strength to successfully fight the resistance of the ultracold lubricants. And it's a real fight. I haven't bent the door yet. And I haven't broken off the steering wheel. But every time I leave work on these intensely cold nights, these and other problems seem on the verge of occurring. Just getting home is a workout. Pushing in the clutch requires considerable strength, and after letting it go it takes so long to come back that I often wonder if it's going to do so at all. But, after the engine has warmed up with the clutch out and the transmission spinning in neutral for five to ten minutes you're as ready as you're going to get. Ordinarily flexible plastic and foam seats turn into largely inflexible, hard, heat-sucking benches. This is the only thing that makes me feel cold—this and the steering wheel. A heavy wool blanket over the seat and heavy gloves solved this after day one. Still, I stand outside a little ways off enjoying the night while, after ignition, my personal mechanical lapdog becomes accustomed to the thought of moving.

When the temperature gauge shows upward movement, the engine is ready to join in the fight to get the vehicle home. It's a show of brute force. The door, tough to open, is impossible to close. And, of course, one of the few things that seem to work pretty well is the whining, "door ajar" alarm. It will keep me company for the whole journey—that and the whistling wind. I slowly get the clutch in, get it into reverse, then, with an unavoidably slow return on the part of the clutch, the vehicle starts a painful lurch backwards. If I'm lucky, I can budge the steering wheel (this old model does not have power steering). Sometimes I have to seesaw back and forth a few times to get headed in the right direction—the steering has limited play (and none at all when the vehicle is stationary). Because it is so difficult to turn and to shift, the best parking spaces are those that leave the car pointed home after backing out from a plug head. Many drivers back into the space and use longer extension cords. But most of us usually have to take corners and shift gears, and each is an event. Steering is so tough that I feel great satisfaction at turning out of the parking lot, but the feeling leaves instantly as I try to horse the wheel back around so that I'm going straight again.

Wide, poorly controlled turns are unavoidable. (A bad place to park would be near parking lot entrances.)

In first gear, the engine has little trouble getting the vehicle moving and keeping it going. But that's too slow for public roads, and I have to at least get it into second. Here the cold-delayed clutch return becomes a serious problem, because as soon as it's disengaged those exceedingly stiff lubricants in the wheel bearings work like a well-set parking brake. I'm lucky if the vehicle is still moving when I get it into second and the clutch finally comes back out. (Later, inertia makes the shift from second to third go a little better.) This is where some people regularly get hot, burning smells as the clutch fights with limited success to get and keep the vehicle moving. But for now, if I didn't come to a complete stop and kill the engine in that first shift, I fly down the road in second gear. Maybe it's only my speedometer, but something about this intense cold makes it go crazy—it tells me I'm going about 80 mph in second gear.

Even in the state of high concentration that this driving requires, I enjoy this first screaming straightaway. The tires have lost essentially all flexibility, and they've also lost air volume and have become squared up with the cold. On this perfectly smooth, flat, well-paved road, it feels like I'm driving on square wooden blocks. In second gear, the engine is seriously working, the cab's fan keeps giving off intermittent protesting shrieks, the speedometer proudly states incredible speeds, my head is bouncing rhythmically off the roof in time to the square tires, the cold wind of an open door begins to make itself known, and the door ajar whiner is doing its thing in the background. I find that the radio breaks the tranquility of the moment, so lately I've just been leaving it off.

Out on the open road, ice fog is a new hazard that arrives with the intense cold, added to the ever-present icy winter roads. Ice fog is a consequence of burning fossil fuels under conditions of a thermal inversion; the exhaust of furnaces, vehicles, woodstoves, and power plants is trapped in the low-lying cold air mass, and the prevailing calm conditions keep the trap closed. In town, this causes a dense fog, and the air smells like big-city air. Outside of town this fog is almost absent, but in town it requires caution and headlights in midday. My jostling, windy ride home takes me clear of this fog. That and the heated garage (a truly wonderful feature of our house) make coming home an even greater pleasure than usual. I pity the poor souls who have to go through, in getting to work each morning, what I have to go through to get home. Fighting a vehicle like mine in both directions would be very discouraging. And, in fact, down around -50° F you find that vehicles begin dropping like flies. It just becomes too cold to get many of them to function at all.

On our first -40° night, I went out to do some celebratory grilling. Boy—and I thought the knobs on the gas grill were stiff at -20° and -30° F. But even after sloooowly twisting them open, I had tremendous difficulty getting the thing lit. When I finally succeeded, the pitiful result was a few tiny blue flames, which remained tiny even when the gas was turned all the way to high. Carefully, and without much hope, I laid two hamburgers on the grill and took the rest inside to fry. Ten minutes later I found that the two grilling burgers hadn't even gotten warm. A rare grilling lesson: liquid propane (LP) remains in the L phase when it's -40°.

The moose seem to get restless at these low temperatures, too. Sightings go up dramatically, at home and on campus. Nobody knows what brings them out of the denser woods to hang around people and buildings. The chickadees come in to the feeder as usual, tail feathers bent from roosting in small holes, but their movements are a little sludgy, and they tend to hop back and forth from one foot to the other when perched on metal. The red squirrel is conspicuously absent, choosing to estivate[12] for a while. A lot of people wish they could just sleep through it also. Down at the airport we can hear jets "idling," because all too often those who shut their engines down can't get them going again once they've cooled. Small aircraft mostly give up and wait it out. Creative solutions to heating things keeps the fire department busy. Some people have actually started small fires under their vehicles to warm them up—and watched them go up in flames when the lubricants really loosened up. We learned the hard way last week that it's a boom time of year for furnace repairmen, too. An important water flow valve in our heating system chose a night of -40° to fail; we were lucky to get someone out before any pipes froze.

As of my writing, there was no letup predicted; in fact, lows of -50° F and below hit. But that gives us more opportunities for observation. They say that if you throw a cup of boiling water (100° C, 212° F) out horizontally at -40° that it will hiss and fall in frozen droplets. Well, somewhat skeptical, at -40° I conducted an experiment: At 98.6° F, water thrown in a more natural manner (i.e., as urine) hits the snow in liquid form. Always glad to use scientific methods to resolve these burning issues!

---

12. Estivation is a state of dormancy often used by species that do not hibernate so that they can sleep away periods of environmental extremes, when being active is simply too costly. It is a state of torpor in which metabolism is slowed to decrease energetic costs, the better to wait out—in this case—extreme cold.

9

Changing the Channel — Going South

BELOW-ZERO TEMPERATURES ARE the winter norm here in Alaska, and they are nothing to get worked up about. But the spring semester can bring with it a pace so frenetic that seventy- to eighty-hour workweeks do nothing to dent the massive and growing piles. Whoever thought of spring break should be recognized by declaring the Monday after it a national holiday in his or her honor. At least that way I would only have missed one lecture . . .

Studying Neotropical birds in addition to Nearctic birds requires travel, and when you're coming from Alaska it's a long way to go to hit tropical rainforest. But I've been doing this long enough that the varied inconveniences of having distant field sites are just part of the job. This year I was worried about being able to sample the nonbreeding bird community in southern Belize before spring migration began. Our spring break offered the last opportunity to do so, and I took it. Lecture on 8 March was fifteen minutes shorter than usual, and I went straight from there to the airport. Wednesday's class session was the midterm, administered by Garth Spellman, my teaching assistant. During the midterm I was in Belmopan, the capital of Belize, working on getting a scientific research and collecting permit. That was after more than twenty-four hours of airplane and airport travel: Anchorage, Los Angeles, Houston, Belize City, and then a bus trip to Belmopan. In Houston, I saw the first green landscape I'd laid eyes on since things froze up in Fairbanks last October. In Belize it was green and hot. It had been -15° F when I left Fairbanks. Standing outside in sandals and shorts in +90° F temperatures was a distinct change.

The permit people in Belmopan received my proposal well before my arrival, and the only delay in issuing a permit for my study came from a general power outage. The next morning I boarded the 7:00 bus to Punta Gorda for the approximately seven-hour trip to the southern end of the country. The first part of the journey is pleasant, with good scenery and a pleasant breeze as the bus pokes along, picking people up and dropping them off wherever they choose to be. South of Dangriga (Stann Creek), however, the "Southern Highway" is a two-lane dirt road that simply must be endured.

The last time I'd taken this bus was truly one of the Rides from Hell. It was the Christmas season of 1997, and a lot of people were traveling. I had to transfer buses at Dangriga amidst tremendous confusion. It had been no trouble to get my gear aboard the correct bus through the rear emergency exit door, but the conductor told me at the front door that I had to go inside the depot and get a seat number on my ticket, which I'd purchased up in Belmopan. There was a long line inside the terminal, and after getting through it and stopping hastily in the bathroom, I found that the bus had already left—with all my stuff on it. And it was the last bus of the day headed all the way to Punta Gorda. Everyone in Belize is a nice, helpful person, and a guy who'd helped me load my stuff and steer me to the right line in the terminal saw me looking for a bus that wasn't there. He asked me where my bus was in a tone that left no room for doubt that I was a serious inconvenience, but then he cheerfully went and found the keys to a small pickup truck out back. We piled in and raced after the bus, catching up with it about six miles out of town. Despite the ensuing bus ride, I still consider the generous tip that I gave this guy to be some of the best money I ever spent. But that's probably because being reunited with irreplaceable field gear lingers on in the glowing memory bin far longer than the aroma of fresh vomit. But I get ahead of myself.

The bus fleet of Belize seems to be sustained entirely by used school buses from the United States. They just don't make these things for adult-sized people. It is physically impossible for me to sit in a normal position in these seats. After recently spending so many hours in airplane seats, I recognize that it is this seat spacing model that airplane manufacturers are working so successfully to emulate. But spending about seven hours in a seat that's far too small is just a little piece of this school bus experience. To my delight, the bus we caught up with was not full, and I had a whole small seat to myself. Sitting sideways for leg space, I enjoyed the breeze from the open windows as we raced down the washboard dirt road at a pace guaranteed to shake apart even the best US bus-building craftsmanship. At least that's what my hindquarters suggested.

There was a fifteen-minute rest stop in International Village at the Café and Hotel Hello, and when we pulled up hours later we saw that due to the heavy traffic of the season the bus line had sent two buses on the route instead of the usual one. As we had our Cokes and small snacks in the tropical night, rumors were flying that the drivers were considering sending just one bus the rest of the way to Punta Gorda. Our reasoning that there were simply too many people to do this was apparently not the same reasoning followed by the drivers—for when our fifteen minutes were up, there was a mad scramble as people on "their" bus tried to regain their seats; and people on "our" bus tried to get themselves and all their stuff aboard "their" bus.

Now that was a full bus. The aisles were packed with as many people standing as there were sitting. In the spirit of the season, there was a lot of joviality as we pulled back out onto the dirt road for the final three hours of the trip. We were soon racing, weaving, bouncing, and rattling down the road; and with the cabin lights on, it was not too difficult to carry on a loud conversation. But then the driver turned off the interior lights. The joviality went off as quickly. It was very dark, and we were pitching around like a shaken can of living human sardines. It was also hot—too many windows had been put up because people didn't want their hair ruffled. Or it might have been because the cool breeze coming through the windows also bears an amazing load of coarse, gritty road dust. Anyway, in this shaking, hot can of humanity, someone barfed. And during the next hour you could smell it rolling up and down the pitching deck. After that first hour its importance dwindled as other sensory input took precedence. You noticed by severe cramps in lower leg muscles that it really was important to try to stand on your toes to help absorb some of the rattling road shock. And you noticed that the schoolchildren of the US and the engineers that build buses for them have no concept of adult height and just how important it is to have hard metal ceilings placed well above nostril level on a hunched-up, standing, and frequently airborne adult male. What a ride.

I've done that same trip three more times now; and, in contrast, each one has been infinitely more pleasant. The seats are still too small, and the dust is still thick, but to my relief I haven't seen a bus packed so full since that first unpleasant ride. This year I arrived at the end of the seven-hour journey in midafternoon. I was dropped off at the end of a nondescript road just north of Big Falls—the road in to Mr. Don Owen-Lewis's "Missouri Farms." My 150 pounds of gear didn't seem all that heavy as I carried it the mile in to Mr. Owen-Lewis's place in the ninety-degree heat. The sweet scent of abundant orange blossoms in the surrounding groves was energizing, and it was good to be back. Since I'd left fourteen months ago, I'd thought often about the place. Here I'd experienced the highest winter capture rates that I'd ever seen, and I was looking forward to seeing whether these conditions were maintained right up until spring migration began. It is a tremendous pleasure to work in a very dense and diverse nonbreeding bird community. That was why I was back.

Don Owen-Lewis is a British expatriate who came to British Honduras in the 1950s to work as the Kekchi Maya Indian agent in Toledo District. He stayed on to become a farmer when Belize gained its independence from Britain. His farm, which now produces oranges mainly, provides a diverse array of habitat types, including primary rainforest, which is the source of the abundance and diversity of the birds I had so much enjoyed sampling last time. Don's home sits in the middle of an orange grove,

Figure 9.1. Don Owen-Lewis on the front porch of his home on Missouri Farms, Toledo District, Belize, Central America.

and it's a model of independence. His roof collects all of his water, and his limited power needs are delivered by solar panels out back. In the evenings he talks with friends all over the world via ham radio. His farm animals consist of chickens, turkeys, and guinea fowl.

One needs a reminder once in awhile of just how successful we've been in breeding intelligence out of farm animals. Don's confused rooster who crowed at 4:00 a.m.—long before daylight—was a daily reminder. But even better was his duo of amorous tom turkeys. When I first stood still in the yard with my boots on, these boys slowly got themselves pumped up and began displaying toward me—or rather my boots. And then, without any say-so on my part, one of my boots (it was the left) suddenly gave the impression of a submissive female turkey, and boom—one of the toms was having his way with it. I shook him off in surprise, and thought I'd better be more careful about what boots I wore. But later I saw one of the boys leap in and give Don's shoes the same business. Domestic turkeys are dirt stupid.

My visit coincided with a spell of idyllic weather. Moderate heat, tolerable humidity, but, importantly, light breezes and sun predominated during my stay. When your days in the field are tightly limited by commitments back home, having perfect weather helps enormously. Each morning I got up and out at dawn, picking a couple of perfect juice oranges for lunch and hiking on down to the "bush" (rainforest) to open nets. Capture rates were just about as high as they'd been over a year before in December and January, which was a pleasant surprise. There was no sign of migration, nor were there the cold, wet weather systems that I thought had had some positive effect on last year's capture rates. Thus, despite the lateness of the season and the very pleasant weather (which usually keeps capture rates down), I was kept very busy every day from dawn to dark. A kaleidoscope of birds passed through the nets and my hands, and it was easy to lose track of time with the bustle and wonder of it all. On one of the hot days when it got up to around 95° F, I remarked about how cool it was when

I got back to Don's house in the evening. When I saw on the porch weather dials that it was 88°F with 87 percent humidity, I realized I'd become truly acclimated. The next day, when the thought crossed my mind, I found it difficult to even imagine snow.

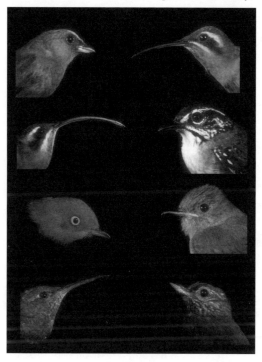

One day I had the rare privilege of watching a Black-faced Antthrush feed in the leaf litter at very close range. I'd heard the rustling on more than one occasion, but hadn't had the good fortune to get close enough to obtain a good look at this robin-sized bird of the dark forest floor. It walked very purposefully, a master of its small world, tail cocked and head thrust forward like a gallinule. It vigorously threw leaves from side to side—they really flew. In a couple of places the

Figure 9.2. Portraits of some of the important birds in the Belize study, from top to bottom (left column): Olive-backed Euphonia (Euphonia gouldi), *Long-billed Hermit* (Phaethornis longirostris), *Red-capped Manakin* (Pipra mentalis), *Rufous-tailed Hummingbird* (Amazilia tzacatl); *(right column) Stripe-throated Hermit* (Phaethornis striigularis), *White-breasted Wood-Wren* (Henicorhina leucosticta), *Ochre-bellied Flycatcher* (Mionectes oleagineus), *and Wedge-billed Woodcreeper* (Glyphorynchus spirurus).

bird burrowed itself well into the leaves to a depth of half its height, and it was clearly catching things that were too slow. This is a bird that walks boldly into the fray and takes no prisoners.

As each day in paradise rolled by I was treated to other wonderful birds, both old friends and new ones: truly Neotropical birds like the Ivory-billed Woodcreeper, Bare-faced Antthrush, White-necked Jacobin, American Pygmy Kingfisher, White-collared Manakin, and Stripe-throated Hermit; and wintering migrants like the Worm-eating Warbler, Gray Catbird, Wood Thrush, Orchard Oriole, and Kentucky and Hooded warblers. These nonbreeding bird communities are endlessly fascinating. I was pleased to find no evidence yet of migration, even though a couple of the residents were already beginning to nest. The days flew by.

Norm Koenig, from Cleveland, Ohio, was down visiting southern Belize, and also staying with Don. Keith and Rebecca, two graduate students in archaeology working with Peter Dunham on a site in the Maya Mountains, were staying in the nearby archaeology camp. Each evening seemed to bring together a different combination of us in Don's kitchen for dinner and highly varied conversation. Don and Norm are connoisseurs of the pressure cooker. Both bachelors, this implement straight from a medieval torture chamber or a terrorist's lab enables them to quickly whip up their gourmet bachelor's meals. "Ten minutes!," they each exclaimed in rapture. It does seem to work as advertised; the lentils were mush after the allotted time. One night Don had a party for family and friends in his kitchen. Everyone brought something to the feast. Don brought out the smoked salmon that I'd brought for him from Alaska, and conversation turned naturally to that distant land. Young Richie, Don's grandson, asked me how big grizzly bears are. Before I could answer intelligently, Don answered, "Bigger than a tapir," to help him visualize it. A very meaningful, but to me incongruous, comparison.

My work went better than I imagined it could have, and after eight long, hard days I was ready for a break. So when Norm formed a small group to go out to the cays for a day, I was happy to go along. We all met down in Punta Gorda and went out with Jackie Young, son of Wallace Young, in a boat named "Permit." Jackie's father, Wallace, bade us good day as he and Jackie went down to launch the boat. Apparently, back last century after the Civil War, a group of Confederates moved down to Toledo District. Wallace is the last descendant of this group, and he speaks with a basically American accent. Jackie, his son, speaks a creole that requires concentration to understand. As we held onto the crumbling pier, waiting for everyone and everything to get aboard, my natural history skills were tested by some scat that had been deposited near a crack in the concrete. My hand was right beside it, so the question was more than academic. It had been washed by rain, it seemed, which raised the challenge level a little, but the telltale sign turned out not to be the scat itself, but rather something beside it. It was no challenge at all, really: only one animal would have left what were now the weathered remnants of toilet paper there.

Although it hadn't rained at all while I'd been netting, we set out to sea toward a black horizon, and soon we were motoring along in a heavy downpour. It showed no sign of letting up, so when we got to a turquoise blue bay off of a small cay, into the water we went. It felt a lot warmer in the water, at least for the first half hour, and snorkeling showed that the coral formations hosted a dozen or more species of interesting fish. When we climbed back into the boat, Jackie headed out to Snake Cay, where we planned to eat lunch. The rain stopped and it became moderately warm again by the time we reached the cay. This was very welcome; everyone was dressed for a sunny day. I was the only one who'd brought a raincoat, and it leaked. This cay had seen some private development; there were two defunct homes. And, judging from the historic bottles lying near one of these abandoned buildings, this cay had been used for recreation for at least a century. Explorations had to wait a bit, though. The many empty conch shells lying along the beach

Figure 9.3. Strangler fig, Toledo District, Belize, Central America.

demanded assessment for souvenir potential, and there were a lot of scampering hermit crabs that had to be played with. It was a long way from Alaska, teaching, and even the rainforest understory.

Shortly thereafter I found myself back in Belmopan, getting a specimen export permit; and a short bus ride after that I was back in Belize City, waiting for an airplane. Imagine my surprise at crossing paths with Bob Dickerman in the airport. The waiting went by quickly with good conversation and a few beers. Getting a flight back to Alaska right after spring break had been difficult, and as a consequence I wasn't able to get back until Wednesday afternoon. When I got back to Fairbanks, spring had arrived before me. I'd left an icebox but returned to rapidly melting snow and long, bright days. Belize and tropical birds rapidly faded into the background as the barrage of a shrinking semester reached a crescendo and segued into the busiest field season yet planned.

10

Adak—Birthplace of the Winds

DURING MAY, MILLIONS OF BIRDS are migrating to Alaska and eastern Asia to breed. The Aleutian Islands offer a unique base from which to monitor and sample this migration. These islands also host their own diverse avifauna, and it was to sample both the migrants and the residents that I went to Adak.

This is an island with a long history. Occupied by the Aleuts for thousands of years, and predominantly by Western peoples since World War II, Adak possesses an untold story that would make fascinating reading. I am only a transient, though, and so can give just a fleeting account of the island from the perspective of someone interested primarily in its birds.

Adak is centrally located in the Aleutian archipelago, and the settlement there—the town of Adak—is the southernmost in Alaska. The island is a convenient Aleutian destination, because there are still regular commercial flights in and out (twice weekly), unlike the great majority of Aleutian islands, where access is much more limited. This access does not come cheaply, though. At this time, Reeve Aleutian Airways is the only game in town, and travel to remote locations in Alaska is generally expensive. My ticket from Fairbanks, including the Fairbanks–Anchorage leg on Alaska Airlines, was an astonishing $1,200. For a few hundred dollars more I could have gone to Johannesburg. Working in the Aleutians is as or more expensive than it would be for me to work in any developing country—even when I am based in the same state as these islands. To my knowledge, there is no other state where scheduled in-state air service reaches such international-scale proportions. But there is no other state with such geographic diversity. I went from a fine spring in Fairbanks to the dying gasp of an Aleutian winter. But the birds were doing their thing. The resident Song Sparrows were hatching while I was there, and the migrants were migrating, singing, and displaying.

Most of Alaska operates in the same overstretched time zone, but in the Aleutians some sense prevailed and folks decided to set their watches back an hour, putting the region in the Aleutian/Hawaiian time zone. But the north Pacific and Bering Sea give no Hawaiian illusions. Ambient temperatures during my visit tended to be in the thirties and forties Fahrenheit, usually with wind and often with rain as well. Snow still covered the highlands and was present to low elevations.

The Aleutian Ridge, whose peaks are the islands, was formed through volcanism, and there are a number of active volcanoes in the range—it is part of the Pacific Ring of Fire. Our flight to Adak went by an active volcano after leaving Cold Bay, but I was unable to see it due to cloud cover. Earthquakes are also common among these islands.

The US Navy maintained a very strong presence on Adak from World War II until just a few years ago, when the Naval Station on Adak was shut down. Although the Navy is essentially gone, final closure of the base has been extended on a year-by-year basis for the past few years. On the ground, the change has been profound. From the sixth- or seventh-largest town in Alaska, Adak's human population has dropped an order of magnitude to about 500–600 people in summer. When I arrived, I estimated that 10 percent or more of this diminished populace was in the small airport, either leaving or greeting new arrivals. There were about thirty-five people aboard the Reeve 727 that brought us out, which is a surprising number of passengers given a twice-weekly flight schedule to such a small, end-of-the-line destination. But there is a lot of cleanup activity going on here. Apparently, fifteen million dollars has been budgeted for the naval station cleanup. There is a crew of sixty or more doing asbestos abatement on one of the housing divisions being demolished, and there is another crew removing landmines and other unexploded ordnance (UXO) from portions of the island. Also, a group of people on this flight appeared to be Southeast Asians coming to work at the island's fish processing plant.

By the looks of the now mostly empty houses, naval housing on Adak was pretty nice. The attached solarium concept was used extensively in the newer housing, which seems a great idea for a gray, northern location. One truly Aleutian feature is the wind guard placed on the windows. These guards allow a window to be opened outwards without exposing it to the chance of being ripped off or damaged in strong winds. The doors on the vehicles have been reinforced with strapping to prevent them from blowing open too far and bending backward. These precautions are fully warranted. The nostalgic descriptor for Adak as "Birthplace of the Winds" doesn't do justice to the fact that these winds can be born as raging, screaming monsters. Last March, just after an earthquake that registered 6.8, a storm blew for nearly two days with sustained winds of 120 mph and gusts to 160 mph. By all accounts it was one hell of a storm. Included in the fun was a four-day period without power, which meant no heat as well. During my stay, however, there were no winds over 30 mph.

The human atmosphere here is one of a grossly underpopulated small town. Residential streets are empty of people and traffic; children's swings and playgrounds lie still; and everyone waves when passing on roads or sidewalks. It's all very friendly, but it almost seems as though people are reassuring themselves and each other that the ghosts of this ghost town are being held at bay. Since the closure of the base, food is available on Adak either through purchase at the store, open at limited times, or at mealtimes in the high-school cafeteria for eleven dollars per meal. Some people airfreight their food in and cook in their homes. As a transient, I often ate dinner in the cafeteria, getting by with granola in the field during the day and when it was inconvenient to get back for dinner.

Eating in the cafeteria is like being part of a large family. To my surprise, the "clean up and shut down" status of the island has not resulted in just a skeleton crew of men being present. While there is a strong male bias, women and children are common; many families have come here for the cleanup work. A substantial number of people on the cleanup crews are from the Pribilof Islands. Conversations at the long tables are quirky and perfectly ordinary, ranging from the price of land in Las Vegas to working crab boats in the Bering Sea. The people working on the asbestos abatement crews have a grueling job. They wear Tyvek suits and respirators all day long and work six-day, sixty-hour weeks. They're well paid for it; they make more per hour than I do (why again did I spend all those years in school?). But I still wouldn't trade places. I'm having more fun. Same with crabbing in the Bering Sea: one guy made $15,000 in a month of work as a crew member on a crab boat last year (working twenty-hour days), and he'll take time out from asbestos abatement to do it again later this summer. The Bering Sea crab fishery is one of the most dangerous jobs in the world, though, with a remarkably high fatality rate. Together, bad weather, freezing waters, brutally hard work, and fatigue put a steady stream of human bodies into the Bering Sea.

Shortly after arrival on the island, I had to go through an orientation briefing—a half-hour, double-video education on the perils of walking the hinterlands of Adak. This briefing is required if one intends to be on the island for more than one week and/or to go off of the road system. Following the briefing, one is issued a "blue card" that must be presented upon request. This is an entirely new permit in my experience. The main focus of the briefing is unexploded ordnance (UXO). Judging from the videos, UXO is everywhere, ready to spoil your day. It is a little difficult to take fifty-year-old landmines seriously in this wet climate, however, and I must admit that I was not impressed by the videos. Near the end of my stay, though, I had the chance to see the UXO display near the post office, and the physical presentation of perfectly functional, fifty-year-old antipersonnel mines had a much stronger effect, especially when I realized that I had actually been in an old minefield.

This wasn't my first time. That had occurred on the Falklands in 1990, when youth, churning tidewater, and really neat birds made it a simple decision to casually cross into a fenced-off minefield. This time on Adak, however, I was a little less informed—or perhaps a little less serious about the signals. There are signs over much of the island stating that, when hiking, you venture off of the trails at your own risk. Well, I never hiked where I saw any trails, and the thought of corroded, fifty-year-old explosives didn't slow me down. I didn't know it at the time, but the rusty old sharp fenceposts that I had used as handholds to get up a very steep seaside bluff (twice)—and the very short sharp ones that I had to avoid putting my feet on—were Rommel stakes: remnants of a Rommel Line of posts, barbed wire (still evident), and landmines. I would have been far more careful if instead of the videos they'd shown me the display that the de-mining crew had put together showing some of the ugly things they'd found. After fifty-plus years in the ground, many of these mines are still ready to go. I'm glad I didn't meet one.

*Figure 10.1. Old World War II-era Quonset hut buried in heath,
Adak Island, Aleutian Islands, Alaska.*

When walking across the tundra-like heath, you often encounter a stovepipe emerging from nowhere. As often as not, you've stumbled onto a buried WWII-era Quonset hut, whose entrance is a steep hole in the ground that is not evident until you're up close. A number of these huts and more traditional cabinlike structures were maintained through the years as cabins for recreational use by individual Navy personnel. Consequently, there are a lot more WWII-era structures still standing on Adak than there are on Attu, where winds and a much smaller human presence have taken their toll during the past half century. It was several days before I stopped at the small graveyard beyond the north side of town beside the tiny grove of conifers named Adak National Forest. I was surprised to find that it was a pet cemetery, with crosses and plaques in remembrance mostly of family dogs, but also a few cats. As far as I could tell, no humans have been buried on the island in the past fifty years.

In 1998 the Aleut Corporation began making a serious effort to privatize the Port of Adak and make it into a viable civilian town and enterprise (see www.adakisland.com). The Navy has left an excellent infrastructure, which it is natural to try to use in some way. But rumor has it that it costs a million dollars per month to run the power plant alone, and it has yet to be demonstrated that a local economy could support this level of sustained infrastructural cost. There is a fish processing plant on the island. I saw them hauling in crates full of beautiful halibut from vessels at the dock, but the local fishery is not yet operating at a very large scale. At present, humanity exists on the island under a one-year grace period from the federal government, associated more with cleanup than anything else. The future becomes uncertain again this fall. A proposal came out of the state government in Juneau to resettle some of the Kosovo refugees on Adak. While it is true that there is a lot of quality housing out here, standing empty, people from a landlocked, temperate, agrarian society would receive a very rude shock if transferred to this remote, treeless island in an arctic environment.[13] Some Westerners really like it out here, but others hate it and can't wait to get back to the "real world."

The natural history of the island is every bit as fascinating as the human history. Clam Lagoon, for example, hosts the highest density of sea otters I've seen. On most days at low tide you can find small groups of them hauled out onto land at the water's edge. They are not particularly shy, and

---

13. Arctic is used here in the sense of Congress and the National Science Foundation, not in the strict geographic sense. Strictly speaking, the Arctic consists of the area of the globe north of the Arctic Circle at 66° 33′ North latitude. Arctic habitats occur well south of that geographic line, however; so agencies such as the National Science Foundation recognize the Arctic as, essentially, the distribution of Arctic-like habitats. In Alaska, this distribution roughly follows tree line, and so it includes much of western Alaska and the Aleutian Islands, which lie well south of the Arctic Circle.

you can approach to within twenty to thirty meters before they slowly get back in the water and swim to a safer distance (the road frequently passes so close that such approaches are inevitable). Mothers grab their pups by the scruff of the neck and haul them in—and these are last year's pups, getting quite big. The pups ride on top, cradled in their mothers' arms.

I've never before had the chance to watch sea otters so closely. One thing that puzzles me is their propensity to swim on their backs with their front feet held together as though praying. I wonder if it might be an attempt to minimize heat loss through the palms. This water is bone-numbingly cold. You'd never guess how cold it was watching these animals go about their lives looking happy and carefree, lolling along on their backs, feeding on mollusks in the shallow waters. Apparently the Aleutian populations of this species have declined substantially in recent years. It is now thought that this may be due to prey switching by killer whales, which, due to large-scale declines in Steller's sea lion populations, are forced to

Figure 10.2. Clam Lagoon, Adak Island, Aleutian Islands, Alaska.

feed on alternative food sources. This has to be tough on killer whales, too: for me it would be like going from salmon to guppies.

One of the birds I'd come to meet was the Pacific Wren. They are resident here, and they reach a size about half again as large as their migratory mainland relatives. In the absence of trees they occupy cliffs, making them difficult to obtain. I'd brought a tape of the species' song to play and thus draw in territorial males, but it didn't work very well. I stumbled along the rocky bases of these seaside cliffs at low tide and played the tape, and territorial males came out and sat at the very tops of the cliffs, hundreds of feet above me, singing cheerily. I had the same problem last year on the Queen Charlotte Islands in old-growth forest, where they'd sit singing on the highest available perch—the tops of old-growth conifers. Here on Adak, my only chance was to climb the cliffs and go after them, which I did. It was generally tough going. Once up there, I found myself stalking shy birds along the cliff edges. At moments it was fun working the cliff tops; I was often playing the tape from within the decaying remnants of World War II cliff-top lookout posts. But one day I went up and down the damned cliffs eight times chasing just two lousy birds. The tape I was carrying also had the Gray-crowned Rosy Finch's simple song on it, and I found that these birds were almost pests in their zealousness to find and drive away this artificial intruder.

There are two things to keep in mind when working cliffs. One is your sense of balance, which can be messed up both by watching birds and by winds that can eddy, wax, and wane suddenly and dramatically. The other thing to keep in focus is the friability and generally unstable nature of the substrate. I've found that climbing cliffs with a shotgun and pack is always entertaining, but that retrieving birds collected on cliffs reaches the proportions of a refined sport. And I was reminded that one should probably practice this sport in pairs for safety—although even in pairs I recall that safety is not always foremost in consideration. But that's another story that John Klicka could tell as well as I.

After a long, knobbly hike along a boulder beach one day, I reached an abrupt headland that prevented further progress. I hadn't obtained any birds for the tiring foot-bruising, but as I stood there contemplating the end of the beach, three remarkable birds came along feeding in the nearshore waters. I'd been waiting a long time to see this species, which bears my favorite scientific name: *Synthliboramphus antiquus*—the Ancient Murrelet. I was forced to laugh while I watched them feeding, merrily diving and resurfacing as they progressed around the headland. The next day I stood on the shore of the harbor in Kuluk Bay and watched two gray whales sporting about amidst more than a hundred Ancient Murrelets. And the day after that I found the legendary Smew, an Old World duck that is a rare migrant in the western Aleutians. This female was very skittery, though, and I had only a short look before she flew off. Nevertheless, seeing two such remarkable birds more than made up for the season's slow migration.

Aleutian Terns arrived back on the island during my stay. But despite long days pounding the accessible areas, I encountered few Old World migrants. This just wasn't a good year for them on Adak, due mostly to a lack of westerly winds, unlike last year—a rare one—in which hundreds of usually scarce Old World migrants had appeared. I did get to see a Wood Sandpiper, though, and a flock of Whimbrels of the Old World flavor (*Numenius phaeopus variegatus*), but no unusual passerines or other shorebirds.

Glaucous-winged Gulls are a trash bird here. One quickly puts *Larus* gulls out of one's mind when there is anything even marginally more interesting around, but on this trip these birds caught my attention twice. Once was when I was going through a cloudy pass with a cold, wet wind urging me on. As the moving clouds thinned for a moment, I caught a brief glimpse of a head-to-tail row of about a dozen gulls standing strung out on a snow field just above me. Perhaps it was because the wind was so cold, but it seemed strange that they would choose to stand on snow when snow-free tundra was so close at hand. Who knows, perhaps if one is a gull, cold feet aid the digestion of beach-washed spooge. Several days later in the same pass, this species gave me a surprise. As I worked my way along, a flock did a slow retreat in front of me. All of a sudden as the back of the flock lifted off to move to the front, an all-white gull was standing right there in front of me. This is a time to shoot first and ask questions later—all-white gulls shouldn't be here. It turned out to be an almost completely albinistic subadult (second- or third-year) Glaucous-winged Gull.

Bald Eagles are also dirt common on Adak. Perhaps this is why the door exiting the high school cafeteria is posted with what must be a unique sign, stating that "Several people have recently been attacked by eagles as they left the cafeteria with food in their hands . . ."

Lapland Longspurs were just completing their long Aleutian migration while I was there, and the tundra was covered with singing males. Rock Sandpipers were scarce, but I found a few here and there. They were beginning to defend territories on the high heath as it became snow free, and I occasionally heard a male's song drifting down on the wind. Shorebird songs and displays, given only on the breeding grounds, were a wonderful surprise to me upon first coming to Alaska. Away from their breeding areas shorebirds are quiet, rather unobtrusive birds. But on their tundra territories, they become fascinating creatures in their displays and songs, completely dominating the local avifauna with their presence. So many birds. So little time.

Some of the other everyday sounds out here included the loud croaking of displaying Rock Ptarmigan, the mewling of sea otters, and the pleasant popping sound made by walking on the flotation bladders of intertidal seaweeds. The latter seems like walking on slippery bubble wrap.

Aleutian weather is typically cloudy, windy, and wet. And the cloud cover is generally low, so the local mountaintops and neighboring islands are invisible more often than not. But we did get one full day and another partial day during my visit when the sun was out much of the time, and the regional scenery was in its full spring glory. Adak is a beautiful island. Its beaches are strikingly clean, and it has an often rugged three-dimensionality. On this day, Mt. Moffet, the island's volcanic peak, shone down brightly on us few humans scurrying about on our business below. And the majestic, snowy peak of neighboring Great Sitkin Island reared out of the sea like

Figure 10.3. Great Sitkin Island appears beyond Adak Island, Aleutian Islands, Alaska.

some artistic beacon. It's easy to see how the full Aleutian chain became settled many thousands of years ago. If I had a kayak and some free time I know I'd be in the water, paddling over to the next island to see what was there.

Vernon Byrd, of the Alaska Maritime National Wildlife Refuge (AMNWR, headquartered in Homer), says that Jeff Williams has the best job in the world. Jeff has been the biologist on Adak for nine years, directly responsible for the Aleutian Islands Unit of the AMNWR. Comprising 200 islands and spanning over a thousand miles, this is a marvelous portion of an amazing National Wildlife Refuge. Between them, Vern and Jeff have covered the birds of the Aleutians for the refuge for most of the past three decades. It is a lot of fun working with these guys, although both are so busy during the season that it's tough to get much time with them. We're hoping to put together an effort next year that will throw us all together on board the refuge's vessel *Tiglax* (Aleut for eagle), with Kevin Bell, one of the most enthusiastic men in the north Pacific (and a keen seabird watcher), and captain of *Tiglax*.[14]

One of the twice-weekly flights scheduled to arrive while I was on Adak wound up coming in a day late. Upon arrival, Steve Ebbert, who I had never met before, had a message for me. It was bad news from Attu: our research trip scheduled to go there in mid-to-late June had run into a serious snag. There was no way off of the island, and there were no available accommodations for the two people we'd already booked to send there. This was a real kick in the head for an important endeavor, but after a long talk via satellite with the commanding officer of the Coast Guard LORAN station on Attu (with noticeable satellite delay), the problem was indeed

---

14. This project proposal, submitted twice, was rejected both times, so we continued working with Vern, Jeff, and Kevin on a catch-as-catch-can basis as funds permitted. Kevin Bell has unfortunately died in the interim, and Vern has now retired.

unresolvable. I had to begin making alternate plans for our two intrepid travelers. The logistics had been compromised by a construction project—apparently due in part to the March storm damage. To make contingency plans, I had to get back on the phone and speak via satellite to Dan Gibson on another Aleutian island—Shemya, over 400 miles away to the west, and right next to Attu. Dan was having a better migration than I was, with species such as Black-backed Wagtail, Common Pochard, and Rustic Bunting making appearances.

Reeve's delays played hob with the *Tiglax* schedule, especially when the mate was bumped from Tuesday night's delayed flight from Anchorage because it had been overbooked. As a consequence, the *Tiglax* crew had to pull a couple of days' worth of work from farther along in their schedule and work locally instead of heading off to Buldir and Attu. Unfortunately, it was during this local work that they accidentally struck a rock and damaged the vessel. Dan Erickson, the deck hand who dived on the vessel to examine the damage (who, incidentally, had been bumped from Tuesday's return flight due to overbooking), found a hole in the bow large enough to crawl into and also learned that the left rudder had been torn off completely. This was bad news for a ship with a tight schedule and whose movements affected a large number of people. The domino effect was immediate and painful. Ian Jones and his group from Memorial University in Newfoundland had no way to get out to Buldir, where they have been conducting long-term studies of auklets (*Aethia* spp.). And seven archaeologists waiting on Shemya for a ride to Attu had to find another way home instead.

Steve Ebbert, head of the Alaska Maritime National Wildlife Refuge's fox trapping efforts, was scrambling to figure out how to get Attu finished this season. *Tiglax*'s grounded schedule threw the year's efforts into jeopardy. Arctic foxes were introduced onto most Aleutian islands from Russian times well into the 1900s by enterprising trappers and businessmen. Fox populations grew quickly on the seabird-rich islands, and their pelts made these ventures well worthwhile. But, as a consequence, island-nesting birds took a real hit. The Aleutian Cackling Goose (*Branta hutchinsii leucopareia*) eventually became endangered, and, independently, the islands became a national wildlife refuge (in 1913). So the introduced foxes lost their desirability, and efforts have been made to eliminate them from thirty-five islands so far. Attu is the thirty-fifth, and it is a credit to these hardy trappers that they can be so successful on such large and rugged islands. There seems little doubt that regional seabird populations will see an increase in the near future.[15] The Aleutian Cackling Goose is doing so well on fox-free islands that it's becoming a bit of a runway pest on Shemya.

As everyone was working out the short-term future of *Tiglax* and its effects on their field efforts, I was winding up my visit. After cleaning up the bunkhouse, doing laundry, and spending a few more hours in the field, I was just waiting out the hours until the (again delayed) Reeve flight. About ten people had been bumped from the previous flight, so it seemed likely that some would be left behind again this time. Consequently, there were a lot of people there at check-in time, hours before the flight. This uncertainty about travel is the norm in the Aleutians, whether from weather or from mechanical problems. And it did not improve. Arrival of the flight was later than the scheduled delay.

Instead of the usual 727, they had sent the four-engine, turboprop Lockheed Electra on the route. This plane holds more passengers (much of the 727 passenger cabin is devoted to cargo), so nobody was left behind. Thus, when we finally got aboard and had our seatbelts buckled, people were in good spirits despite the half-day delay and the total loss of

---

15. And they did!

connecting flights in Anchorage. But as the flight attendant ran through emergency procedures, I noticed that the right inside engine was being shut off, rather than accelerating. We sat there for a while longer before the pilot announced that they were having trouble starting engine number three. He said, "We have a procedure for starting it, but this requires that all passengers and flight attendants deplane." It's the last time I'll count on flying somewhere when I'm sitting in my seat with the belt buckled. I, among others, wondered whether the mysterious procedure involved push-starting the damned thing. Inside a windowless room in the small airport, we listened to revving propellers as the plane raced up and down the runway using wind speed to air-start the recalcitrant engine. We could hear a difference when the craft eventually pulled back up to the airport—engine number three was running. Upon reboarding, I learned that the plane had been first commissioned in 1961. I guess it's no surprise that it needs a little boost now and then. Nobody chose to remain behind, and we were soon thrumming our way across the ocean toward Anchorage.

The plane landed in Anchorage shortly before 3:00 a.m. Bleary-eyed with on-flight reading and the late hour, I collected my bags on a cart and wheeled first for the Alaska Airlines counter (closed!), then for the nearest bathroom. But as I creaked along, I thought I saw—no it wasn't possible—but it seemed that—yes—walking toward me and the same bathroom at the same ungodly hour in Anchorage, Alaska, was Robert W. Dickerman, ornithologist. Amazing. The last time I'd seen him was in the airport in Belize! He remarked that he'd have to take notes on "Strange airports where I've met Kevin Winker," and we spent most of the next three hours exchanging tall tales while we waited for our respective flights to leave, he for Kodiak, and me for Fairbanks.

Back home, I found the house still intact, the plants still alive, the trees fully leafed out, and a Hammond's Flycatcher singing in the yard (Rose had been gone, too). The Aleutians are a remarkable archipelago, and these islands are a wonderful region to visit. But I have to admit that it's also a pleasure to return to tree country. Trees have a smell that you don't notice until it slaps you in the nose after you've been away for a while. And after a few days back in the woods, a Townsend's Warbler and Swainson's Thrush were also singing in the yard.

Among my backlogged hundreds of emails was a warning that the Anchorage airport had installed one of these new super x-ray machines to keep our skies safe and our film ruined. It remained an open question for some time as to whether the many Adak images I had taken were only to be lodged in the shifting sands of my memory.

11
Copper River Reds

IT WAS HIGH SUMMER here in Fairbanks, with twenty-four hours of daylight and idyllic weather—light breezes, constant sun, and temperatures in the seventies. June here is noteworthy for this incredible climate. But this year, for me, it had raced by in a sucking morass of what seemed to be largely proposal deadlines, funding snafus, and other crapola that is difficult enough to face when Alaska isn't just out the window, beckoning so seductively. To be fair, June hadn't been all bad, but neither had it involved stomping around neat places looking for birds that hadn't met me yet. Instead, I had to send emissaries. They carried out their scientific ambassadorial missions with distinction, and they had a good time doing it.

All I had to show for the month was one long string of words dripping from my fingertips onto various keyboards. Needed words, but not fun words; there is a big difference. So I was cranky. And it wasn't just the run of stimulating office work, either. Suffering from photostimulation can be a real drag here in the north. There seemed to be no time for sleep. Even in artificial darkness, the subconscious knows that, hey—it's light outside and you should be up doing things. The never-ending days can be incredibly productive, but sleep deprivation prevents one from deriving much cheer from that.

So when I went to get a fishing license and a Copper River Personal Use Fishery dip-net permit, I was really ready to get the hell out of the office and have some fun. Rose was, too. We had a great time fishing down there the previous year, and we had thoroughly enjoyed the proceeds since then. It was time to restock the freezer. This year's salmon run hadn't been very good so far, and there had been a series of closures of the fishery to ensure adequate escapement, but we were optimistic nonetheless. This year we got a second net to boost our chances (last year we took turns using a single net), and we set out on a Wednesday afternoon in hopes of catching the tail end of a slug of fish picked up by the Miles Lake sonar, down near the river's mouth, two weeks earlier. We've heard that it takes the fish about ten to fourteen days to get from the mouth of the river to Chitina, and we timed our effort to roughly hit the first decent bunch of fish detected.

The drive down to Chitina was stunning. The familiar Alaska Range grows closer and more striking as you follow the Richardson Highway down to Delta Junction. The road often skirts the shoreline of the blasted-looking, highly disorganized Tanana River. With its extensive open bars and drift-cast timber this isn't what one would normally describe as a beautiful river. In fact, it's pretty ugly on first sight. It's not like "real" rivers; it always looks like you arrived just after a huge flood ripped everything up. But after two years up here, the beauty of this type of river had time to sink in, and it was one of the impressive sights along this drive. South of Delta you climb smoothly up into the Alaska Range, driving among mountains and alpine tundra before just as smoothly descending again into lower elevations. The pipeline also follows this route, and it is a familiar sight along the Richardson Highway south of Delta.

Upon descending from the Alaska Range, the spectacular Wrangell Mountains to the southeast began to dominate the view. They were out in full splendor, and the spectacular scenery continued making the six-hour drive go very quickly. A gas stop in Glennallen barely broke our scenery watching. Soon enough we were in Chitina, poking just a little down the road to McCarthy and Kennicott to get a first look at the Copper River from above. A few scattered people were dip netting from the gravel bars. It became windy in the steep valley, and a light rain began to fall as we pointed our way down the narrow gravel road south of Chitina. For us, this road ended at the bottom of a steep incline at a small, windy campground squeezed into a small creek valley at the river's edge. For people with four-wheel-drive vehicles, the road continues on down the river, narrow and often very steep, mostly following an old railbed whose trestles are now just broken memories. As we chose a camping spot, we watched several vehicles attack the very steep climb up the southern side of the O'Brien Creek valley. During the netting season this traffic goes on twenty-four hours a day.

Two years before, my old tent took a real pounding in the strong Bering Sea winds on St. Matthew Island, and we only used it now for places that aren't windy. Its replacement was still new in the bag when we began to set up camp here. Thank goodness the rain stopped and we only had wind to contend with

Figure 11.1. People cleaning salmon at O'Brien Creek, Chitina, Copper River, Alaska.

as we opened up this new tent and tried to figure out what some weird tent-making genius had in mind in its design. Puzzles like this are a lot more fun when it's not late at night and windy. At least it was still light out, and the rain had stopped. Once we had the tent up and well staked out, with rocks piled on the tent pegs, I went down to the river to see how the day's activity had been. It was 11:00 p.m., and the sun was still out on the nearby mountaintops.

There were more people here than we'd seen last year, and there was a lot of netting and fish cleaning still going on. The day's run had been good. The most interesting netting was being executed by four people with Russian accents. In a place where the river was roaring by right next to the shore, two of them were standing up to their waists in the cold water and making long sweeps of their nets out into the maelstrom, dipping deeply to sweep the bottom. They were wearing neoprene chest waders and were well tied off to shore. It looked like what it was: cold, brutally hard work. The other two guys were minding the ropes, pulling the netters back when they lost their balance, and standing ready to take nets or fish when necessary. And they were resting up for their turns. On the bank lay an impressive catch of king salmon; they hadn't caught a single red salmon here, and they were just one king away from their limit (which is four each).

Back at camp we had a late dinner and then took a quick stroll back through the netters and fish cleaners. We watched one hardworking guy pull two reds out of the river as he swept the strong current. Despite the hour, seeing all those fish and active netters had our blood pumping. We were ready to go! But sleeping first was a priority, and this spot wasn't a particularly good one for netting. We finally went to bed at midnight, listening to the roar of the river, a Hermit Thrush trying to sing over it, and the occasional vehicle climbing up out of the little valley on the steep dirt road.

At 6:00 we got up and began packing up for the day's fishing. The charter boat operators were open at 7:00, and we were on the first boat out, with Sam McCallister. Most dip netting is done in Wood Canyon, where the mighty Copper River surges through a narrow area of steep cliffs and bluffs. Dip netters cling to accessible surfaces and hold nets in the raging current. On the west side of the river, the netter density is highest because the old dirt road allows access to that side. The east bank has no road access, however, and it is actually part of a wilderness area of Wrangell-Saint Elias National Park. The people fishing this side have to be dropped off by boat, and these are the places that are the predominant niche of the charter services. There are also good spots on the west bank that are only accessible by boat—we'd had one of those last year. O'Brien Creek is just north of Wood Canyon, and we roared off in Sam's boat downriver into the canyon with four other people. The water was fast, cold, and utterly opaque. The silt load was incredibly high, giving the surface a churned, gray-and-tan look. Sam made three drops; we were the last, being placed on the east bank at the base of the narrowest point of Wood Canyon.

As we pulled up to our spot, we found that there were two guys already there. We were a little confused—it didn't seem like a good place to put so many people. But it quickly became apparent that they were waiting for pickup. They'd been out all night, and it looked like both had gotten their limits of reds. This was a good spot. A small rock finger projected out from the bank to the edge of the fast water, and the small downriver embayment had a nice eddying backwash that kept a net billowing out upriver, perfectly opened to receive fish swimming upriver and taking advantage of a brief stretch of water flowing with, rather than against, them. Moreover, this finger of rock was comparatively flat—we didn't have to wedge ourselves into a crevice and cling to a steep bank all day. The forest even extended to the bank here.

We broke out the nets, extended the handles, and got them into the water. And so began the dumb luck part of the exercise. The river is a big one, and a thirty-two-inch net on an eight-foot handle is a decidedly puny instrument with which to filter the water for fish. And, because we couldn't see more than a millimeter into the water, we just had to feel the rocks and current and try to guess where to hold our nets so that fish bumbled into them.

As we sat there, waiting excitedly for the first bump of the net, the peacefulness of the area settled in. To the north, the snowfields of Mt. Wrangell reared majestically over the Wood Canyon scenery. To the south, the snowy peaks of Spirit Mountain played with a few clouds all day. We also happened to be on a Hermit Thrush territory. The male sang beautifully nearby all morning, and the female foraged past us periodically. Later in the morning an American Dipper came in close to inspect the quietest part of the shoreline, and a pair of red squirrels boldly inspected our stuff to see whether we had brought anything for them. An adult Bald Eagle hung out in a spruce about thirty meters away. We continued sitting on the increasingly hard rock, waiting for sunlight to warm the place up a little and for fish to strike our nets. The glacial meltwater component of the river must have been very high, for as the water swirled around our rock we could hear it effervescing with escaping gas. The bubbles must have been minute, because they weren't noticeable in the rushing water.

Eventually, the bumps began, and we started hauling in beautiful red salmon, wriggling mightily as we lifted them out of the water. We gave them a conk on the head with an oosik to stun them into slower movement so we could clip off the corners of the tail fin (a state legal requirement) and get them out of the net and onto a stringer. By the time they hit the water again they were usually very full of life; the stringer thrashed about in the water.

In the first four hours of netting we averaged about three fish per hour—not bad. But then it dropped off to about zero. One hour went by. Then two. There were a few bumps, but, frustratingly, no fish were getting into the nets. I figured that many must be cutting obliquely across the current and getting their heads briefly caught in the outside of the billowing nets. But the drop in catch also coincided with full sunlight striking our peaceful little spot on the river.

Well, it had been peaceful. Several boats were fishing in a different manner just below our spot. They'd roar up to within thirty meters of our position, put the boat crosswise to the current, then drift rapidly downriver with everyone but the driver hanging over the upriver side with a net held as deeply as they could get them. And they were still catching fish. Earlier, we had caught a couple of fish that looked like they had been hit by boat motor propellers. It seemed somewhat improbable, but the wounds were very fresh. These fish were a little unsightly, but still very vigorous and perfectly good for food, so we kept them. When things dropped off in the early afternoon, we were glad to have them. We later heard another theory—that these were fish that had escaped seal bites.

Periodically, brief breaks were necessary to allow for needed butt stretching, to have lunch, and to visit the woods for relief. In the woods I'd noticed that one of the overnighters had not had a pleasant gastrointestinal evening. Rose later stated succinctly, "It looks like someone had a medical condition."

Then, suddenly, a spurt of fish began at 2:15, and we caught ten beauties in the next hour—the best fish of the day—nice, big, silvery, lively fish that really lit up the afternoon. We'd noticed a similar pattern last year: a lull in midday with things picking up again later. It's a common pattern in birds, also. We were in sight of the household limit of thirty fish, but none were king salmon yet. I kept hoping for one, but we weren't in a king spot, apparently. Fortunately, the reds kept coming along, so by 4:45 Rose pulled in the last of them. As the day's fishing wound to a close, our arms were shaking with the protracted strain of keeping the nets straight in the water, and it was a real effort to pull them in to check each bump. And back strain? Wow. All worth it, though, when we looked at the long stringers of fish. Even breaking the oosik when a fish moved too fast and I hit the rock seemed a minor inconvenience. Although later, when I was reminded that an oosik of this quality with some Native art on it sells for $300, this particular inconvenience seemed a little larger (non-natives can't sell them). I'd picked this one up on a beach in western Alaska in 1990. Sadly, it won't be clubbing fish again.

While waiting for pickup, we began cleaning our fish, just gutting them and putting them back on the stringers to keep them cold in the river. Many were still alive, despite the hours of being tethered to the shore. We threw a lot of

Figure 11.2. Clients returning in Captain Sam McCallister's charter vessel from a successful day's dip-netting for salmon, Chitina, Copper River, Alaska.

the guts onto the rocks for the gathering gulls. Three species consumed them with gusto (Mew Gulls, Glaucous-winged Gulls, and Herring Gulls). It was amazing how much the adult Herring Gulls could hork down. By the time our ride arrived, we'd gutted all the fish and the local gulls were sated. On the way back upriver we picked up three guys who'd had a great day just above our position. They had caught several very large king salmon in addition to reds, and it was a lot of work to get their barrels of fish aboard. They were even more cheerful than we were.

The river's silt load is so high that fish on stringers get loaded with dirt; it especially plugs up the gills. Back at O'Brien Creek we thoroughly rinsed each fish before laying them in coolers, layered with ice we brought along. The coolers full of ice and fish were so heavy that we filled them in the truck so we didn't have to lift them. After this, we took the tent down, groaned with the building stiffness, and then set out for home. It was 8:00 p.m. A brief stop at Fritz's Alaska Deli in Chitina for hamburgers to go was the last stop before heading fast for the north. Hours later, we watched a spectacular, protracted red sunset as it sank obliquely into the Delta River valley just south of Delta Junction at about 11:15. In Delta, all the gas stations were closed, but, fortunately for our nearly empty tank, we found a pump that worked on a credit card. No ice was available until we reached Fairbanks. Bringing thirty salmon down to ice temperature used up a lot of what we'd brought, and we needed more to keep the fish cold for the rest of the night. So at 2:30 we found ourselves standing in line at the grocery store, buying ice and, as long as we were there, plastic bags to pack the fish in when they'd been cleaned. One would think that shopping at 2:30 a.m. would be fairly wait-free, but this was Fairbanks in summer: there was a lot of activity all night long. The radio advertised all night golf. It was beginning to get a little dusky, and we got a rare glimpse of the moon as we headed home.

We dropped into bed exhausted at 3:00 and slept all too little before getting up and cleaning the fish. Steaks, fillets, and even whole ones for grilling filled the freezer, and our muscles slowly began to feel normal again. Copper River reds were selling for $5.98 a pound in the grocery store ($3.98 a pound for whole fish), and it was satisfying to have a freezer full that we hauled in ourselves. They sure tasted good. On one hand, one could look at a trip like this (as some here in Fairbanks do) as driving a lot, sleeping a little, getting sand in your eyes from the wind, and working over a net until every muscle aches. On the other hand . . . well, I'm ready to go again!

12

A Cracking Good Life

WE AREN'T ALWAYS OUT on exciting Alaska adventures. For most of the year we just have to live and work like everyone else. Well, maybe not quite like everyone else. Being in Alaska is a little different from being in other places. Living just a hundred and fifty miles or so from the Arctic Circle can bring atypical experiences. And not just cold winter nights, either. There's an eclectic assortment of humanity, for example—enough to keep anyone entertained. Even before moving up here we could see from the newspapers sent in the mail (the *Fairbanks Daily News Miner*, nicknamed by some the *News Minus*, or the *Nose Miner*) that we were relocating to a different sort of place. The letters to the editor were particularly noteworthy for their oddity. It was explained to us that you get all kinds washing up at the end of the road. Too true (including us?). The quirkiness level does seem higher here than elsewhere. But at the same time, the tolerance level also seems pretty high, so, everything considered, it's a great town to live in, remote as it might be from elsewhere in the US.

Despite its remoteness, Fairbanks is not altogether bizarre—nor impoverished. Heck, there are even a couple of McDonald's in town. Or Taco Bells, if that's to your taste. And that's not the pinnacle of Fairbanks' social environment, by any means. For example, we may live in Fairbanks, but we can have Wensleydale cheese any day of the week. Anyone who's watched the Wallace and Grommit claymation movies knows that Wensleydale is "cracking good cheese." It does make a good omelet. And in a quirky, *Nose Miner* kind of way, its presence here shows that we're not just a bunch of pokes living out in the sticks in some boreal-forest backwater. Well, at least we like to think so.

But, like elsewhere, we sometimes seek a little diversion. In the lab, mindless music with a steady beat tends to be preferred over more sappy stuff. Preparing bird specimens goes a lot better with stimulating music. So when ZZ Top came to town, Rose and I had to go. It seemed like a great idea to see live what we'd heard so often on CD (well, at least I'd heard it often). And immediately afterwards, we went Outside for intensive visiting. It was fun, but when we got back ten days later, I think I'd spoken with about 400 people. It's always fun to visit, but it's also good to get back home.

A couple weeks ago, as it grew dark at the astonishingly early hour of 9:45 p.m. in a light rain and with a few yellowed leaves falling, I stepped out into the backyard and found that our moose was back. She'd been gone all summer, so it was a sign that summer was really over. She stopped her leaf munching for a couple of seconds, but she must have recognized me, just forty feet away, because she quickly went back to trimming our yard in random mouthfuls. A few nights later, Rose heard a shot at dark (which doesn't seem as uncommon in our neighborhood as it perhaps should be), and we were left for a week hoping that some neighbor didn't put our yard pet into their freezer. But Rose later spotted the moose again nearby, so who knows what was shot?

After the manic summer, it's pretty neat to see real dark again in September. And when it coincides for a brief week or so with sleep schedules, it's just amazing. Dawns and sunsets are new experiences. But, losing daylight at seven minutes each day, we quickly cruise through this comfort zone and head on into the dark season—crisply dark skies with stars so close you can almost touch them, and, when you're lucky, a silently screaming aurora borealis rages overhead. The temperatures get cool again at night.

Smoke often taints the summer air up here, especially in dry years. Between the smoke and the increased humidity, the Alaska Range's appearance is a welcome sight in summer. Once fall is here, the mountains are visible much more often, and you find yourself looking out on them frequently. So for Labor Day weekend we took a couple of days and went down along the Denali Highway to get a closer look at them. We hadn't been this way since the summer solstice of 1997, and seeing this spectacular road in September is well worth the trip. The weather was picture perfect, and the colors at these higher elevations were farther along than at lower elevations. The mountains were out in snowy splendor. We moseyed along slowly, stopping often to look at scenery, gawking along like tourists. It's an idyllic time of year. The spaceships (large recreational vehicles) have pretty

Figure 12.1. Susitna River valley near the Denali Highway, Alaska Range, Alaska.

much left the planet as far as we're concerned, leaving the summer's dregs to the year-round inhabitants.

That night we had bratwursts and a campfire (having brought our own wood up to this treeless elevation), and we watched a long sunset and the night's first stars come out before going to bed. There was not a light to be seen in any direction. After dark, two wolf packs began howling from a mile or more on either side of the tent, the first sounds after dark in this wilderness. But later during the night an occasional Willow Ptarmigan made a few loud cackling croaks. Next morning we woke to a clear, frosty landscape and went for a walk along the road.

Afterward, we were sitting on our campstools on the Denali Highway, eating Wensleydale cheese when a fine looking brown bear (grizzly) on the mountain met its end at the hands (trigger finger, anyway) of an Alaska hunter. We'd stopped and talked with him on the roadside for a minute before he set out on a long stalk up the mountainside, where the bear was minding its business in full view, eating blueberries about a mile and a half away. The road is a jump-off point for hunters in the fall. We saw about an equal number of hunters and tourists like ourselves on this trip. Caribou and moose were the usual game, but bear and sheep were also being hunted by those who didn't mind climbing. Boats and four-wheelers seemed to be the favorite jump-off vehicles; there is little game readily accessible near the road unless you just happen to catch a herd of caribou crossing (we didn't).

One of the really great aspects of autumn in Fairbanks is the crane migration. Thousands of Sandhill Cranes and Canada Geese mill around in the few fields in the area for a few weeks, flying around and staging in large flocks. The sounds of migrating cranes—a haunting, beautiful sound—can be heard all over town. And on most days I can look out my office window and watch flocks just down the hill. This stimulating sign of autumn goes by all too fast, though, and soon the familiar flocks just up and disappear. This year it was at about the same time that the leaves really began to jump off of the trees.

Another bit of autumn ambience descended upon us as September meandered along in full color. Pockets of decidedly putrescent air drifted around, occasionally assaulting unwary nostrils. We call it snork. Clouds of it creep around at this time of year. It must be some vegetative decomposition process, and it stinks in a rotting, snorkish sort of way. Rose and her friend Judy Friedrich came up with the name last year when it seemed to hang around outside the house. I have no idea what it is, but doubt that knowing would make it smell any better. It just seems to be a part of the moist, autumn, boreal forest environment. It makes you look for a dog turd mushroom sort of thing. As common as they must be, I have yet to spot one, but I'll keep looking (someone later told us that it is highbush cranberry senescence).

13

Autumn Migration to Mexico

JUST AS AUTUMN BEGAN to look serious—most leaves had already fallen in Fairbanks—I geared up for my first trip to Mexico in almost two years. While I used to spend a lot of time doing field research in Mexico, since coming to Alaska there hasn't been as much time to spend there. But Mexico is crucially important for wintering North American migrants, hosting a higher density and species diversity of wintering long-distance migrants than any other country. So, to someone studying North American migrants, Mexico is an important destination.

This trip combined two independent events: a big international meeting on Neotropical birds (held just once every four years) and the chance to continue making progress on a project that Patricia Escalante and I had begun years earlier. Patricia is the curator of Mexico's national bird collection, and we've been working together since 1993. This project is examining population-level differentiation among Mexican forest birds on the Atlantic coast. My recent Belizean efforts are tied to this study, and on this trip to Mexico I hoped that we'd be able to begin acquiring necessary samples from the west coast. And, as long as I was there, it seemed like a good idea to bring up some of the samples obtained from our previous two field efforts so that we could make more progress in the laboratory phase, getting DNA sequence data to see how subspecies-level differentiation is reflected in genetic divergence.

Our ultimate goal was to understand how closely related these different populations are, and how frequently they exchanged individuals in recent times. Now that remaining habitat is largely restricted to isolated reserves, we needed to know whether the birds associated with them are pieces of formerly widespread populations or remnants of populations that were isolated. It's likely to differ among species, so we were sampling broadly to get some sense of pattern among many species. It's a slow process, requiring just as much patience in waiting for the right birds to hit the mist nets as for getting the permits to collect and export the samples. We tried for gun permits early in the study, but the Zapatista rebellion in Chiapas seemed to result in a resounding "NO!" to requests to use shotguns to collect the specimens we needed. So it was mist nets all the way, limiting the species we could effectively work with and requiring a lot of patience when in the field.

The VI Neotropical Ornithological Congress in Monterrey was scheduled to be going full blast for six days. I couldn't stay so long, and so had just two great, long days meeting and re-meeting a lot of friends. It was fun, and one thing was clear: Mexican ornithology had come a long way since my last attendance—the second such Congress, held in 1983.

While it was good to be a small part of this meeting for a couple of days, it was just as fun to get away and into the field. Since fall semester began in Fairbanks, my daily calendar had been too clogged with the piecemeal conduct of day-to-day University and Museum business. Although it's all important, this business becomes downright tedious when it collectively grows beyond a certain point. It had definitely gotten beyond that point before my departure, and changing the channel to something different seemed like a very effective sanity balm. If only you could bottle it.

An itinerary that had me bouncing from Mexico City, to Monterrey, Mexico City, Jalisco, Mexico City, then home doesn't sound like a lottery ticket to sanity, but I have to say that even this traveling seemed like a nice change of pace. And I had good connections from Fairbanks—both going and returning took only about sixteen hours. Back in Mexico City after the meeting, I took care of some business, picked up an Instituto de Biología truck, and drove down to Colima, arriving at night in a rainstorm at Jorge and Cecilia Vega's house. Rose and I and Jorge and Ceci had been neighbors for three years at the Smithsonian's Conservation and Research Center in Front Royal, Virginia.

After finishing his PhD in Virginia, Jorge got a job on the coast of western Jalisco as a researcher at the Estación de Biología Chamela of the Instituto de Biología, Universidad Nacional Autónoma de México (UNAM). Out of schooling concerns for their daughter Debhora, they lived in Colima, about three hours from the station itself. It was great to see them all again. Colima looked like a very pleasant place to live. The next day Jorge and I drove on down to the coast—the steamy lowlands of the west. It's a striking region, with rolling forested hills coming right down to sandy beaches. But it was very hot.

For the first couple of days at Chamela, my head felt like a throbbing, three-hundred-pound bowling ball. Adjusting to such heat always takes me a few days, and the first couple of days are particularly rough. Aspirin and a lot of water help. But by days three and four, and gallons of sweat later, it's possible to feel how relatively cool it gets after sunset. Just getting through a day in such heat is quite exhausting, so I found myself sleeping very well each night. Within a couple of days, I was set up at a field site just over eight kilometers from the station, cutting net lanes in some private second growth forest near a papaya plantation carved into the surrounding forest.

This is tropical dry forest, although in October it's all still green, lush, and hot. I was not able to measure conditions while I was there, but the daily humidity seemed to be 80–100 percent, with temperatures in the nineties (at times pushing 100° F). The ceiling fan over the bed provided nocturnal respite, but during the day I was constantly soaked—and I was only rained on once. Tropical dry forest is interesting. At this season it's tough to imagine it as a deciduous forest, but you quickly notice large cacti of several species scattered among the trees—like trees themselves, but waiting for a season when they're less smothered by all the surrounding leaves. The presence of thorns and spines seemed a little higher than in the rainforests of the east.

Figure 13.1. The author waits between net checks, near Chamela, Jalisco, Mexico.

In addition to this being the hottest field work I'd ever done, I had the pleasure of hosting the most enthusiastic biting insect fauna I'd ever experienced. Speciose, too. I used more DEET than ever before, having to smear on a new coat after each net check. But there was a species of biting fly that bit through DEET like candy. These buggers really liked my elbows.

The champions at biting me, though, were wasps. In clearing a net lane one day I was suddenly whacked on the side of the head—hard, as though someone had hit me with a stick. Fortunately, it didn't take me long to figure out what had happened, and I backed out in a hurry. I left that new net lane alone and went on to make another. Imagine my surprise to get whacked on the head again! This time I ran out of there in a hurry, and with two swollen, throbbing wasp stings on my head, I began to do thorough visual checks for small hanging wasp nests.

Capture rates here were so low that I was cutting two new net lanes every day to keep my activity and productivity up. I soon had fourteen nets out, and even moving two each day just kept activity at an even level. The avifaunal densities here seemed to be adjusted to the lower productivity of the forthcoming dry season, when all the leaves fall off. Interestingly, activity patterns here did not seem typical, either. Jorge had told me that the forest here lacked the dawn chorus that is typical for the eastern rainforests, which seems quite odd when you experience this absence. Early morning activity in general is off—the first net check of the day is not the most productive; and the second one often is not either. There are late morning and late afternoon peaks, but neither is sharp or deep.

I was able to see some neat things on this trip, stuff you could wait a lifetime to see and miss, but that you might just happen to catch with a bit of luck. The first was a tarantula hawk wasp with a paralyzed tarantula. It was busily dragging this thing, probably ten times its size, to some secretive location where its single egg could develop and the larval insect could grow up, consuming its still-living prey from the inside out. I've seen a lot of tarantula hawk wasps in Mexico, always looking ferocious while out hunting for prey. The kind I'm most familiar with is about two inches long, metallic blue with deep orange wings and yellow antennae. The Chamela area is rich with a large, handsome tarantula species, and I'd never seen so many of these spiders or the wasps that prey on them.

Figure 13.2. A large tarantula (Mexican pink, Brachypelmides klaasi) *walks along a fallen tree, near Chamela, Jalisco, Mexico.*

Pulling a toad that weighs more than a pound out of a mist net is an uncommon and interesting occurrence. After I let this ugly bugger go on its way, though, I found something completely new for me just a few feet away: a gila monster had stuck its head through the net and twisted around a few hundred times and strangled itself. Because uneven terrain or rain-soaked sagging can sometimes cause mist nets to touch the ground, I've caught a lot of things in nets besides birds (e.g., frogs, turtles, crabs, snakes, squirrels, etc.), but this was a first; and, pickled, it made a good specimen. Fortunately I didn't have to wait long to see a live one.

On one net check I heard some very high-pitched squeaking nearby. Moving carefully, I found the back half of a gila monster sticking out of a small clump of forest litter. Upon moving the clump of litter away carefully with my boot, I found the front half of the gila monster busily consuming squeaking baby mice. It barely paused upon being exposed, but slowly and deliberately grabbed each squeaking little mouse (eyes still closed, but acquiring hair) and swallowed them down as they squeaked, using crude, slow, deliberate jaw motions, opening and closing its mouth. One little mouse's squeak was partially cut off each time the mouth closed as the gila monster horked it down. The monster licked its reptilian lips between baby mice. Finally, after a crude, nose-down rummaging through the nest to be sure it hadn't missed any, and after some lengthy lip licking, it hightailed it out of there, finally showing some concern about my presence. They must be rather deaf (and mice rather stupid), because there was one still left squeaking in the nest I'd moved aside with my boot. I put it all back— one survivor. If dinosaurs still walked the planet, we'd have justifiably bad dreams.

One night, the last day on which it rained while I was there, I was kept later than usual picking the nets clean before closing them. Now, I'd been later than this before and had had no problem, but on this day I found that the gate to get out onto the road was securely locked. Damn. I'd been told that the people in the house near the road had a copy of the key. Fifteen minutes later I learned this was not true, and that I was going to have to leave the truck behind the locked gate overnight and find my way back to the station on my own. I threw the critical stuff into my backpack, parked the truck out of sight, and walked over the bridge into Chamela to see if there was a cab or something that might be taken to the station six kilometers away. No, but although I'd just missed one, buses came along every half hour or hour. With darkness approaching rapidly, I did the calculations and reasoned that I'd almost be able to get back by walking fast before the next bus came along.

So, in a light rain, I began hoofing it down the twisty road. Darkness came on very fast, and it continued to rain. People who live near highways in hilly country will recognize the deep, roaring, blatting sound that semi-trailer trucks make when they're braking with their motors while going fast downhill. I'm here to tell you that one doesn't fully appreciate that sound until one has stood on a steep, shoulderless Mexican road on a dark, wet night and had one of these thousand-decibel braking events take place just inches away in a maelstrom of bright lights, buffeting winds, and a soaking splash. I paid a great deal more attention to what was driving up behind me after that.

Although avian densities were among the lowest I've yet worked with, the birds were exciting. Many were just western forms of species I was already familiar with, but many others were new, like the Golden Vireo, the Red-breasted Chat, the Yellow-winged Cacique, the Orange-breasted Bunting, and more. And even some familiar birds became much more familiar. On one net check, I caught a Pale-billed Woodpecker, a very large, strong, and astonishingly loud bird that I'd never had in the hand before. That hand was quickly bloodied by extremely sharp claws and a deftly wielded, chisel-sharp bill, but I was too busy to notice, being stunned by the sound and admiring the magnificent fiery red head and crest as I worked to free it from the net.

After just two weeks, the time finally came when I had to leave the field. On Sunday morning I watched what appeared to be a full moon set just before dawn into the Pacific Ocean, beyond undulating, mist-enshrouded coastal hills. That night, over 900 kilometers later, as I plunged down the surrounding mountains and saw México open out before me— the largest city in the world—what clearly was a full, huge, yellow moon rose up beyond this big sea of lights. I didn't have time to gawk, though. The autopista comes barreling in, winding through the mountains in a manner that encourages Sunday evening drivers to go very fast. Of course, things only get worse upon hitting Mexico City proper. This is the one place in the world where I hate driving.

If you can imagine giving millions of people cars with horns, dropping them into a poorly signed maze and telling them to do whatever they want to do, you can conceptualize driving in Mexico City. The last time I'd driven here was in 1990, and we'd been stopped four times by the police, who, attracted by our foreign license plates, were looking for "tips." At that time, the AAA guidebook had boldly stated that if stopped in Mexico City you should pay the officer something like five dollars and just be on your way. That doesn't sit right with me, so it had taken us a little longer to get on our way each time than it might have. But this time I had the advantage of camouflage—a Distrito Federal license plate—and a rather imposingly large pickup with a big cap on the back. Plus, it was dark. These advantages only put me in the category of a stranger in the mix. I think that what makes driving in Mexico City work is that everyone seems to know where they're going. Take away that simple ingredient and you have a moron feeling his way along in a rather imposing truck among a group of people who know their way and seem to want to go much faster. Lacking a copilot to read the map, I made a couple of wrong turns and so prolonged my pleasure cruise. But eventually I made it to Paty's house and was soon unloading gear and putting birds in her freezer.

Paty has a piece of art on her wall that is truly spectacular. It's a piece of "yarn painting" done by a Huichol Indian in the mountains of northern Jalisco, and it's better than television. How to describe a vibrant, colorful, four-by-four-foot piece of art that seems to move with animals, people, and spiritual beings all over the unusual canvas? I spent a lot of time staring at it various times over the course of several days. I'd read about the Huicholes in Carl Lumholtz's, *Unknown Mexico*, but it hadn't prepared me for such rich artistic expression. Another current style is to colorfully bead carved, three-dimensional wooden figures such as jaguar heads. They use beeswax and some sort of resin as a glue for this art, giving the pieces a faint, exotic aroma.

The next day we had to face the major student strike going on at the Universidad Nacional Autónoma de México. The *paristas* (active strikers) had been threatening to close the research institutes to apply a little more pressure. They had already prevented classes from being held for six months for something on the order of 250,000 students. I don't pretend to understand the issues, which seem to center on raising tuition to something like sixty US dollars per semester, but it is clear that a paternalistic government (city and national) is willing to let things go remarkably far without intervening. Forthcoming elections and bad memories of students being killed by law enforcement people in 1968 have thus far worked to the *paristas'* advantage, but they are getting very annoying (e.g., blocking major city thoroughfares), so some solution is likely to emerge before too much longer.

On Monday morning the *paristas* weren't letting people drive onto campus, so we had to park outside and walk in carrying our stuff. The Instituto de Biología had not been shut down yet, so we were free to walk there. My memory of the strike will be dominated by arms made slightly longer by a long walk with a liquid nitrogen tank in one hand and a five-gallon pail full of pickled birds in the other. It's a huge campus, and at a high enough elevation (2,240 meters, or 7,350 feet) to make you feel exerted when carrying stuff. But the weather was nice, and the Instituto graduate students and faculty were all working, so it was a pleasant day to give a presentation on some of my work and to talk with a diverse and interesting group of fellow biologists. That evening we picked up an export permit for the samples I wanted to bring up to my lab in the far-off north, and the next day I underwent the painful metamorphosis back into someone with an office full of work in a different language.

Back home after a long series of flights, I found Fairbanks firmly locked in winter. It may be just as rough a shock to go from very hot to pretty cold, but I find it easier to make the latter adjustment, and just a few days later Rose and I were out skiing. And, as November got underway, it looked like a Christmas card outside, and winter grilling was going very well.

14

Mexico—Cha, Cha, Cha!

Relax, rinse, repeat

Last summer, which seems like a lifetime ago when the days are just under four hours long, Alaska Airlines had a sale "to Mexico." My first question was how far into Mexico they went. Answer: Zihuatenejo, Guerrero. And on a nonstop flight from Los Angeles, no less. Rose got us tickets for a seemingly distant date in early December. As the pressures of a busy semester ground their way into the carpet of life, this distant date began to loom welcomely closer. We finally boarded a nonstop flight to Seattle at 1:30 a.m. on 4 December and were on our way to sunny Mexico.

Unless you're the one doing it, there is something almost obscene about escaping below-zero temperatures on an overnight flight and swimming the next day in warm seawater with a brilliant sun overhead. It seems especially incongruous when you're also very sharply cut off from the seemingly endless array of details that kept your calendar full for ten to twelve hours per day every single day for weeks on end. I understand conceptually that this is what the term "vacation" is about, but it hadn't happened to us since we visited south Florida in 1996. As we puddled around in small tropical Pacific waves just thirteen hours after having left Fairbanks, we made firm plans to come down every weekend.

We spent two-and-a-half days in idyllic Zihuatenejo. There wasn't much to do there other than lounge on the beach, eat, drink, read, and sleep. But as we engaged fully in each of these important vacation chores, we

Figure 14.1. The idyllic seaside of Zihuatenejo, Guerrero, Mexico.

agreed that a few days of this might not irrevocably corrupt us. The beaches were very nice, the water was warm and tame, the food and drinks along the beaches were excellent, and we had the good fortune to come before the seasonal crush, so there weren't many people.

Zihuatenejo is a small Mexican city with a thriving tourism business, catering to national and foreign vacationers who want to spend time on a sunny beach. Our hotel room overlooked the Playa Madera, and when we weren't on the beach we were very close to it, reading books and eating fruit on our porch, eating great seafood and drinking cold beers and margaritas at beachside restaurants, and sleeping to the sound of the mild surf. The weather was perfect: clear, fairly low humidity, and temperatures in the eighties. Our frequently replicated skin-baring experiments revealed no biting insects. And at night it got just cool enough to want a light blanket.

Our daily routine naturally settled into what we considered a perfect vacation plan, which we would repeat to ourselves to keep on schedule: relax, rinse, repeat.

Schedules

But we did have real schedules to keep. Back when we purchased the tickets, our notions of what we'd actually do in Mexico were pretty vague. We'd entertained the idea of renting a car and driving from Zihuatenejo to Oaxaca. Oaxaca is a charming city that we'd visited several times before, and we looked forward to returning. But the estimated driving time on the coastal and mountain roads from Zihuatenejo turned out to be excessive, so we decided to fly instead.

There was another important reason for me to be in Mexico in early December: I needed to accomplish another bird specimen export. These things are sensitive and important enough that they have to be done by hand, and our genetic labwork has been hung up because we lacked critical samples that only needed to be brought up to Alaska. This was a good time to get this done, so it was a core part of our plans. And we had even tacked on an auxiliary trip to Chiapas in hopes of getting small pieces from recently taken skins of a rare Middle American bird to complete one of these genetics projects. This was a lot to try to pack in. The result: Eleven flights in eleven days, four cities in ten days, and over 9,500 miles traveled.

So we left the tranquility of Zihuatenejo behind and boarded a jet to Mexico City. There were no direct flights from Zihuatenejo to Oaxaca. It was a clear, bright day, and the view was spectacular until we reached the bowl of México itself. After unopposed views of the landscapes below, we swung in around the volcanoes Iztaccihuatl and Popocatepetl, and then dipped down into the brown smog of México. It was a putrid day in Mexico

City—very poor air quality—so we were glad to be just passing through. The smog was so thick that we could see the haze in looking down the length of the large airport Sala B, where we sat waiting for our connecting flight. This flight was delayed an hour, but we made it out and flew on to Oaxaca in the dark.

During the wait we pondered our options for the coming days. In our pre-trip vagueness we hadn't put a lot of thought into just how we could spend time in both Tuxtla Gutierrez (in the state of Chiapas) and Oaxaca (in the state of Oaxaca). With just a few days in which to do this, time was a big issue. Here again, we'd thought about renting a car and driving between the two cities, but we had no idea how long such a drive would take. Distance alone is not a good index of driving time on mountain roads. The distance between the two cities was only 550 kilometers, but knowing this fact was not helpful. There is not an autopista (toll highway) between the two cities, just the usual two-lane, no-shoulder, Mexican road. Without having been on it, or asking someone who had, it was impossible to estimate how long the drive might take. So our plan became very simple: ask upon arrival and react accordingly.

As Rose waited for our baggage to arrive on the belt in Oaxaca, I walked through the small, largely vacant airport and found that the only person in the transportation industry still on duty was the guy selling tickets for taxis. He responded cheerfully that, Oh!, that was a ten to twelve hour drive! Ugh. My worst-case scenario—it was a bad road. We didn't have two days to spend driving there and back. So, Plan B. Was there a first-class bus that went to Tuxtla Gutierrez? Yes, and yes again, the buses left at night. Very well, two tickets to the bus station, please. With no time to waste, we got our bags and ourselves into a taxi and headed to the bus station, arriving at about 9:45. And what luck—the last first-class bus of the day was leaving in just thirty minutes, and they had seats available. We bought tickets and congratulated ourselves on how well this was working. Then we shuffled our bags across the street to the row of street food vendors and had delectable *tacos al pastor*—our first for the trip.

As we stood there on a busy street in gastronomic bliss, it seemed odd to be stopping in Oaxaca only long enough to get *tacos al pastor* on the street across from the bus station. But there wasn't time to dwell on it; we'd be back. In the meantime we had to get aboard for our overnight bus ride.

Oaxaca (the city) is in the Sierra Madre del Sur, and some of the roads I'd been on before in the state are the memorable kind that require three-dimensional driving skills and have rows of crosses at some of the more exciting corners—or at places where the road has just slipped off down the mountainside. As it turned out, this was that type of road. The scenery can be spectacular on these roads, but it was dark, so we saw nothing. Instead, a poor movie played on and on—something eminently forgettable starring Jodie Foster in the French resistance in World War II. We tried to sleep, but it was impossible before the movie ended (the volume was too loud), and even then the best we could do was a bad doze as the bus labored up and down and around endless sharp bends.

Sometime in the night we crossed the Isthmus of Tehuantepec from west to east and then began climbing up into the Sierra Madre de Chiapas. The whole thing felt like a bad boat ride in an uncomfortable chair. It reminded me of trying to sleep on rough trips across the Drake Passage and in the Bering Sea, only then I'd been wedging myself into a bunk instead of a bus seat, and the rocking had been somewhat regular. In the bus there was no predictability to the rough jostling, and no matter how well I wedged myself, my head still rocked back and forth on the headrest. To top it off, the roadbed itself and the bus's shock absorbers were both in terrible shape. Dawn found us in Cintalapa, where the bus driver, probably thinking he was being kind, killed all further hopes of sleep by putting in another movie—this one in Dutch with Spanish subtitles and, again, too loud. All in all, it was a memorable bus ride. Ten-and-a-half hours, and one of the worst I've been on. The only way it could have been worse would have been in a second-class bus, which would have stopped at every small town along the way. Or if someone had barfed.

But, hey, here we were in Chiapas. It was a new state for both of us, and we were eager to see a small part of it. So after checking into a hotel and calling to set up an appointment with Eduardo Morales (curator at the Instituto de Historia Natural), we set out walking through the city. It seemed to be just like any of a number of other southern Mexican cities, but we did find an artisans' market that carried some of the beautiful native textiles.

After a short meeting in the afternoon, we went up to the zoo, which was established by (and is now named after) the late Miguel Alvarez del Toro. We were very impressed. They have an amazing variety of animals on display in large cages and fenced areas spread through a large tract of native forest. We just walked along paved trails and marveled at animal after animal. The setting was perfect. We saw Resplendent Quetzals, Scarlet Macaws, three species of toucans, Crested Caracaras, Horned Guans, Ocellated Turkeys, Great Curassows, a King Vulture, and many others. The mammals were equally interesting—we were even able to scratch a pair of tame Baird's tapirs behind the ears. They seemed to enjoy this more than any dog. Mexican agoutis, Plain Chachalacas, and mantled howler monkeys roamed wild on the zoo grounds.

Next morning we went to the building that housed the Instituto de Historia Natural's collections. It was under reconstruction, and the collections were closed, but Eduardo Morales was a superb host and brought the few specimens I wanted to see to his office. As I took small pieces of skin and a couple of body feathers from invisible places on these museum skins (which I had arranged to do with Eduardo beforehand), we talked about the work they were doing in avian inventory and monitoring throughout the state. They have a good group there doing some really exciting field ornithology in this unique Mexican state, and it was a pleasure to hear about some of the things they were finding.

The bus schedule back to Oaxaca was not particularly favorable, and neither Rose nor I was overjoyed with the thought of the return journey. Consequently, we'd enquired about flights back to Oaxaca and found that seats were available. This seemed like an excellent way to spend the money we'd saved on car rental, so that afternoon we flew back to Oaxaca on a small, dramatically underfilled AeroCaribe jet.

"We won't have to be crimpled on the bus tonight" was a happy little song that Rose repeated for three days following the Oaxaca-to-Tuxtla Gutierrez joy ride.

The flight took just thirty-five minutes—ten hours less than the bus ride. It was a nice, clear day, so we could see most of the ground below. If it hadn't been cloudy on the Atlantic slope we would have been able to see both oceans across the Isthmus. There was still a striking amount of forest in the Chimalapas region on the northeast side of the Isthmus. The deforestation in the lower elevations of the Isthmus itself was fairly complete, as we had seen from the ground in 1990, but from the air that day I was impressed with how much forest was left on the northwestern side of the Isthmus also. This region is a fascinating part of North America.

Back in Oaxaca, we checked into a hotel on the *zocalo* then headed for the big city market. Our first efforts were to fill home needs in the "*ches*":

Figure 14.2. The proprietress bags my order of a half-kilo of chapulines (toasted grasshoppers) in the main market of Oaxaca, Mexico.

chilpotles, chapulines, and chocolate. A chilpotle is a jalapeño that is picked when ripe (red) then smoked as it's dried. It seems to have been shortened to "chipotle" in contact with Western civilization, or at least outside of rural Veracruz where I came to know them. The name is of Native American origin, and in being translated from probably Nahuatl to Spanish and then to English it was inappropriately shortened. Chilpotles add incomparable flavor to foods and salsas, and we were completely out of them at home. Chapulines are grasshoppers, captured locally, and lightly toasted to crisp dryness with lime, chile, and salt. They're like a high-protein corn chip in their crispy flavor, and they are sold as snacks in large heaps throughout the market. Tasty little rascals. I'm eating some as I write this. Finally, chocolate for making hot chocolate is made with incomparable flavor in Mexico, and nowhere does it seem better than in Oaxaca. We watched it being milled, and then we sampled some of the fresh, sticky mix before buying several kilos already processed into tablets. The ingredients are simple: sugar, cocoa, cinnamon, and almonds. The flavor secret comes from the amounts of the last two ingredients.

The next day we walked down to the market and caught a bus out to Mitla. The ruins there are always worth seeing for their intricate brickwork designs, but we really wanted to shop among the artisans' stalls. Woolen weavings (*tapetes*, rugs, and blankets) are a regional specialty that we enjoy looking at, buying, and hanging on our walls. Mitla is a good place to go to get started, and we were able to get a quick idea of current styles and prices. I was pleased to see that Picasso-style weavings were finally essentially gone, and that only a few degenerate Eschers were still around. The traditional, Mitla-ish designs were still quite common, together with some new stylish twists. Large blankets were decidedly uncommon, while long, narrow hallway runners had made a strong appearance. It is enjoyable to see stylistic changes when you find something likeable in the new. But you can also really miss the old.

I'd first been to Oaxaca in 1982, when Dwain Warner had brought a few of us down to do some bird censusing. It has changed quite a bit since then. There were many changes noticeable just since the last time Rose and I had been here in 1992. It was bigger now, of course, with more people and more traffic. But what struck me most is the diminishment of basketry and hand-woven goods in the markets. There were no longer any woolen weavings that we could find in the main market, and the basketry section was half the size it had been in the early eighties (and with less variety). To me this suggests that the city's people are no longer routinely using these traditional products. If only they understood that plastic carrying containers and mass-produced blankets and jackets lack even a hundredth of the style of their regionally-produced predecessors. (Yes, the new stuff is probably cheaper and easier, but the local craft and handiwork has, I think, a greater value.)

Nevertheless, we did find plenty of what we were looking for in *tapetes*, first in Mitla, then the next day in Teotitlan del Valle. Teotitlan is a weaving town, and we had picked up some great things there the last time we'd been down. After a quick circuit, we went back to the same family we'd bought things from in 1992. They are a very pleasant weaving family whose products are of very high quality and whose artistic style is one we like (despite its having changed a great deal from 1992). We spent a couple of hours there looking things over, bartering, and finally buying several pieces.

We had to have a private moment to pull together enough cash to pay for everything. When you travel, you worry about where to stash money to prevent theft. You hear a lot of stories, but I haven't had any really bad things happen to me (yet). I was pickpocketed once in Mexico City, and on this trip in Zihuatenejo some young punk thought he'd get a nice pair of Teva sandals while we were in the ocean (I ran him down just after he'd rounded corner number three. What he thought he'd do with size fourteen sandals escapes me). But theft is a constant threat, and where and how to carry cash, traveler's checks, passport, and credit cards is a never-ending puzzle with limited solutions. It had been so long since I traveled with someone else in Mexico that I'd forgotten what a pain this is; it's just part of doing business. My usual solution is to split the stuff up among places and pockets, keeping only what I expect to spend at hand in a shirt pocket. In field work I've found that lockable Action Packers (clunky, large plastic boxes, great for field gear) help a lot—you can leave stuff in your sleeping quarters and not worry too much about it disappearing. And since being pickpocketed (from the front right pocket of a pair of jeans on a crowded subway) I don't trust things to unbuttoned pockets. Traveling with Rose brought back to me just how much time and thought can be placed into worrying about where to put all this stuff.[16] As the trip progressed and we spent our money, this concern diminished considerably. We were particularly carefree as we walked out of Teotitlan, and repeatedly congratulated ourselves on having successfully converted our cash into goods.

It was pleasant to get out of Oaxaca and into the countryside and rural towns and walk around. This is a very pleasant region, almost desertlike in the dry winter. Oaxaca itself was an all-too-hectic city. The streets and narrow sidewalks thrum with heavy motor and foot traffic. At night the *zocalo* was booming with Christmas festivities, and the sidewalk cafes and vendors were doing a brisk business. We took a spin or two around the *zocalo* each afternoon and again in the evening to watch people and admire the black Oaxacan pottery, the brightly colored, carved *alebrije* figures, and other handicrafts for sale. Here is where we picked up our "smalls," the few little things we just couldn't live without. Our visit happened to coincide with the Feast of the Virgin of Guadalupe, a day on which young girls are immaculately dressed in native costume. We watched one two-year-old sedately trying to walk down pigeons in front of the church in her holiday clothes. A budding young ornithologist.

Some sadistic genius had built our hotel room so the interior walls didn't quite meet the windows on the exterior wall. These windows were

---

16. It is surprising to me how quickly cash machines and international banking networks have made much of this moot just over a decade later.

shared by the rooms on either side, and the glass served as a perfect sound reflector. We were just glad that the deaf people who liked TV on one side of us and the cranky family on the other side had civilized bedtimes. Despite this construction quirk, our room was surprisingly quiet given the level of activity on the *zocalo*, just across the building. For two people from the peaceful town of Fairbanks, it was good to have a temporary, quiet refuge from the intense city life. But the place that best qualified for that on this trip was Zihuatenejo.

We'd squeezed in all we could in Oaxaca and Chiapas and had just two items left on our schedule: pick up bird specimens in Mexico City and catch another day and a half of seaside time in Zihuatenejo. We flew into Mexico on a clear, relatively pollution-free Sunday morning and took a cab to Patricia Escalante's house. The student strike was still on at UNAM, so Paty had brought the specimens to her home. And all the tissue samples had been cut already, so we had time to goof off. We spent a pleasant day with Paty and her daughter Fatma (who was two), talking and eating and strolling through a popular holiday market. Even Fatma had fun, personally greeting every small dog and small child.

In the evening we flew back to Zihuatenejo, where there was just time to have a good seaside dinner before bed. The next day, as we lounged on the porch and at the beach, we realized how good it was to be back in the relax, rinse, repeat mode. It was an excellent way to cap off such a busy trip. That evening, sunburned despite ample use of albino sauce (sunscreen), we had the best dinner of a long series of excellent dinners, putting us in a good mood for the long return flight home to darkness and cold. The flight up to Los Angeles was spectacular. Our route went directly up the coast, and we were able to see a lot of the impressive western Mexican landscape, even Copper Canyon away toward the interior. And the good vacation mood lasted well past the delayed, 2:38 a.m. Fairbanks arrival time and our reacquaintance with four-hour-day lengths!

Turismo gastronomico

Even if you don't care for any of the multitude of handicrafts and artworks available in Mexico, you've got to love the food. As we experienced great meal after great meal, I began to think that it would probably be worthwhile touring Mexico only to experience the cooking.

In Zihuatenejo, you'd be a fool not to eat seafood every day. It's brought in fresh daily by the local fishermen (or you can go out and catch it yourself), and it is served up in any way you like. We had such things as red snapper fried in butter and garlic; octopus, shrimp, and sea snail cocktails; shrimp tacos; and *filete al tamal*. This last was a new dish for me; it's very good. They put peppers in the bottom of an aluminum foil dish, then the fillet, then onions and tomatoes, then cheese, and then bake the whole thing. Our last spectacular dinner here, which we had planned beforehand, began during happy hour with two-for-one beers and margaritas with fresh chips and salsa, then shrimp *al mojo de ajo* (sauteed in butter and garlic), *filete al mojo de ajo* (which that night was fresh tuna), and finally the *botana marinera* with more beer and margaritas. The last dish is a seafood platter of octopus, sea snail, shrimp, and fish sauteed in butter and garlic. Wow. Spread a feast like that out over nearly two hours on a starlit night in the sand by a gently lapping tropical ocean, and you've encompassed one dimension of paradise.

Our inland travels brought us heart and soul into *mole* (pronounced "molay") country. Oaxaca is the source of *mole*, and it comes in many varieties. The most famous are the darker *moles*, which are rich blends of herbs, spices, chiles, and chocolate. Broiled chicken smothered in *mole negro* with a pile of hot, fresh tortillas on the side is incredibly good, as are pork chunks in a green mole soup. Enchiladas smothered in mole (*verde* and *negro*) are another superb dish, and we had them all. On the days when we took a bus out to Mitla and Teotitlan del Valle, we started with breakfast on the *zocalo* and accidentally hit upon a superb breakfast menu, having hot chocolate (it was quite cool at night in Oaxaca), freshly cut fruit cocktail, and *tamale Oaxaceño*, a tamale filled with beans, chicken, and *mole negro*, and served steaming in its banana-leaf wrapping. Superb!

Even in our short visit to Mexico City, I learned something new about Mexican food. I'd always thought that *quesadillas* had to have cheese in them, but we learned that this was not the case—the name applies to the style of the food, not to the tortilla's contents. The woman making them on that fine Sunday afternoon took a handful of sticky *masa*, slapped it on a press to flatten it into a rugby-ball-shaped tortilla, tossed a handful of appropriate mix onto it, folded it over, sealed the edges closed, then tossed it into a big, shallow pan of boiling oil, where each *quesadilla* was watched and turned with a wooden paddle until done. There were a lot of things available to fill your *quesadilla*. We had *huitlacoche* (black corn fungus), brains, squash flowers and cheese, peppers and cheese, chicken, and barbecue. Delicious.

As we walked out of Mitla, we stopped at a mezcal shop and sampled some of the many types of that biting liquor made from the roasted heart of the maguey. Here we learned that a maguey worm is not always put into bottled mezcal; but "*con gusano*" was one of the many flavors one could buy. I couldn't readily taste the differences, but we picked up a couple of bottles so we could repeat the experiment at home.

Even the snacks we had on the run were great: *tacos al pastor* whenever we found them (sheets of pork that are flame-broiled on a vertical spindle and shaved off into a tortilla, served with onion, cilantro, and salsa), *tortas de milanesa* and *chiles rellenos* for lunch on the *zocalo* in Oaxaca (hard-roll sandwiches with various fillings), and fruits and breads from the markets. Boy, this makes me hungry. It's hard to believe I actually lost weight on this trip.

15

Pigpolls Need Glasses!

WELL, WE BROKE INTO THAT idyllic part of winter when the temperatures stay above zero and the days zoom upward at seven minutes per day through the eight-nine-ten-eleven-twelve-thirteen hours of "possible sunlight" phases. It was beginning to dawn on us that, gee, it's been winter for quite awhile. But then we were too busy working and admiring the great outdoors again to give too much thought to winter's seemingly long stay. And hey, the skiing was great! To top it off, we rocketed past twelve hours of daylight, passing up all latitudes to the south.

During the Dark Times—now a distant memory—we learned that a driveway triples in length when you drop a couple feet of snow on it. We were coming home early (by six!) to spend a solid hour shoveling the driveway every evening. Talk about sore! But during this time I learned from a new perspective that I married well. Rose is an excellent snow shoveler. Seriously, though, the ugly word "snowblower" actually entered our vocabulary a couple of times during some of those evenings of grunting snow onto growing piles. Just when it seemed as though we would be shoveling every night without being able to drive up and down the driveway, it finally stopped snowing! Woohoo!

We did have some biting cold weather during the Dark Times, though. And when this cold weather descends, it seems like the moose become much more building-friendly, dropping in more frequently to eat trees and bushes near the house. We were pretty much housebound over the holidays because of crisply cold weather. Those -30° to -50° F temperatures don't stay fun very long. It's just really good that we don't get wind.

It's not clear what brings the moose in closer to civilization during these cold snaps, but we do enjoy watching them. Mostly we're just glad we're not out there living such a miserable existence with them. Maybe it would be okay if we ate sunflower seed kernels like the birds and the squirrels, but geez, sticks? No way.

These yard moose are large, rather unintelligent creatures. Last year we thought it an odd fluke that one had walked off with our outdoor Christmas lights, but after this past holiday season we're thinking it's a brainless conspiracy. This time we were at home, watching as the theft occurred. Oh, at first we were fooled by the intelligent-looking nonchalance with which the big female ambled up to the neighboring tree, bent it over, and bit off a tasty wad of frozen sticks. It was the perfect cover for her next move, which, "oops," caused her to turn into the string of lights and drag it protestingly out of its little spruce-tree home, killing in the process all of the innocent little lights of holiday joy. Yes, at first it looked like a very good act of feigning stupidity, but when she'd succeeded in killing the string of lights, there was no look of delight in her eyes. So here she gave herself and all her kind away as rather dumb, sometimes-yard animals that occasionally try to spice up their plain meals and dull, freeze-your-ass-off winter lives with a little prank on the two-legged bozos in the holey boxes.

This bozo shook his head at the large, ungainly creature and later went out to check out the dead, cold little lights in the deepening snow. At least the bozo had had the good sense to tie off everything this year so that it wasn't all dragged away, cord and all, somewhere into the woods to lie with last year's lights and extension cord.

The moose don't just take, though. They also giveth. They leave jewelry in the yard. Now, if you haven't been to Alaska you may be getting some very strange images of the state's largest quadruped, walking around eating frozen sticks, bedecked in jewelry. It's a good image, but it doesn't fit. No, the moose make jewelry deposits, but not from anything they wear. You see, the tourists visiting the state will purchase just about anything as a reminder or souvenir of their Alaska trip. And so a rare and wonderful thing has occurred: The state's greatest artists have created a jewelry fashion statement catering especially to this tourist dollar. And they express this statement in varnished moose turd earrings. So our yard moose may be playing pranks on us, but they are at the same time bestowing upon us untold wealth. This year we may harvest this wealth and "cut" these diamonds in the rough, instead of just mailing off boxes of "Alaska Cheerios" to our friends and families. Jewelry—we can make our own!

Shortly after coming out of the Dark Times each year, we become inundated with other wildlife visitors—pigpolls. Actually, they are normally called Common and Hoary redpolls. But they are real pigs when it comes to shelled sunflower seeds, porking down phenomenal amounts of seed every day. So we consider pigpolls to be the best name for them. They are fun to watch at first, with twenty to thirty often descending at once to munch on the seeds. But they're sure skittery. The slightest thing sets them off. They take flight at the drop of a hat, or the wiggle of a squirrel tail, scattering in all directions and often bouncing off the window like soft hail, with a quick series of little taps. Why they can't see as well as the chickadees and woodpeckers is a real mystery.

Rose summed it up perfectly: "Pigpolls need glasses!"

It's an excellent theory that their behavior seems to support every day (it's light enough when we get up to see several bounce off of the windows before we go to work). But we have yet to really put the theory to the test and put little glasses on an experimental group.

Rose notes also that ravens can't read. The other day we drove by a dumpster that was fenced off and blatantly labeled "Private Dumpster," but there was a happy raven feeding on the dumpster smorgasbord. I suppose that it could plead innocent by reason of language inequity, but this widely respected bird is definitely losing its charm. We prepared a salvaged individual as a specimen last year, and it had McDonald's hamburger wrappers in its stomach. We didn't save the stomach contents for posterity.

This was our fourth year of attendance at the Native Arts Festival, and we also made it to the International Ice Art Competition this year before it melted. The arts festival is different every year, and this year we didn't find anything that tempted our wallets. We did, however, find several tempting items at a later festival, and I went back to get a fur ruff for my ruffless winter coat while Rose watched the dogsled races as the animals and their humans sped through town on the frozen Chena River. The ice carvings were amazing, as usual. It's really impressive what these carvers can do with the "Arctic diamond," fashioning from large, clear blocks of ice larger-than-life art forms and fantastic figures ranging from *Alice in Wonderland* scenes to a rather cubist mammoth, to abstract human forms.

I went skiing just one last time—on sheer ice—before calling it quits. I was so sore from trying to remain upright on the lightning fast, frictionless trails that I hung up my skis for the season and just waited patiently for the snow to finish melting so we could start biking again. With the days growing so long so fast, it wouldn't be long before the birds came back and it greened up again. After a long winter, that is an unusual color!

16

Walking Wild Shores — Among the Eastern Aleutians

THE ALEUTIAN ISLANDS MAKE UP the longest island archipelago in the US and one of the longest in the world. In the lower forty-eight states, these islands would extend from west Texas to central California. If one includes the Commander Islands, geographically part of the island chain but politically Russian, the archipelago extends even farther—about 1,400 miles in total length. The islands extend from 51–55° N latitude and 172° E to 163° W longitude. Ostensibly covered in ice during the last glacial maximum, this chain is a rather complex oceanic range of mountains and volcanoes. Topographically challenging, poorly charted, and surrounded by cold waters, this island chain is a dangerous one for humans. On the other hand, among birds these islands represent both seasonal and permanent homes for a diverse array of species. The complex geographic variation that these birds exhibit has only been described, not examined in great detail, and the migrants that pass through make it a region unique on the North American continent—a combination of factors that make it a playground for ornithologists intrepid enough to venture into this rich yet austere region. We've been very active out here over the past several years.

Field work in the Aleutians is much more expensive than in other places I've worked. I could go to the tropics and spend weeks in the field for the cost of just a couple of days in the Aleutians. At times the contrast is appealing—one must enjoy (or at least be extremely tolerant of) horizontal rain and temperatures in the high thirties and forties when venturing to the Aleutians. But when the weather is decent and the fogs and low clouds lift, the Aleutians provide a spectacle unlike any other I've witnessed, offering a rare and magical beauty to the visitor. One can easily become attached to these wild islands.

I left Fairbanks at the close of a brutal semester, ecstatic to be leaving behind eighty- and hundred-hour weeks of classes, committees, and other obligations that combined to bleed my juices of enthusiasm to a dangerous low. My mental dash lights had been flashing "Get into the field!" since March, when I had to cancel a Belize field effort to deal properly with (yet another) grant proposal. But, by early May, spring, leaf-out, and avian migrants were in the air, and life fluids were waxing once again as I set out for an exciting opportunity to collect bird specimens in the eastern Aleutians. With Rose's expert help in getting my diverse field junk packed into minimal space, I boarded a plane for Unalaska: the second big island in the Aleutian chain as one goes west from the Alaska Peninsula, and the largest of the Fox Island group. I was to be picked up there several days later by the Alaska Maritime National Wildlife Refuge vessel *Tiglax* for an important cruise out to Adak—a cruise that would stop at two rarely visited islands: Bogoslof and Amlia.

At Unalaska, the mean annual temperature is just 38° F. As we landed, I saw that there was still snow to the waterline—the fine spring in Fairbanks would take awhile to reach here still, despite its being more than ten degrees more southerly in latitude. Nevertheless, a lot of melting had occurred, and the birds were singing and displaying on territory. More immediately noticeable, however, was the harbor and related industry. These north Pacific and Bering Sea waters support much of the largest fishery in the US, and Dutch Harbor is the fishery's hub. Mary Schwenzfeier and Ted

Spencer of the Alaska Department of Fish and Game were good enough to set me up in the ADF&G bunkhouse. Two years earlier, Mary had been one of the most enthusiastic ornithology students I've yet had, and she was posted on Unalaska to monitor the shellfish industry. Although she was off of the island for an annual vacation, she was kind enough to let me use her vehicle for my short stay. After meeting Ted when my delayed flight finally arrived, then getting my junk into the bunkhouse, I took a stroll around the nearby road system to begin to get acquainted with the island, its humans, and its birds.

This happened to be a low point in the annual seafood season in the Bering Sea, so there wasn't a high level of activity. But it was easy to see that the scale of industry here often reaches what must be crazy levels. The ability to handle large numbers of containers for shipping frozen seafood is amazing. These containers (reefers) are semi-trailer sized, insulated boxes with independent refrigeration units—internal combustion engines driving freezer units. They were stacked around in the many hundreds if not thousands, mostly empty, but with some full and their engines running. Local folks said it gets real loud during the busy season, when most are running. Apparently Dutch Harbor hosts the world's largest apparatus for loading and unloading these containers. This is not surprising given the volume evident in the waiting container stacks and the waiting space devoted to even more stacks. High-pressure water-service posts are spaced through these stack areas to assist in cleaning the containers. The volume of shellfish that this harbor is set up to handle is mind-boggling. Large metal crab pots are also stacked around by the thousands.

My stroll ended at Ziggy's, the restaurant I was referred to when I'd asked whether there was a place nearby where one could have dinner. A subadult Bald Eagle feeding at the restaurant's dumpster found the food good enough to allow me to approach to within eight feet before it flushed, giving me some confidence in the quality of the cuisine. Upon finding a table, my first question was what kinds of beer they had. When the waitress said it was difficult for her and handed me a menu with the beer list, I asked where she was from. To my surprise, she was from the valley of Mexicali, Baja California Norte, Mexico, and she'd lived on Unalaska for eight years. So we spoke in Spanish. I asked her what the best things were on the remarkably diverse menu. She pointed to two as being the best, and I decided to try one of them: the "Burrito Mexicanisimo."

When incongruities reach grand proportions, it is difficult to weigh subtle differences, so as I ate the best Mexican food I've yet had in Alaska, I couldn't decide whether the fact that I found it here on Unalaska was less likely than meeting someone of such fortitude to move to a climate impossible to even imagine in Baja California—and then live there for eight long years. It seemed equally puzzling that the restaurant was named Ziggy's on the outside but Amelia's on the inside. While I did not find an answer to these ponderings, even at the bottom of a $3.50 domestic beer, I did find immense satisfaction in the final result, and returned there on each of the next three nights to alternate between the two best items on the menu.

Being on Unalaska offered an unprecedented opportunity to collect topotypes—specimens from the "type locality," the place from which the original specimen(s) known to science were obtained. A number of North American species were first described by Russians, whose expeditions to what has since been named Alaska furnished them with biological material new to science. For example, the common North American species Savannah Sparrow was described from specimens obtained on Unalaska.

Several birds presently considered subspecies were also described based on Unalaska specimens. The type concept of species (and subspecies), based on the idea that a taxon (e.g., species) can be represented by a single immutable type, is no longer accepted. But comparative biology and biogeography do nevertheless benefit from reference specimens that represent the described bases for organismal diversity and distribution. It thus remains useful to obtain topotypes when possible, for they provide us with a touchstone when asking questions such as, "How does this compare with the organism described by so and so?" or "To what degree does this population differ from another elsewhere?" These are, of course, fundamental questions of biodiversity and how it varies through time and space. And we were plowing entirely new ground with our efforts because genetic material (tissues) had not been historically preserved, so anything we were able to obtain promised to shed new light on how biodiversity and corresponding genetic diversity were distributed among Alaska's bird populations.

My first stop the next morning was at the Ounalashka Corporation, an Alaska Native corporation overseeing much of the island—in fact nearly all of the land easily accessible by road or boat. To collect on these lands, I needed a permit from the corporation in addition to the state and federal permits that I already possessed. It took half a day, but the folks at the corporation were quite supportive of research. By midafternoon I had a permit for the few days I would be on the island, and I was soon walking along a seaside road that was closed by multiple avalanches. To my delight, topotype Savannah Sparrows were feeding and frolicking along the rocky beach, and, although they were shy, I soon had some of these prizes in my backpack.

In the Aleutians, wind is a constant companion. You assess its direction and strength constantly and choose where to go, how to get there, directions of approach, how to work the land and sea, and how to shoot birds in order to retrieve them in relation to this seemingly unremitting and constantly changing force. You need to carry rain gear and a compass to accommodate the sudden weather changes that it brings (rain, snow, and fog), and you feel tired at the end of every day from battling its unrelenting pummeling. As I rounded the corner of these avalanche cliffs and pushed headfirst into a strong wind funneled down a valley and along more cliff walls, the sand and gravel that it flung up caused me to have to walk backwards with my raincoat hood up. It felt and sounded like walking backwards in a horizontal hailstorm, and there wasn't much active bird life in that valley. Following my perambulation of this valley, I was glad to turn around and head back to the comparative peace of the earlier avalanche walk.

Figure 16.1. Snow melting along the cliffs of Unalaska Island, Aleutian Islands, Alaska.

These avalanches completely blocked the narrow road at the cliffs' base, but passage was comparatively easy along the sea's boulder beach at anything but high tide. In the lee of these tall cliffs a very little afternoon sunshine had warmed up the avalanches enough that they were smoothly flowing. I'd always thought these things were sudden, uproarious affairs, and so was puzzled at first to hear what sounded like a waterfall as I approached one of the big avalanches. It wasn't a waterfall, but instead a steady flow of granular melting snow from high places to low, slowly building up at the bottom portion of the avalanche flow. When I got back to where I'd left Mary's truck, I found that "slow" was relative, and that if I didn't get out of there soon I was going to be embarrassingly stuck behind several avalanches that had been only temporarily plowed clean. In fact, if I'd parked at the end of the plowing effort, I'd have been in serious danger of seeing Mary's truck pushed over the edge into the ocean. Fortunately I'd given that some thought, accidently reaching the appropriate conclusion from a rapid-snow-slide perspective and parking outside of the avalanche zone. As it was, I had to weave around some growing flows on my way out that were impassable by the next morning.

The next day the wind was a bit less, and the rain remained only an occasional spatter, which made an all-day hike a pleasant prospect. As I walked much of the avalanche road again—a much greater distance because of new avalanche closures—it seemed that my friends the Pacific Wrens also thought that it was a pleasant day, for there were now several singing among the towering cliffs. This species is an important one in its geographic variation, but they can be particularly difficult to obtain in spring among the cliffs of the Aleutians. Not only do they occupy terrain that is mostly impassable to humans, but even after you walk miles of seaside and finally find one, they do not respond to tape playbacks of their song as do territorial males of most other bird species. As a consequence, you find yourself straining for even a sight of these remarkable songsters, often either not getting a sight or a shot, or getting a fleeting, long-distance 12-gauge shot when a wren happens to flit briefly to a place from which it would be retrievable. Chasing after Aleutian wrens has repeatedly put me in the most precarious of cliff situations, and our sample sizes have been only slowly and grudgingly pushed upward. Although these particular cliffs were quite tall and the rock very friable, on this day I was fortunate enough to get three of the little buggers: our first for all of the territory between Adak and Kodiak, and consequently worth their weight in gold as modern specimens.

I walked the shores of Unalaska all day in search of coastal avifauna. The rocky beaches yielded up a few shorebirds, but they were few and far between, as were the Song Sparrows, another resident species with pronounced geographic variation. After undulating my way along the coast to a small river flowing into Humpy Cove (humpies are so called after their characteristic dorsal shape and are more formally called pink salmon), I was astonished to see horse manure. There are few things I would less expect to find here, but it looked as old as last fall. After hiking up over a very windy pass into the next valley over, I began finding more horse manure, and after rounding a hill and coming out into a flat valley I found its source—ten horses, including two new foals. Someone must have thought they needed some horses out here, and apparently these exotic animals can overwinter here just fine. A nice gray seemed glad to be scratched by a human. Later, as I fought my way back up to the windy, snow-clad pass, an arctic fox stopped to watch me, and we rested and mutually inspected one another from just fifty feet apart.

The next day was windier, and I went out to a different area with Ted and Ryan. We walked a lot of beach, along which birds were just as sparse as the beaches I'd walked before. Spring migration in this in-between region is rather spare (and this was proving to be a slow year), and the rocky beaches are not particularly high in productivity. On a walk across the high country to cut back across the peninsula we'd just rounded, we came across a lot of worms that had crawled out of the heath onto melting snowbanks and died. We also experienced what for me was likely to be the last snowfall of the spring.

Horizontal rain and similar weather ugliness came in the next day. It was not going to be a nice day to go out and work the shores, but it was to be my last day on Unalaska and there were some wrens I still wanted to meet. As I put on my gear, however, the phone rang with the news that *Tiglax* was in already and was just waiting to get a group of us aboard before getting underway to Bogoslof Island. A little over an hour's scramble later, the boat's complement was aboard and Captain Kevin Bell was giving us a training rundown on such things as survival suits, fire hoses, and life rafts. Soon thereafter we were off, glad to be headed for wild places and to be getting away from a large tour vessel regurgitating passengers onto the dock before us.

Bogoslof, a small island west of Unalaska and north of Umnak Island, arose from the sea in 1796, and it has been a volcanically dynamic and changing piece of land since then. In sight of both Umnak and Unalaska islands, and of such recent origin, it seemed unlikely that any endemic subspecies could be here. The goal in stopping was to drop a seabird observation camp that would later be occupied in mid-June. After a circumnavigation, we anchored up for the night just offshore. The reason for dropping the camp now was that by mid-June something on the order of 20,000 northern fur seals would crowd the island's beaches, making passage very difficult.

Next morning, after a hearty breakfast, we began offloading the camp. Dropping a camp is real work, and all hands worked hard for hours until it was done. Shorter spines and longer arms seemed an inevitable consequence of this human mule labor. The seemingly innumerable skiffloads and human transport loads were made a little easier by knowing that we had been able to land on the beach with the smaller boulders, but it was no picnic. Waders and hip boots take up a lot of valuable space when packing for an air trip, but they can be mighty nice for those moments between skiff and land. Having come by air, I'd opted to use "poor man's waders"—duct tape at the bottoms of my rain pants to stick them to my rubber boots. This time they didn't work so well, and the cold seawater soaked me during the first offloading in the crashing surf. This was a small point in a very busy day, but by the end of the day the backs of my legs were chafed raw by my boots. After offloading the camp, Steve Talbot and I were freed up to conduct our sampling efforts. Steve was here to collect mostly mosses, and I had a few birds to collect.

As soon as I shed my Mustang suit and assembled my gun (brought ashore in pieces in my pack), I was off to meet a local Song Sparrow; there was one singing from up on one of the naked volcanic blast piles. These formations made the small island's shape unusual, and it seemed odd to me that each of the several thrusting projections of rock were so different in compositional detail—at least the rocks' shapes differed. As I made my way up one of these piles, carefully going around sharp, projecting boulders, it quickly became apparent that I was in the middle of a thriving Tufted Puffin colony. These handsome seabirds nest in underground burrows, and this hill of boulders provided excellent subterranean crevices, many of which required little or no digging. The birds' presence was revealed by the soft patter and shuffle of feet running deeper into the burrows, by fleeting glimpses of surprised faces at burrow entrances, and by the occasional escapee—birds deciding that the burrows did not offer sufficient protection from this bipedal threat and flubbing their way clumsily into the air. Once I had my Song Sparrow, I pulled out my camera, put on my telephoto lens, and stalked some of these elegantly clownish puffins. Some proved very cooperative. But our limited time ashore made it important to move along quickly; I wanted to cover the whole island before our departure.

Figure 16.2. Tufted Puffin (Fratercula cirrhata), *Bogoslof Island, Aleutian Islands, Alaska.*

It seems inevitable that accidents should happen when one is pushing the limits in remote areas, moving fast to obtain rewards that seem important at the time but which dim in memory as they become overshadowed by the stronger memories of the consequences reaped—or the potential consequences that thankfully didn't materialize. As accidents go, this one wasn't so bad, but it was unprecedented in my experience. When in the Aleutians and working shorelines, you become of necessity a boulder dancer. As I leaped from boulder to boulder to retrieve a beautiful Wandering Tattler I was happy to have run across, the boulder upon which the tattler lay proved to be the only one that was as slippery as snot on a doorknob. I went down instantly, and five things happened at once. The first to register was something skittering off across the boulders to my right into the crashing surf. The second was the firing of the gun—my first ever accidental discharge—into another seaward rock. The third was a piece of the gun stock lying on the rock beside my hand, and the fourth was the delayed registry of pain in my left leg. Fifth was the damage to my camera lens (I'm afraid I left my camera dangling from my neck after those puffin shots), which made me realize that the initial skittering object was the lens cap, now quite irretrievable. I grabbed the tattler and the gunstock fragment and noticed the ricochet mark of the gunshot on a nearby rock as I gingerly leapt to better rocks farther from the surf. Only the .410 barrel had discharged, and that explained why I hardly noticed the noise over the sea. I reloaded and took care of the bird, putting cotton down the throat to prevent internal fluids from leaking onto the plumage and placing it in a bag of corn-cob dust to keep any other fluids from soaking the feathers before placing it in my pack. It was a damned nice bird (made perhaps more so by the cost of obtaining it) and almost certainly the first of its species ever taken on this island.

For weeks later, most of my upper shin for six inches below my knee remained very painful to the touch, but the gun—still broken—bore the brunt of the accident. Thank goodness, it remained functional. I can limp, but a nonfunctional gun would have put a sudden and disastrous end to a very rare collecting opportunity in a region where there are no other practical means of obtaining specimens.

There were a number of northern fur seals hauled out at various points along the beach. Among the larger boulders we would occasionally surprise each other; they would roar belligerently or retreat, and I would just retreat.

Only now do I wonder why I didn't try roaring also. It might have been interesting to see the reaction, although I couldn't match their guttural bellows. At the time I just didn't want to disturb them. On the western end of the island a lot of Steller's sea lions were hauled out. I gave these large animals a wide berth. Their populations have crashed in western Alaska in the past decade, and they need all the help they can get. It is always a pleasure to see them, though. I sat above them on a low bluff to watch them loaf, and a pair of puffins appeared, fighting hammer and tongs, with bills locked, wings beating, and bodies rolling across the sloping beach.

Another area of the island that demanded avoidance was a long, sloping, grassy plateau that ended abruptly at a cliff. Covering the turf were legions of Common and Thick-billed murres and Tufted Puffins, all out standing on and near their nests. Murres make only the roughest of scrapes on open ground or cliff ledges to lay their large, blue, speckled eggs, and this island, free of terrestrial predators, provided some excellent expanses for murre nest gardens. The contrast of dense stands of puffins and murres made quite a spectacle.

The island wasn't predator free, however. A pair of Bald Eagles in all their splendor, far from any dumps or dumpsters, had been soaring about all day; and in my perambulation I found a pair of colorful puffin mandibles—all that was left of a large predator's snack. Not long afterwards I found the eagles' nest. It was placed in an unusually accessible spot—on the open turf at the edge of a small, sandy bluff. I slowly approached to within ten feet of it to see whether they'd laid eggs yet. They hadn't, which is probably why they let me get so close, although both members of the pair kept a close eye on me and gave occasional screams as I passed through the core of their territory.

There were a fair number of Song Sparrows on the island, so I took a second male to better document the population before heading back to the camp. The hardworking refuge crew had assembled the weatherport and put most of the camp's gear inside, and we were soon rounded up and headed back out to *Tiglax*. And as soon as people and boats were back aboard we were off—headed farther west for the legendary island of Amlia.

Our sailing time to Amlia was going to be about twenty hours. After the Bogoslof workout and with the rocking of the boat it was not difficult to sleep, despite a moving bunk. For most of the next day we were still underway. Taking notes, reading, and watching seabirds from the wheelhouse and deck were pleasant ways to pass the time. By midafternoon, Amlia was off our starboard bow: first some white surf, then small rocks, then a big headland. We kept going along the south side to about the middle of the forty-mile-long island, where there's a good deep harbor—Sviechnikof Bay. We pulled in here just as we were finishing a leisurely dinner. Then everyone scrambled to get ready and go ashore.

Amlia is probably one of the least-visited large islands of the Andreanof Islands group. Refuge personnel hadn't been here for years, and in our slightly longer than two days here I didn't see any evidence of humans, aside from the usual beach trash (and there wasn't much of that). Even World War II seemed to have pretty much passed the island by, judging from a lack of sign. We were here to reconnoiter for arctic fox trapping as refuge personnel continue to remove this introduced predator from many of the Aleutian islands on which they had been historically stocked for their furs. The Aleutian Cackling Goose was one native prey species negatively impacted, and it has only recently been de-listed (removed from the federal threatened and endangered species list) following many years of recovery efforts. Steve Ebbert, head of the fox-trapping operation, was aboard to choose three or four locations on Amlia suitable for base camps, which would be dropped in September. It was this important purpose for our visit upon which our scientific efforts were piggybacked.

One of the pressing ornithological questions of Amlia was what subspecies of Song Sparrow occurred on the island. My first shot on the island answered this longstanding question (*Melospiza melodia maxima*), and I solved the puzzle four more times before completing my walk along a beach at the base of a cliff. (When documenting populations, one strives to obtain statistically useful sample sizes, so we usually try to get series of individuals when sampling.) A cliff-dwelling Pacific Wren proved far less tractable, however; despite time both at the top and bottom of the cliff with my tape playback unit, the little rascal remained safely out of sight, occasionally singing from unseen crevices to toy with me (and presumably to attract a mate and defend its territory, but toying with me seemed more likely at the time).

In general, for all of their wildness, the islands did not offer up dirt-stupid birds that stood there unafraid as I, the supreme predator, approached. On the contrary, I've rarely experienced such skittery birds; few remained in 12-gauge shotgun range at my approach. We had a great desire for Rock Ptarmigan from Amlia, but they tended to flush from 500–1000 meters away, going fast and usually with the wind. The first one that I was able to get was like pass-shooting fast waterfowl, and it skipped at least sixty feet across the heath when I dropped it on a snapshot. Dean Kildaw had led me up onto the highlands for this bird and a couple others he saw that first evening ashore. As we headed back toward the pickup point, we could see Steve Talbot high up on a slope, stalking the wily rock-dwelling mosses. It was cold (probably in the high thirties) and windy, so I put on my Mustang suit and found a comfortable spot out of the wind to await his return. It was nearly dark when he made it back to meet us on the shore with the news that he found a plant previously known from only two islands. So it was a late and productive evening on Amlia. The fact that my bunk didn't move that night made my six hours of sleep blissful.

Next morning two zodiacs headed off in opposite directions to scout the southern shores of the island, and we set off in *Tiglax* to keep pace with and eventually pick up the boat covering the southeastern quarter. The island is about forty miles long and only a few miles deep, and oriented east to west. Kevin Bell dropped Steve Talbot and me back off in Sviechnikof Bay as we passed back that way to pick up the crew covering the southwestern portion. Steve and I hit the ground running just after lunch, looking to cover as much country as humanly possible before the vessel's return in the evening. It was a gorgeous day, with excellent visibility and even a little sun. My course took me first along the eastern shore of the entire bay, then back up over and through the high country. Song Sparrows were cooperative along the shore, but the only Pacific Wren that I found was at the very end of the walkable beach. He was entirely uncooperative and is no doubt still singing from his rocky crevices. Shorebirds were also sparse along the rocky shoreline.

So I went up into the highlands, where it was beautiful, but also windy and cold. I was glad once again to have brought an insulated rainproof jacket, rather than have trusted to noninsulated gear. Bird-wise it was pretty sparse up there. The only ptarmigan I saw were too shy to approach closely, so after putting up the same pair three times over long distances I pushed on, higher and higher. The long march back took me over and through some wild and windy country. I'd set myself a long, looping course to cover before *Tiglax* returned, and I really had to hoof it to accomplish the entire loop before the vessel's return. When I topped out and looked out over many miles of Amlia with my ten-power binoculars, I could just make out *Tiglax* returning from the western shores, and I could see that Steve had also just topped out near the big waterfall at the bay's head. I hadn't counted on battling a strong north wind the whole way back, but you can move fast across the hard, fell-field habitat of the highlands.

After a round trip just short of six straight hours of hard marching, I was back at the pickup point. I was exhausted when we got back to the boat, and it seemed a good idea to eat dinner before sitting down to the hour or more of specimen duties in store before I could quit for the day. Usually birds come before food, but I needed the sort of energetic and motivational boost that only food can give. Bob, the cook, invariably prepared a delectable spread for each and every meal—one of the many factors that makes life aboard *Tiglax* so enjoyable. It is a sign of the extreme land-based physical effort that I actually lost weight on this trip. Bob's cooking would certainly cause one to predict that the opposite should occur with every voyage. But that night, Bob felt really bad that nobody had told him that two of us hadn't made it to dinner, and in cleaning up after leftover night he'd thrown out the remains. No matter to me: the slop pail was right there beside the galley counter, and when Bob wasn't looking I was able to fish out some of the best of it. I was very happy to have warm food at all, and some of the selected contents became delectable after a couple of minutes in the microwave.

The next day we had the northern shores to cover, so we left the calm bay where we'd anchored for the night and went around to the northern side. In rounding its eastern end the island presented a memorable sight— it's remarkably narrow end-on. As we moved around to the Bering Sea side, the island showed a much more foreboding face. It was no longer the island of the past couple of days, but rather a wild place of brooding cliffs and pounding surf. This side did not have a bay like Sviechnikof. There was a poor bay along the northeastern quarter that we went into at around midday. As soon as we began the approach a school of Dall porpoise began sporting around and alongside us, and they kept up their play until we stopped. One of the skiffs went in to shore for a quick look, but we neither anchored nor stopped for long in the rough water. Much farther along the northern shores the island became less rugged. There was still plenty of topography, but fewer cliffs met one at the shoreline. Here there was also a better bay, and after gingerly going in, charting depths electronically all the way, we found that we could anchor up for a trip ashore. After dinner we had a fast few hours on the island—our farewell visit.

My goals on this final lap were to obtain any wrens or ptarmigan possible in a rapid tour of the nearby highlands. The first pair of ptarmigan that I put up, still in sight of the ship, were as skittery as the others had been; their rapid wingbeats and a croak from the male bade me a fast (and too distant) farewell. A wren surprised me in a grassy seam at the top of a cliff, and I had no choice but to take a quick shot with ptarmigan load in the gun. The shot gave us both a surprise: he flew out of the center of the pattern completely unscathed, and I was left with a poignant reminder of why we use 7-1/2 shot for ptarmigan and 9 or 12 shot for wrens and other small birds. To my satisfaction, I was able to find him again on the jumbled cliff top, and this time I was able to obtain him with the correct load—to my knowledge the only existing modern specimen of an Amlia Pacific Wren.

Up on a broad, undulating highland, it was windy again. I went on a long, roundabout loop looking for birds. It was wildly beautiful, an amazing wilderness rarely seen and rarely experienced. As I rapidly marched over and through it, the hand of man seemed far, far away. The sun was shining, and visibility was superb. A dark Aleutian Peregrine Falcon circled and

Figure 16.3. Amlia Island, Aleutian Islands, Alaska.

screamed at me from a distance, annoyed at my presence near its nest. But this country yielded few birds—perhaps in part because of the peregrine's presence.

After covering the high, windy country and finding no ptarmigan (and very little else), I had to descend to cross a small, marshy valley and creek before I could get back up to other highlands and use those (i.e., their easier surface to walk on) to head back to shore and ship. As I neared the bottom, another pair of ptarmigan flushed, once again at a great distance. But this time I walked in well below them on the steep slope where they had landed and was able to approach close enough to obtain the pair. Thus concluded the last, and very successful, stop on Amlia Island for bird collecting. I hoofed it back to the drop-off point, and the shore parties were soon picked up at their respective spots. As soon as the people and skiff were aboard, Kevin Bell weighed anchor and headed for Adak. Jeb Stuart had caught a seventy-five-pound Pacific halibut from the fantail while we'd been ashore, and the fox trappers had found good places to put their camps. We were a happy group.

That night as we made for Adak, I had one of the most bizarre nightmares I can remember. In my dream I was just trying to conduct myself in ordinary day-to-day business; I can't recall any details, but in its thread it was just a real-life sort of dream. The nightmare part was that I suffered some sort of strange and horrible affliction: unseen forces were pushing me and pulling me in different directions, unpredictable both in direction and in time. At one point I remember saying to someone in my dream, "Oh no, here it comes again," before being whisked backwards from pressure on or in my chest. The forces seemed internal, and the general attitude was one of fatality. The banging of dinner plates in the nearby galley woke me, and, although I'd slept poorly, I was happy to be awake after that dream. Its source was immediately clear. When you're used to sleeping on a bed that doesn't move, nights aboard ship can be very trying. On the nights when we'd been anchored, I'd slept like the dead, to my knowledge utterly dreamless.

Adak was a sharp contrast to our previous island stops. We were back in civilization. A large group helped offload gear and supplies. After getting set up in the bunkhouse and changing into my "dancing shoes" (rubber boots), I joined Christy Pruett and Deb Rocque, students working under my supervision at the University, for an afternoon of bird collecting. They'd been on the island for a few days, covering this section of the Aleutians for spring migration. We were lucky enough to find some Bar-tailed Godwits passing through. Amazingly enough, I was able to get two and keep my feet dry. At dinner I found that things in the dining hall hadn't changed— they still served high-quality food very much overcooked. The group at

Figure 16.4. Christin Pruett and Deborah Rocque as PhD students in the field collecting birds, Adak Island, Aleutian Islands, Alaska.

dinner was smaller than last year, however, and few women and children were evident. The asbestos abatement and demolition work seemed to be finished. That night I slept like a rock on a bed that didn't move.

Next day we began doing the circuit, looking for migrants that might have come in during the night. A Tufted Duck proved uncooperative on a long walk, but we were able to get several Song Sparrows to increase the sample size of modern specimens from this important island. The weather was Aleutian—windy, rainy, and cold. Birds were generally laying low, and we were happy to be doing most of our cruising in a vehicle, rather than on foot. At one stop for Song Sparrows, a Pelagic Cormorant became the object of our attention. For population-level documentation, we wanted ten from the island. Deb was a little uncertain of the gun she was using, which was new to her, and so asked if I would collect the bird. It stood on the last piling of a row of them left from an old World War II dock, and it proved overly tame. At my shot it fell into the water, and I had to move fast to retrieve it before the wind took it out into the bay.

As I neared the last piling, I was sure that the old concrete I was running on just under the water would also give out, and I was right. But I could see some good rocks right there and so continued on. The first step went fine, but the next one, the one that had me just one step shy of the bird, put me up to mid-thigh in remarkably cold water. The water was instantly numbing, and the next step proved no drier. I latched onto the bird and turned back. But that first step back proved to be a tough one—I tripped and went down, stopping myself only when I was down in up to my chest, trying desperately to hold my gun above water. I tasted salt water in my mouth as I gasped and huffed and puffed in that *freezing* water and struggled back out. Once out, the air felt positively *hot* in contrast to the frigid water. I stood by the vehicle, dripping, while Deb and Christy went after the Song Sparrow we'd stopped for. It was an excellent lesson in how not to get cormorants, and I couldn't help but remember that the last time I'd gotten a cormorant I'd done the same damned thing. It took an hour to clean the gun, which had taken a little seawater after all, perhaps in a splash.

My final day on this trip was a long one, filled entirely with travel. Reeve Aleutian Airways has long had a reputation of remarkable dependability, often flying in weather that would ground other pilots and airlines in a region renowned for its bad weather. But lately their fleet has been plagued by mechanical difficulties, and flights have not been very dependable. Cancellations and delays were frequent. The check-in procedure at the small terminal on Adak bordered on the ridiculous; it was the product of the combination of federal regulations and a small airline staff at this remote outpost. On "plane day" (only two each week), passengers must bring their baggage to the terminal to be checked between 7:00 a.m. and 9:00 a.m. Then you have to show up again at about 11:30 to check a hand-carried bag (only one is allowed) and to pick up a boarding pass. When you've finished going through this second line and are back in the small terminal waiting, the plane lands (provided it's on schedule), and you mingle with and greet the arriving passengers (it's a small world, so you're likely to meet people you know). Finally, one last line is formed for passing through a security check, and you're allowed to pick up your checked handbag on the way out to the old, four-engined, propeller-drive Electra. The 727 was not able to make the run that day, adding an hour to the journey each way. After learning this at check-in in the morning, I'd gone back to the bunkhouse to try to change my connecting flight from Anchorage to Fairbanks, but the phones were out.

Later, when the phones came back up, I learned that there was no space on later evening flights from Anchorage to Fairbanks. So the delay of the Electra was costing me the chance of making any connections in Anchorage. The best I could do was to fly standby that night and have a confirmed flight out the next morning. Ugh. It was gold rush season again—tourists were flocking to Fairbanks to buy moose-turd earrings. After a long wait in the Anchorage airport, I lucked out and made it home in the last seat on the last flight of the day. And here it was green, green, green.

17

Summertime, and the Living is Easy

AFTER A COOL, WET SPRING, summer seemed to be brewing up as more of the same. There had been a remarkable amount of office work to be done, keeping my nose pressed to the old grindstone. I sat down to write this out of desperation for something different to do in the middle of reading a massive pile of theses—six students were defending in a two-week period, and I was on all six committees. But it was a great time of progress, so after a little diversion it would be back to the theses.

Rose and I decided we'd have to get out and have some fun a couple of times this summer. On the solstice we went canoeing after work. We parked Rose's car at a pullout on the Tanana River near home, then took the canoe on top of the truck to Cushman Street in downtown Fairbanks. We put in on the Chena River right in downtown Fairbanks, near the best and the worst of it. We hadn't seen Fairbanks from this angle before, and we looked forward to a peaceful paddle with the river's current to inspect this historically important side of our town.

The Cushman area can be both reputable and disreputable. We got off to an action-packed start. Within twenty meters of shore, three things happened in quick succession. A small, flat, racing boat began whining, spinning, and throwing up a roostertail; the driver had to lie facing forward just in front of the oversized outboard motor. It did not look fun. As he sped off downriver, something could be heard approaching the river from the left bank. As we turned to see what was crashing toward the river, a woman came rolling out of the narrow patch of woods with her pants down around her ankles. As she struggled to pull them back up, a pair of dogs and their owners also stepped up to the bank. The fast, loud boat and the approaching dogs must have caused this woman to lose her balance at a critical point in taking a leak. Close to some of the area's low-rent bars, a few minutes earlier this must have seemed to be an out of the way place to get some relief. Surprise! Rose and I held off talking and laughing until we were down the river a ways.

Canoeing through an urban and suburban area is interesting. We were repeatedly passed by Jet Skis piloted (usually) by overweight young males—a combination that Rose charmingly termed "jet dinks." Their most acrobatic zooming seemed invariably to be done where they could be observed, such as in front of a big outdoor restaurant deck. Farther down we were passed by the riverboat, Discovery III, a large paddlewheel vessel used for tourist rides. Eventually we hit the Tanana River, which was quite a transition: from the relatively clear and calm Chena River to the faster, roiling current of the Tanana, with a high silt load and a bubbling effervescence of escaping air bubbles.

One of the human dramas of this summer has been "Our man in Watson Lake." A new student, Andrew Johnson, had been driving up from Michigan to start here at the University as a graduate student under my supervision. Unfortunately, his transmission went out in the small town of Watson Lake, Yukon. And, just as unfortunately, there wasn't another transmission available anywhere nearby. Andy's dad sent one up from the US, but it took an inordinate amount of time to arrive despite the UPS guarantee, and Andy was stuck in Watson Lake for about two weeks. The rumor mill concocted a good story that he'd fallen in love and had decided to stay in Watson Lake. But the truth was that he found a temporary job at a resort where he could work in exchange for room, board, and some salary while waiting for that errant transmission to arrive. Andy did eventually leave Watson Lake, and upon his arrival here we learned from others at the University that Watson Lake is the Bermuda Triangle of the Yukon—many have been stranded there en route to Fairbanks.

One Sunday afternoon as I went in to the office to catch up on some work, I saw smoke moving in from the west. Several hours later, the whole region was heavily inundated with a strong, thick pall. The forests of the Interior have been on fire ever since. The odor of smoke only varies from light to heavy, and during the heavy periods the sun ranges from deep orange to flaring red. After a couple of weeks of this, we were ready for a change back to clear air.

One fun thing about summer is going to the movies. It's neat to go into the googolplex, sit in a dark theater to watch a great movie, then emerge at ten or eleven in the evening into full glaring daylight.

After one movie, we stopped at Wendy's to have a small shake, and I was surprised when the clerk snapped out what seemed an absurd question: "Want to piggie size that?"

"What?"

"Want to piggie size that?"

It still took a second to realize I was hearing "piggie" for "biggie," but the caloric interpretation was the same. I don't think most people eating at Wendy's should want to piggie size anything further.

Every day as we drove home this summer, we were confronted by subtle mailbox humor. On our route home the main road comes to a "T," and just across the road from the stop sign there used to be a wooden stand with a row of mailboxes on it. One night during the peak of winter (or is it the nadir?) somebody went through the stop sign at great speed and used their vehicle to bowl over the mailboxes, continuing to plow on into and up the bank behind them, scattering boxes and their stand all over the snow, and leaving pieces of the vehicle's front end on the embankment. Somebody rearranged the wreckage at one point, but—perhaps under the influence of alcohol—somebody again went mailbox bowling with their vehicle. The embankment, once again littered with vehicle debris and mailboxes, looked like a real frame bender. (Alcohol consumption is apparently high in the winter.) Well, once the ground was thawed, one frustrated mailbox owner rebuilt a nice stand, lengthy enough for all the former box occupants, and put their one box back in place (not even in the center). And there it sits all alone on a stand big enough for the whole neighborhood—a far less tempting target for mailbox bowling next winter.

This thesis season fell right across our usual salmon dip netting on the Copper River. That was one thing Rose and I were really looking forward to doing, so we kept a close eye on when the season was opening and closing (they leave it open only for a few days at a time) and also on the numbers of fish passing across the sonar station at Miles Lake, which is a ten- to fourteen-day fish-swim from Chitina. Right in the middle of the thesis onslaught, the season was open and the fish numbers seemed decent. So on a Wednesday afternoon we left work early, threw our gear into the truck, and headed south on the six-hour drive to Chitina. It's a beautiful drive, and we listened to a book on tape as we took in the Alaska scenery. Upon arriving at O'Brien Creek at about eight that evening, we pitched our tent, fixed dinner, and went on a stroll through the fishermen down by the river to see how things were running before retiring to our spacious and comfortable tent. It was not raining, the creek was running loudly right beside the tent, and we had a great night's sleep.

We arose early and got everything ready for going out on the river all day, packing up a box of equipment, having breakfast, and packing away the tent before going down to meet the charter boat. We were one of two couples going out on the first drop-off at 7:00 a.m. The river was high and rising, and the success had been mixed the day before. Well down into the throat of the canyon, where the Copper River roars at ferocious and turbulent levels, we were dropped on a steep little crack beside a raging back eddy. In our three years of dip netting this was certainly the wildest spot we'd been placed; the water boiled up like a 747 was coming to the surface. We wasted no time in tying ourselves off to small trees on the steep bank. If you fall into wild water like this, there's a good chance you won't live to tell about it; having a way back to shore increases the odds.

The current here was very strong, and holding our nets in it all day proved a constant muscular trial. The river was high and rising, and the fishing was slow. But there was enough activity to keep it exciting. Our fourth fish hit my net very hard—not something you relish when wedged precariously on a precipice with deep, wildly roiling water splashing at your feet. I knew it was a king salmon as soon as it hit, and I hauled in for all I was worth. Sure enough, out of the opaque water came this giant beauty of a fish, bashing and splashing me furiously as I tried to maintain my balance and prevent its escape. Rose went for the club while I stood there wrestling with this fish, knowing that with my adrenalin levels (and my ability to breathe) it would get tired before I did. So I held it suspended and thrashing until it slowed down and I could climb up to better footing, then we were able to subdue it and get it onto a stringer. Wow. My first king. I think the adrenalin rush kept me going for the rest of the day.

We kept at it for 10.5 long, hard hours, and averaged just barely over one fish per hour, finishing the long day with eleven fish. It was the first time that we hadn't caught our limit. But we had calculated the night before that based on the price of salmon at the grocery store it would take ten fish to break even on the trip, so we had done just fine. I had gotten a second, smaller king—another great adrenalin rush—but this year we were only allowed to keep one, so I had to let it go. It was painful then, knowing that we wouldn't come close to catching our limit, but now, after having partaken of king number one, it hurts even more. Last year, when we were allowed to keep four of this species, we hadn't caught a single one.

Both Rose and I were very tired and sore when we quit for the day and went back to the campground in the charter. Dip netting is a lot of hard work. The beauty of the canyon gradually diminishes during the day as your arms and back get sore and you aren't catching many fish. But it had been a pretty fun day—certainly a welcome break from the office.

After gutting our fish and putting them in the cooler layered with ice, we headed home, expecting to get back at about one in the morning. We were delayed and nearly foiled in this goal by the unexpected. A strange sound on a remote stretch of the Richardson Highway just before ten in the evening turned out to be a flat tire. No problem, we thought, as untold millions of mosquitoes homed in on us and we prepared to change that tire. Thank goodness we had had the foresight to get a real spare after that Haul Road episode a couple of years ago. But, after we got that spare unmounted and out in the open, the stupidity of the driver reared its ugly head in a distinctly unpleasant form: the spare was flat. I had meant to check it before we left. Honest.

We were smearing on bug dope like crazy and looking skeptically at our surroundings; this was a very unlikely spot to camp for the night. Now, both last year and this year, after I'd had my studded tires changed to plain tires for the summer, the boys at the shop had not done a perfect job in mounting the non-studded tires (or so I'd thought). One always had a slow leak (this was not the one that had gone flat). So I'd bought a hand pump to top it off periodically, and I kept this in the back of the truck (some might wonder why I didn't just take it back and have it done right; but others understand that it's easier to just give it a few pumps every few days). Anyway, that pump was surely just the ticket. We had that baby out and hooked to the spare in no time. But the flat spare was not sealed at the rim, and so it would take no air. Looking again at our surroundings, it still seemed like a bad spot to camp for the night. So in a burst of clear thinking, we hooked the pump up to the flat, I pumped like a madman, Rose stowed the jack and spare, and we roared out of there, figuring out the distance to the next outpost of civilization—with Rose hanging out the window checking to see whether the tire was going flat.

Meier's Lake Lodge was just under fifteen miles away, and each five miles I got out and pumped like a madman again before racing off on the next short leg. It would have been humorous if it were happening to someone else, but short, Anglo-Saxon words rolled steadily through my head. Meier's Lake Lodge held out little hope for us in the way of tire repair, but it would at least give us a leg up on it in the morning. The small store there was still open, and I walked in hoping against hope that they might have a can of that tire repair stuff that I'd heard about but never tried. As I asked, my eye fell on a can of it. The last one. Eight dollars seemed a little steep for this stuff, but I was amazed that they even had it, and it was worth a try. I pumped furiously once again before emptying this spray can of goop into the tire. It made a pleasing, sputtering sound when it hit the leak, and we left in a hurry, being careful to follow the directions to drive two to five miles immediately to help it seal.

We were prepared to have to return to Meier's Lodge, but after five miles a careful inspection showed no further loss of air. And it was the same after the next five miles. And the next. A hundred miles later, just at midnight, we hit Delta Junction—this was the only place to get tires repaired. But of course everything was closed. The tire looked fine, though, so we zoomed on the last hundred miles to Fairbanks, arriving at 2:00 a.m. and happy to be arriving at all. When we woke up later in the morning, the flat was completely flat. And, in moving tires around the next day, I learned that the one with the slow leak had both a screw and a nail in it. Now the tires are all in great shape. I'm still working on the driver stupidity problem.

So, luck had been mediocre in the fishing, but definitely on our side in the post-flat phase of the trip. Later that day, after another thesis had been read and the fish were all cleaned and in the freezer, we engaged in the gastronomic phase of the trip, concocting culinary delights unsurpassed in excellence. First was the pile of very thinly sliced raw salmon (sashimi) salvaged from the fileted carcasses. With wasabi and soy sauce this is a rare and wonderful treat. And the wasabi sinus therapy will cure any summer cold. At the same time, using the king salmon head and skeleton, we made up some of the best soup I think I've ever had. We ate that soup for three days straight and could have kept on going if we hadn't run out. And I honestly can't remember which ended first, the soup or the theses.

King salmon bouillabaisse with wild rice and roasted garlic, over baby asparagus with scallions and parmesan cheese.

Simmer one king salmon head and skeleton in water with some thyme, bay leaf, salt, and pepper. Cool, pick meat into a separate bowl, discard bones and skin. Holding meat aside in the fridge, simmer the broth for several hours to concentrate, then add wild rice and barley. After half an hour more of simmering, add carrots, celery, onions, garlic, fish sauce, white wine, V8, and salt and pepper to taste. In the last ten minutes, add the cooked meat and, separately, cook asparagus and place in a bowl. Ladle the hearty soup over the asparagus and sprinkle on chopped scallions and freshly grated parmesan cheese.

18

Of Moose and a Deadman

BACK LAST WINTER, DAD called up with the suggestion that we go moose hunting this fall. Nonresidents can hunt big game in Alaska without the added expense of hiring a guide if they go with a resident family member. It sure sounded good to me; I hadn't been hunting for game animals since coming to Alaska three-and-a-half years ago. That's a long time to go without hunting big game when you enjoy game meat as much as we do.

The trip began for me months before the season. For one, I didn't have an appropriate rifle. For another, having never gone big game hunting here before, I had no idea about where one could productively go. When I inquired about fly-in hunts, I learned that most were completely booked for the year as early as January and February. My colleague Joe Cook had a good hunt in floating the Chatanika River some years ago, and it sounded like a good float trip and an opportunity to get a moose.

Once I decided this was the trip to take, Rose and I spent a day on each of a couple of summer weekends scoping out the put-in and takeout points of the river. Our drive up to the put-in point was on a gorgeously clear summer day, and we found a very nice, small river—clear, cold, and fast-running. We also saw a spike buck yearling moose—a good omen. He didn't want to leave the road as we pushed him along in front of the truck. And he was probably among the first moose to hit a freezer in Fairbanks when the season began for residents on 1 September.

The takeout point, though in mileage closer to home, proved to be a seriously difficult place to go in a small, two-wheel drive pickup. The last fifteen miles of Murphy Dome Road are four-wheel-drive miles, and we were under-trucked to do it in anything less. After bouncing our way for fourteen of those miles, we were stopped by some serious mud. So we walked the last mile to the river. It looked like it would be possible to drive it if only the rains would let up. But they didn't. What a wet summer we had.

Once we knew where we'd be going and I had my rifle ordered, there were a few miscellaneous necessities to acquire. When Rocket Surplus had a fifty-percent-off sale, I picked up a rubber raft and a box of MREs (Army surplus "Meals Ready to Eat"). The raft was to augment our capacity for floating out great quantities of moose meat. The MREs were for quick and easy lunches in the field. Dad was shopping, too, and we coordinated over the phone.

When Dad came up a day and a half before the nonresident season began (on 5 September), we had a bunch of final work to do before heading out on the three-day float trip. Building big piles of gear then trimming them down to portable size is a familiar exercise. This time, however, we were anticipating adding 600–800 pounds of moose meat to our load during the trip. In dropping the truck off at the end of Murphy Dome Road, I found the last mile to be worse than when Rose and I had walked it a few weeks earlier. A big piece of the road had been washed out, and the mud wallows were deeper than ever. I made it to the end, but my hands were shaking as I parked, and I had no idea whether we'd be able to get the truck back out again.

That night we finished packing and did a final paring down of gear. The next morning, Rose dropped us off on the river just off of the Elliott Highway, and our trip began. We paddled for the better part of an hour, then got out and hunted for about an hour. This became our pattern for the next two days, and we saw a lot of beautiful country and moose sign. The colors were at their peak, and we saw very few people.

Figure 18.1. Fred and Kevin Winker set off on a float trip moose hunting, Chatanika River, Alaska (photo by Rose Meier).

The moose themselves seemed to be pretty scarce, though. Each time we stopped to hunt, we saw a lot of sign, but no moose. Dad finally spotted our first in the evening on the riverbank—a yearling female down to drink. We floated silently by her as close as twenty feet while she watched us pass, and we camped on the same bar just around the bend. It was good to be out on a cool evening setting up camp and cooking a hot dinner. We'd packed pretty lightly, bringing only a small backpacking stove on which to boil water for dehydrated food in pouches, but it sure tasted good at the end of a long, tiring day.

The next day was a repeat of the first, with the two of us seeming to always be just behind a lot of moose, judging from the tracks and pellets.

OF MOOSE AND A DEADMAN

We'd left most of the few people behind, though, and we seemed to have a hundred square miles to ourselves. The colors were gorgeous, and in the morning the river was alive with beavers busily cutting small trees and branches and hauling them to their underwater caches. Many let us pass very close to them, and others gave resounding tail splashes when we got too close. Nearly everywhere that we got out, the banks were covered in willows and alders that showed evidence of years of being eaten—bitten off low by beavers or high by moose.

At one point we were lucky enough to see a rare sight. As a Red-breasted Merganser flew toward us up the river, a Northern Goshawk appeared out of nowhere going for the duck. Just as it seemed the goshawk would strike, the merganser barely escaped with its life by making an uncontrolled, gravity-assisted tumble out of the air and into the water. You could almost hear that goshawk go "Doh!" and imagine that the duck was rinsing out its shorts.

As we floated silently along on our second morning, I heard a heavy animal walking along in the forest above the riverbank. The bank was high enough that we couldn't see what was up there, but it was clearly something big. Dad heard it, too. I had been fooled earlier by a red squirrel cutting spruce cones and letting them fall to the forest floor below. The cracks as the cones hit leaves and fallen tree trunks had sounded like a large animal. But upon careful consideration, these sounds had a distinct gravity component (flit, flit, flit, crack!), and they were very tightly located, so one lesson was all it took to prevent my being misled again. It really was a big animal this time. We quickly found a tolerable place to put in on the bank, and Dad was out of the canoe with his rifle out of its case in no time. As he scrambled up the steep bank, I got my rifle out of its case, pulled up the canoe more firmly, and followed him up.

My eyes were ready to see a nice, big moose. But there wasn't one there. There was nothing to be seen! Then, in scanning again, I saw something much lower to the ground moving in the grass beside an ephemeral pond. As a head turned, I realized that it was a black bear, and I flipped up my scope covers and clicked off the safety. Before going hunting I had read the regulations, and I was surprised to find that residents in this hunting zone had what might be termed a "Goldilocks limit" of black bears—we could shoot three of these animals! This seemed astonishing to me, until I realized that I'd heard that one of the major predators on moose calves was bears. Well, with heart pounding, adrenalin racing, and lungs pumping after a steep riverbank climb—what can I say? To make a long story short, that bear stood right up and looked at us, just like in the movies. And I completely missed. More than once. We looked the scene over very carefully, and I followed its tracks for over 200 meters. I still don't know how I could have missed at about 80 meters, but that's what happened.

At one of our many stops I found a yearling female moose a moderate distance from our pullout point and thought I heard another moose nearby. But it was going to take longer than our agreed-upon time to fully inspect the situation, so I returned to the canoe and got Dad so we could both creep around and find out what was in the area. We split up at a small tree that had recently been de-barked by a moose rubbing its antlers on it, and we began to slowly and quietly work our way around a large, open swamp. Not 100 meters farther along, I suddenly spotted a very large moose torso standing at right angles to the path I was walking on. Boy, did my heart start pounding. It was a *huge* animal, and I was sure it had to be a male, although its head was behind a dense spruce and I couldn't tell its sex for sure. I snapped off the scope covers and clicked off the safety and used the scope to try to find antlers through the dense spruce. It took awhile to steady the shaking, but once I had it under control I had no luck seeing through that spruce. And the moose just stood there, not moving. After a couple of minutes of this the shaking began again—this time from arms too tired to hold the gun up any longer. I had a perfect, easy shot at the heart, but I didn't dare take it until I had proof that it was a male. I had seen an ear flick through the spruce, but that was all. I very slowly and carefully eased my way to a fallen log on the trail and sat down to steady my arms. And after several more minutes of this I gave up using the scope and took out my binoculars. I was beginning to think this moose would never move! All of a sudden off to my left, another moose whooshed or barked, and this animal's big head swung around to look. But it was the massive head of a very large cow, not a bull. Damn. It had sure had my pulse going. The whooshing sort of bark kept on going. I wasn't sure what was going on, so I went over that way. After awhile it stopped, and I could hear the animal walking off through the forest. It turned out that another female had come upon Dad waiting at a good point of the swamp edge and had stood there facing him and telling him off.

Before turning in each night, I used the GPS and the topo map to figure out how far we'd gone on the amazingly twisty river. It sure didn't seem very far—those twists added a lot of mileage to a relatively short straight-line distance. The river mileage over our course must have been at least fifty to sixty miles for a distance as the raven flies of only about thirty-two miles. The river exhibited a lot of differences along this stretch, varying from a highly winding, rapidly flowing course through primarily deciduous woodland to a less winding, sluggish course through black spruce bog country, then into a fast, but straighter course through hills.

On our second night it looked as though we had covered only half of the distance. The third and final day was a long one. We had camped for the night in bog country, with little moose sign. Our morning hunts turned up little; we'd left the oxbow lakes and better moose country behind, it seemed. There was still a lot to be seen, but moose densities were sure low. Light rain and heavy dew made us both glad we had good rain pants and waterproof parkas, and we found ourselves wearing our gloves most of the time.

We soon found ourselves paddling a lot more in the sluggish current, and the river became less twisty, so we were making better time. But just when it seemed that the surrounding country was becoming more moosish, we began hitting cabins intermittently along the way. Cabin density increased as we came back into hill country. One must have been built by a helicopter pilot—it was positioned absurdly high up off the river. It seemed that a good portion of Fairbanks liked to have small vacation cabins out on this river. This was a little surprising, because the shallow river provides the only access to the far side (four-wheelers can apparently come down off of Murphy Dome to access the near side).

Once we hit hill country again, the current picked up. We stopped at a few places to hunt, but we really spent most of the day paddling. Dad could probably paddle all day without switching sides; I had to request a switch once in awhile. There is almost never wind in the Fairbanks area, but there were several long, straight stretches of river where we fought headwinds—only to take a corner and find that we were still fighting headwinds! The course of the winds down there must have been well channeled by the surrounding hills. But we made excellent time, and the scenery was beautiful. We spotted a couple of moose on the bank at one point—a cow and her calf—and there were more hunters evident along with the increased cabin density. At one point on the bank we saw a big porcupine just slowly going about its business.

We pulled up at the pullout point in the early evening, more quickly than I thought we could. After working some of the stiff kinks out by standing and stretching, it was quick work to put the canoe on the truck and load up our gear. Another guy was sitting at the pullout on a canoe with a small fire going. He and his partner had been out hunting the same stretch for six days, and, like us, they had not seen a single male moose. His partner had gone walking out to call their ride; they'd reached the pullout point two days earlier than expected. After driving through the mud puddles (barely inching out of one), we bumped along the long road out, first stopping to look for a moose we'd scared off the road, then picking up the hunter's partner farther along. He said he'd had to walk 5.2 miles out to make a call on his cell phone. So much for Mom's suggested emergency gear. I was glad we hadn't figured out how to get one, given that this guy hadn't been able to use his on the whole trip.

I spent a long day in at work the next day catching up, but on Saturday we had planned to do some work on the next phase of finishing off the last room of our house. The previous owners had left one large room unfinished, and Rose and I had decided that it was time to get it done. Over the summer I'd been puttering around wiring it, and we'd just finished insulating the walls and putting up the vapor barrier. Drywall was one thing we didn't want to do, but we'd been having trouble getting a contractor to do it. And it had to be done soon, because it was getting cold, and we had to have the ceiling up to insulate the attic above. Well, Dad's visit sure solved this problem.

There were three parts about putting up drywall that we didn't want to have any part of: carrying thirty sheets of it upstairs and around many corners to get the material into the room; holding sheets up to the ceiling to get them screwed down; and taping and texturing. One of the things that appeared to be keeping contractors from committing to our job was that they seemed to dislike the idea of getting the material into that upstairs corner room just as badly as we did—and I guess they were busy enough that they didn't need the work.

The company selling the material didn't want our puny job, either—you had to buy a lot more drywall to get them to leave the yard with their boom truck. But with Dad here, we had a good team. In no time we had a workable plan in place to pick up the stuff and get it up into the room with little trouble. We built a two-by-four cradle and rigged a rope yoke and a pair of pulleys and hauled two eight-foot sheets at a time lengthwise up through the room's window (which had never been put in). There was a little excitement when the rope broke once (fortunately Rose had stepped back). And when we got to the 5/8-inch ceiling sheets, we were pooped enough to go one sheet at a time. But we got it all up.

The next breakthrough that Dad brought up with him was the concept of the deadman. I remember watching drywall hangers holding heavy sheets, four-by-ten-feet, up against the ceilings with their heads while they screwed them down. Rose and I figured we weren't going to be able to do that very well. But this deadman thing sounded pretty neat—it's just two two-by-fours hinged together at the middle of one of them to form a "T." One of the boards is left at eight feet and the other is cut just short enough to wedge a 5/8-inch sheet of drywall up against the ceiling when it's kicked into place to form the upright "T." The cross-piece supports the sheet across its length. Well, it took all of ten minutes to make one, and the first couple of sheets went up easily. Over the course of four evenings of puttering away, we had the whole ceiling done.

But before that, on Sunday, we abandoned drywall and went moose hunting again, this time on an upper stretch of the Chatanika. It was an incredibly gorgeous day—sunny and with a peak of fall colors. I couldn't remember being out on such an amazing fall day. It had been unusually wet in late summer, and as a consequence we had peak autumn colors longer than usual.

The shoreline was steeper than where we'd hunted before, with fewer wetlands and less moose sign. We did find some sign—but no living moose. There was one area in a huge aspen parkland where, last year, moose had scraped off tremendous amounts of bark up to nine feet and even higher. When I found a place in this woodland of violent giants that showed fresh scraping, I clutched my gun a lot tighter and my head-swivel rate went way up.

We walked a lot at every stop. My left hip complained bitterly about hopping through the second-story window onto the ladder about twenty times the day before. Rose's cracking a joke on one of those leg-up oofs had caused a good strain as I cracked up laughing. Nevertheless, we covered a lot of ground, both on foot and paddling.

This upper Chatanika was a wilder river, and several corners were fairly tricky. Sometimes when we cut corners, we wiped out or came close to it as the front end of the canoe left the rapid downriver current and hit the backcurrent while the rear was still entirely gripped in the fast downriver flow. The water was also shallower, and there were several places where we scraped bottom. On one part of the river, I was pulling hard to prevent a spinout and broke the paddle. Damn. But I just grabbed the spare engine— an aluminum-shafted backup paddle—and we kept going.

Not much farther along, another hunter cruised up behind us. On a Jet Ski. Now I'd seen everything. Although it looked like a good way to quickly get to a hunting spot, we couldn't figure out an easy way to bring meat back out. Maybe, like us, he was getting used to coming back empty. It was a gorgeous fall, though, and Dad was able to get in a train trip to Denali before he had to go home and we had to drag our tired bodies back to work.

Disclaimer: Although we did our best to make it otherwise, no animals were harmed in the making of this story. Two sheets of drywall did get their corners broken in a bit of an accident (when the rope broke), but we had a heck of a good time.

19

Harmonious Cloacal Tunes in Singapore

IN SOME OLD BIRD SPECIMEN preparation guides, the single orifice at the rear-end of a bird is euphamistically called the "vent." Its proper name is the "cloaca," and we wanted a bunch of them. Fresh. You don't see spindles much anymore, but sometimes, when I'm in that vague state between sleeping and not, I envision a spindle racked high with bird cloacas. Not a pretty image, I'll agree. Nevertheless, the avian cloaca is a subject I have begun to know well. Funny—I could not envision being a proctologist, but avian cloacas are to me a philosophically neutral aspect of the universe, falling somewhere between raw sewage and fine chocolates. As neutral as this may be, however, I am careful not to lick my fingers while at work, and I advise all who work with me to follow this lead.

This is not the mindset of the normal foreign traveler, so you can expect that my views of Singapore or any other place I visit are somewhat different from what you would expect to read on the back of a postcard. (Well, maybe not too different from the postcards I send or receive.)

My trip to Singapore in November was one of those pleasant accidents. I had wanted to go for some time, ever since hearing stories about it from our colleague Henry Springer, who had visited there from Alaska a couple of years ago. But our field budget was fully committed to two other trips—Australia and the Philippines—neither of which I could go on. But the Philippines fell through for the season due to protracted permit negotiations, and Singapore seemed like an excellent backup plan. As soon as we learned that the Philippines wasn't going to work for the autumn season, I fired off an email to the only person in Singapore listed in *The Flock*, the directory of the North American ornithological societies. Navjot Sodhi, who had obtained his PhD in Canada and was now at the National University of Singapore, answered back immediately and welcomed our proposed visit. Navjot proved to be a wonderful person and host. It turned out that although he didn't know it (he was interested in other parts of the birds), he was also the king of avian cloacas in Singapore. What luck!

The downside of it all was that I had not planned to go into the field until the first of December. Although I was not teaching in fall semester, my dance card was overflowing with other commitments, particularly with multiple search committee obligations. The gyrations I had to go through to change my schedule were painful, but mostly just to me. In the end, with a sleep deficit and Rose's expert help, I was able to move my travel schedule up two weeks and leave for Singapore on 11 November on the red-eye to Seattle. But it was one of those times that I was packing right up to departure time. Yikes. We've fielded a lot of expeditions out of our garage, but this was one of the most down-to-the-wire so far. The last lid was crammed on and the last duct tape whipped around containers of field equipment just in time for a fast drive to the airport. Off to Southeast Asia—a new region for my own study of birds.

The flight pretty well sucked. It was really long, and leaving in the middle of the night only made it seem longer. An undergraduate in my lab had given me a tip before I left about a certain place in the Seattle airport where it was quiet enough to get some sleep on long layovers. That tip was right on, and upon my 5:45 a.m. arrival I went straight there, lay on the floor, covered up with my raincoat, and slept like the dead for a couple of hours. From there I went straight to the longest airport line I've ever been in—the Northwest Airlines line for international passengers. All I needed was a seat number, but it took almost two hours to get it. In the end I did obtain an emergency-row window seat, so in leg space it was well worth the wait (it was a ten-hour flight).

Somewhere on this flight we crossed the international dateline. I caught a couple of short naps. At one point I looked out the window over a rugged land of pristine, snow-covered mountains. It did not look at all familiar. Although it seemed geographically unlikely for a flight from Seattle to Tokyo, by timing calculations and the crude map in the seat pocket it was clear that we were flying over the Kamchatka Peninsula. What a remarkably desolate region! I saw just one short road that went a little way from the sea; there were neither buildings nor anything else visible. This location diagnosis was confirmed by angle and direction when we hit the coast again, and a comparatively short time later we were flying over Japan. As I sat in the Tokyo airport, waiting for the next seven-hour 747 ride to Singapore, I changed my watch from 11:20 p.m. on the 12th to 5:20 p.m. on the 13th. Crossing the international dateline going west either throws you into the future or costs a lot of time, depending on how you look at it. I was too tired to enjoy the future.

Upon arrival in Singapore at 12:30 a.m., I found both of my checked bags and met Navjot Sodhi, who had come to the airport to pick me up in the middle of the night. Navjot was a real champ—it's rare to have the chance to work with someone like him on such short notice. After we arrived at the National University of Singapore, which is about a forty-minute drive from the airport, we wrestled my junk up to a fourth-floor guesthouse unit on campus and agreed to meet later in the morning.

When I awoke after dawn, I looked out over a neatly architectured, landscaped, and manicured area. About half a mile away, my view of the ocean itself was blocked by colossal machinery and the vast piles of shipping containers that this equipment had been built to handle. After a quick shower, I strolled out into an already hot and humid morning to look for some food. At the nearest university food court I found an amazing array of food shops and stunningly diverse menus. I quickly learned that prepared food in Singapore is abundant, highly varied, delicious, and very affordable.

We spent the rest of the day talking and meeting with people, including Peter Ng, director of the Raffles Museum. It was a lot of fun to meet and speak with such a good group of active colleagues, but by evening I was pooped. Back in my room I found myself nodding off while reading in the air conditioning, and I was asleep by 9:00 p.m., too tired to go out and find dinner. I had to work at it, but I was able to sleep until almost 6:30 a.m., and in doing so came very close to completely overcoming jet lag by my second day.

Several things about the surrounding buildings struck me. The first was that the satellite dishes pointed straight up. That was a new direction to me, but I hadn't spent any time so near the equator before. Next was the ubiquitous distribution of the buildings. While there was a good effort in the architecture and landscaping to keep green spaces among the buildings, there weren't any obvious large green spaces. This island was crowded. But it was also very, very clean and meticulously landscaped, making it a pleasant place to be. I found the campus to be well designed and well equipped. It would be a comfortable place to be a student. The way things were run was a little different from what I'm used to from North American institutions, but they, too, still emphasize quality in education and research.

Tom Braile, one of my graduate students and the one who had been committed to the Philippine gig, was going to join me in Singapore after I had a week or so to get things rolling there. There was no sense in having two of us sitting on our hands during the usually slow initial phase. With Navjot's expert help, though, I was up and running very quickly. There is a House Crow control program in Singapore. This smallish crow was introduced onto the island early in the last century, but in the past few decades its numbers have grown enormously; they've become pests. Navjot was tied into "crow central," receiving hundreds of the carcasses from the control program to examine their parasites and the age and sex structure of the population. This was an excellent source of fresh cloacas for our work. With the USDA, we were looking at the wild-bird virus pool in western Alaska and now also on the wintering grounds of Alaska migrants. These crows were found throughout Singapore in all habitat types that we saw, making them a great taxon to survey for circulating strains of viruses. And with a lot of them being killed in the control program, we were able to get some decent sample sizes.

So we tore into crows and into the dregs of the freezers on campus. Everywhere you find biologists and freezers, dead things get stuck in a bag and frozen. The good stuff usually gets taken care of when there is a museum around, and in Singapore there is the world-famous Raffles Museum. But normally there's a steady accumulation of lower-quality and lower-priority stuff that just languishes. This was the stuff we were good for—because the Raffles Museum hadn't yet begun a tissue collection, even the most common taxa in the poorest condition had scientific value. Tom and I spent our days swabbing cloacas and skinning and skeletonizing birds from freezers. It's fun to prepare new species of birds, even if many of the specimens are rotting road kills or dead and necropsied zoo specimens. And we'd brought along the world inventory of skeletal specimens and found that some of these things in the freezers were represented by fewer than ten skeletons in the world's museums—a consequence of skeletal specimens being a lower-priority preparation type in general and of the longstanding tradition at the Raffles Museum of preserving only skins. Quite aside from our cloacal swabbing, which was our immediate objective, we felt that we were making some good contributions to ornithology by preserving material from species poorly represented in the world's tissue and skeleton collections.

Figure 19.1. Preparing bird specimens salvaged from freezers at the National University of Singapore; Tom Braile and a flamingo specimen.

The lab in which we were able to set up and do our work was a huge room where large lab sections were taught. Our visit happened to fall mostly between semesters, so this lab was pretty well empty. They had a large stereo system set up there that Navjot's students and assistants turned on immediately when they began going through crows. The radio station the students chose to listen to played music I was not used to hearing—rocking dance music with lurid lyrics. We became so accustomed to this dance music, associating it with long days of preparing and swabbing birds (for me a welcome break from the office routine), that when we returned to our own lab in Fairbanks we downloaded a bunch of the better songs from Napster to play while we worked here on less exotic birds.

One of the more promising aspects of working in Singapore was that it serves as a regional center for the captive bird trade. Possessing cage birds is apparently an important aspect of Chinese culture, and there were a lot of birds available in Singapore—both a high species diversity and a broad geographic representation. Henry Springer, a wildlife enthusiast and friend of ours, had been to Singapore before and had told us about the captive bird trade there. One of my hopes on this trip was to make some contacts with people in this trade to determine whether some of the mortality associated with it could be preserved for science. As it is, outside of a few zoos and aviaries, most of the birds that die in the captive bird trade are buried or incinerated. Needless to say, if the bird is of wild origin, or rare, threatened, or endangered, there is substantial scientific potential in the carcass and it's a real waste when these are destroyed.

After first receiving philosophical support for salvaging birds in this way from the Singapore Agri-food and Veterinary Authority (AVA), Tom and I each went to several dealers, but we had little luck in convincing them that we were a good outlet for their dead birds. On average, they seemed very suspicious of us. We were obviously foreigners and interested in something they wished didn't happen. A couple of them even denied that any birds died in their care—one of these while a budgie was quietly dying in an overfull display cage!

While it is clear that birds are in general a renewable resource, and that a healthy captive bird trade can occur without unduly harming wild populations (and in some cases can preserve species going extinct in the wild), visiting some of these dealers was depressing. There was frequent overcrowding in cages, and too many birds had obviously gone crazy after being taken from the wild and stuck into small cages. Some species seem to make good cage birds; others do not. And the level of care and concern for these live animals was on average considerably below the standards I grew up with. Nevertheless, there were many birds that were obviously well cared for and doing very well in captivity, and the variety available was stunning. Mentally prepared for seeing birds from Southeast Asia, I was very surprised to find, for example, a considerable African representation. We were not able to find a cooperative dealer during this trip, but we had some pleasant interactions with some of them just in talking about birds.

Figure 19.2. Captive birds for sale, Singapore.

HARMONIOUS CLOACAL TUNES IN SINGAPORE

One evening Tom and I went with Navjot to a park while he did a crow survey. It was a very pleasant park, but it was like a tame city park, and there were a lot of people out enjoying it. As we walked along, I realized that it must be difficult to get away from it all on this island, and I asked Navjot about this. For him and his wife, Canada is home, and they suffer here from what he aptly termed "urban stress." Apparently, given the population size and the island's area, the average person-to-person distance is something like five meters. That's crowded. I like the label "urban stress." It's a good term for something I usually feel as soon as I get on an airplane to go outside of Alaska.

Our park visit was terminated with a downpour the likes of which I've rarely seen. In fact, on most afternoons it rained profusely, and I heard more thunder in a couple of weeks there than during years in Alaska. That night Navjot dropped us off in a street so flooded that we waded to the restaurant complex where we usually had dinner near campus. Tom accidentally took a little detour through an invisible drainage ditch up to his waist, and we laughed as we sat drinking cold beers and watching waves come sloshing into the restaurant as each car boated past through the rain and the flooded street.

The food courts in Singapore offered such a tremendous variety of food that it was seriously difficult to make up your mind what to have. Stalls served Chinese food, Malayan food, Hindu food, Western food, fruits, drinks, and on and on. And each stall had its own diverse menu, so it would probably take a very long time to get bored with lunch. Always glad to support commercial ornithology, I enjoyed seeing whole roasted ducks hanging in the stall windows, and I had a lot of delicious duck. The fruits were highly varied and delicious. Just for sport one day I had a glass of freshly squeezed starfruit juice. These fruits cost two to three dollars each in the store in Alaska, and I wondered what a glass of the juice might taste like. I watched the lady drop at least nine of the buggers into the squeezer, and it cost only a buck or so. But I didn't have it again; it tasted like I imagine cactus juice might. Mango juice was a lot better; so was pineapple. Dishes such as "deer meat in black pepper sauce," "fish with ginger root in black bean sauce," "Tom Yam soup," "roast duck noodle," and "prawn-sauce chicken," made excellent lunches and dinners, and things like stingray, cuttlefish, prawns, and shrimp kept things interesting.

Singapore seemed like a pretty friendly place, but there was a very serious side that was apparent before landing. The disembarkation form emphasizes in bold red letters "Warning Death for drug traffickers under Singapore law." This brought to mind the news about caning people guilty of writing graffiti on public spaces. Apparently chewing gum is just flat out illegal. And I learned that there was a $100 fine for not flushing a toilet. Talk about legislating the details of everyday life. On the bright side, they have excellent public transportation and make car ownership very expensive. This cuts down on air pollution and keeps the roads passable. Another energy saver I appreciated was the wall-mounted water heater in the shower. Heating water at the point of use and also heating just the amount being used is a considerable improvement in efficiency over the standard US method of keeping a big tank hot and then, through transport, heating all the pipes between the tank and the point of use.

Tom and I didn't have much spare time, but we did get out one Sunday. First we went to Jurong Bird Park, which turned out to be a great place. They have a phenomenal diversity of bird species in a well laid-out park setting, from penguins (in large, refrigerated quarters), flamingoes, and hornbills, to parrots, raptors, and a multi-continent array of songbirds, most in large outdoor aviaries. We enjoyed ourselves immensely here before going on to try our hand at some shopping. It was a lot of fun to see the variety of merchandise available in the country. It varied from silk goods and carved ivory stamps and figurines to Chinese furniture and antiques.

We never did make it downtown, although it was recommended. We were told it was well worth seeing, but that you want to be home before midnight because that's when all the prostitutes came out. I was surprised that in such a tightly legislated country this was legal, but it was. In fact, we were told there is a whole sex tourism industry centered here. One evening as I went through the yellow pages to see whether there was a good used bookstore nearby, I was surprised to find only one small shop listed. Disappointed, and wondering what legal prostitution looked like in a phone book, I randomly paged around to eventually find eighteen pages (!!) of escort services, offering Asian, Caucasian, Malaysian, and Indian escorts. What a contrast to the used book market. This was not a type of shopping we explored.

On a later shopping trip, after I left, Tom went to an herbalist for some quality ginseng. While there, he asked the proprietor if there was some traditional herbal equivalent of Viagra. Of course there was, and Tom bought a container of small black pills called "Golden Rod—Never Touch Ground" in Chinese. The ingredients read like something you wouldn't want to put in your mouth. Tom told me about these little wonders during his brief return to Fairbanks before heading home for the holidays. When I joked with him about being careful taking these little pills, he said he wouldn't be taking them alone. I suggested then that he wait until he boarded his flight to have a memorable trip.

Coming home from distant Singapore was interesting, not the least because it all happened in one day. When you cross the international dateline going east, you gain seventeen hours, giving me a forty-one-hour-long day. After a few hours of sleep, I got up in Singapore at 2:30 a.m. and began getting my junk ready for an early cab ride to the airport. One of the important things to do was to empty the liquid nitrogen dewar of fluid; it's illegal to fly with any liquid nitrogen in these tanks. These dewars are large, expensive, super thermos bottles. When charged with liquid nitrogen, the interior is about -196° C. It is an ideal way to freeze samples in 2 mL cryovials, and we'd been dropping hundreds of samples into this tank during the past couple of weeks. I took the tank down to the ground floor and dumped out the very cold liquid into a concrete drainage ditch, creating an eerie fog in the ditch for thirty meters in either direction. Once poured off, these tanks can retain their contents well frozen for a day or two with no problem as long as the lid is left in place. But once they're emptied of liquid, the clock is ticking, and there's nothing I worry about more than some overeager customs or wildlife agent taking a dislike to us or our permits and confiscating a dewar. An ensuing meltdown would mean the loss of weeks of work and the loss of irreplaceable samples. For this reason, I prefer to travel with the tanks as checked baggage rather than send them unaccompanied. They raise a lot of curiosity, and I've even been tracked down in my seat by airline personnel to verify that the contents are in no way dangerous (they're safe).

Tom helped me wrestle my junk to where the cab came, and I was soon on my way on a 6:00 a.m. flight to Tokyo. Both that flight and the one from Tokyo to Seattle went smoothly—until a predawn fog in Seattle had us circling the airport with the pilots debating whether to go to Vancouver instead. This delayed our arrival enough that I was concerned about being able to get through customs to meet my connecting flight to Alaska. And, sure enough, the USDA and customs people there were not pleased to see me. You would think that when you go to all the trouble to get the proper permits and call ahead to let agents know you will be coming through with museum specimens of wildlife, your passage might somehow be smoothed. Well, in Seattle, unlike most of the other ports I've brought samples through, my passage was in no way smoothed by having done everything correctly. Perhaps it's that this type of event is out of the ordinary; perhaps it's that this group was unusually cranky that morning. Whatever the reason, I got a remarkably thorough runaround from several agents before they finally let me and the specimens go on our way. Once free, I went into high speed in the seemingly vain hope that I might still be able to catch my flight. Bags re-checked, I raced to find the terminal and gate from which my flight was departing. Thanks to construction and poor signage, I had serious trouble finding out where I was supposed to be, and then more trouble actually getting there. Running for much of this had me out of breath as I raced up to the gate to see the last two passengers boarding. A delayed departure had just barely enabled me to squeeze aboard—the last passenger on a packed airplane.

Epilogue: Back home, I was too wound up to feel the exhaustion, and I got a lot of mileage out of my forty-one-hour day. I had five or six meals—mostly on airplanes—and probably all of about four hours of sleep that day. Used to midnight arrivals and departures from Fairbanks, Rose had misinterpreted my arrival time of 12:30 for the middle of the night, and when I couldn't get her or anyone from my lab on the phone, I took a cab up to the museum. There I transferred specimens into freezers and began dealing with the backlog of brushfires that had sprung up in my absence. Feeling awful for missing my arrival (I thought it was hilarious), Rose came over to help when she received the message at work that I'd called from the airport. The very next day, two job candidates for two different position searches were scheduled for interviews. I was on both search committees, so my dance card was once again full to overflowing. The month of December was soon consumed by meetings, committees, emails, and reports. Tom came back from Singapore with some good samples and specimens, and Bob Dickerman had stopped there to help out for a week en route from Australia, where he and Kevin McCracken had also been hunting the wily cloaca. Kevin's return to Fairbanks also brought in a bunch of good material. All in all, a busy, exciting, and productive time, and I was glad to have had this great field interlude.

20

When Whirlwinds are Steppingstones

FROM ABOUT MID-APRIL through the end of July, when darkness goes on holiday here in the North, time becomes a maelstrom through which one passes by leaping from whirlwind to whirlwind. Or at least sometimes that seems a better way to think of it than being just plain busy as hell.

For a whole bunch of reasons, such as the brevity and intensity of the field season, the size of Alaska, and the length of the winter, spring and summer are one long frenzy of activity largely unconstrained by darkness. You need to get a lot done, you want to get a lot done, you can get a lot done. A lot gets done.

The insanity of it all begins as spring semester winds up to its final crescendo, while at the same time the field season gets underway. There is way too much to do, but somehow most of it gets accomplished. Oh, there are the many loose ends that get dropped or neglected. My infamous email "in" box (from which too little gets out) grows to 400 or 500 messages at times, and I begin to get several reminders each day about some ordinarily important duty that's become trivialized and neglected because of larger priorities. But even these things get resolved or blow away as time races by, becoming in a sense just some of the details ground into the dance floor.

Do the Hustle

The heavy activity that comes with the end of the semester combines in a decidedly frothy fashion with spring field work. (The froth is that ugly kind of scum you sometimes find on turgid shores.) The time demands of end-of-semester deadlines collide with the equally inflexible demands of the season's field obligations. So you light the candle at both ends and everybody dances. This year we had a lot going on, and I wound up trying to keep the group informed through broadcast emails, like this:

17 May update:

Dear all,

Things are really jumping. Last night when I got home at 2300 there was a message from Dan to call him out on Shemya Island (it was only 2200 there). Wow, did he have a story to tell. A lot of eastern Asian migrants were "in town" out there. There was even a raptor that he didn't know, and also a very lost Sandhill Crane. I called Deb Rocque and Andy Johnson on Attu Island this morning to urge them not to let their gun barrels cool. To sum up what's going on between Attu and Shemya: Smew, Bramblings, Eastern Yellow Wagtails, Gray Wagtails, Eurasian Bullfinch, Wood Sandpipers, Long-toed Stint, Olive-backed Pipits, Pechora Pipits, Red-throated Pipits, Hawfinch, and Rustic Buntings. No doubt there will be more to come. Most are apparently quite shy and difficult to collect, but some aren't.

I spoke with Bob Dickerman and Dave Sonneborn on the phone yesterday; Bob is on Kodiak now. Sent James Maley off to meet him. They'll be on Kodiak together for a week before rotating in to spell Deb and Andy on Attu next week.

Tom sends his best from the Philippines, where he is on the verge of having all his permit-related wishes come true. It's definitely paying off to hang in there, make connections, and get the Filipinos enthused about this research. Tom will likely be in the field by the end of next week. Kevin and P. J. McCracken came in from Argentina last week and there are a lot of cool duck specimens drying in the lab. Kevin is already in the lab sequencing.

Christy passed her written and oral prelims and is now officially a PhD candidate!

Here at the nexus I get to hear all the neat things going on. Wish I were out! Meanwhile, I got a proposal off on Tuesday and grades in on Wednesday. After a report and another proposal on Monday, I think I can attack the huge piles on my desk and whittle those down a little . . .

4 June update:

Here's what I know:

Me—Gone 5–14 June. In on the 15th (maybe afternoon of the 14th?) but then out again very early on the 16th to Dutch Harbor. Going to get that endemic subspecies of Song Sparrow on Amak! Back on the 22nd.

James and Bob will be Gold-Streaking birds up from Kodiak, probably on the 8th. I'm having the Gold Streak folks call the lab when the birds arrive. To make adequate space in the freezers for this new stuff, we're hoping Bob and James can blow through some seabirds. Most new stuff needs to go to ATCO freezers. Deb will leave a note about the seabirds (wing, skel., tissues, incl. intestine). You—Bob and James—could pull a box of them out when you get the rest of your birds in. I'm leaving the ATCO key on the lab table. You might have to be creative on freezer space in the meantime. I suppose we could plug up the -40° freezer for a couple days if we have to, but it's been pretty full with cryofumigation stuff from other departments.

Bob—keys on the eagle fob in the lab are yours. Our house is your house, and you've got my truck also (which I'll leave in the museum lot tomorrow morning when Deb takes me to the airport). Note at home about Rose's fish (need to be fed a pinch when you arrive and another after about three days). Plants are under someone else's care.

Bob and James: You need to begin the paperwork on the Ketchikan trip as soon as you return so you can leave with money in your pockets. I've begun the travel form so I can be reimbursed for the ferry trip (Haines-Ketchikan and back: 0130 22nd to 1830 4th of July). You can ask Marie to help a little if you have to, but try to get it done yourselves—she's stressed with the workload right now. I figure you'll want to leave on about the 19th. I still need to call Steve Heinl, but there's freezer space available in Ketchikan and probably also on Prince of Wales. You may not need dry ice, but I don't know. Let's see how Christy and Andy fare on the Haul Road trip. That will tell us how useful it is on a longish trip. My guess is that your trip will be too long for it to last if you leave here with it.

On the 15th I have to spend almost all my time figuring out budgets so we have things clean for the end of the ridiculously scheduled fiscal year (which ends 30 June).

Dr. McCracken is off on his own, beginning that fabled tenure track. We look forward to continuing to work with him, but don't ask him to do much for us—anything he's kind enough to do is a favor. Thanks for picking up the boys on the 10th at 1918 h, Kevin!

Oh—and can you guys figure out how to leave my truck at the airport on the night of the 13th? Looks like Rose and I get in at 0045 on the 14th. We could just walk out to short- or long-term parking, drive home, and surprise Bob. And so we will be in on the 14th. Good. I need two days on those damned budgets.

Dan should be back from Shemya on about the 15th also.

Tom is lining up another couple of permits and waiting for The Big One from PAWB, which should be finalized "any day," as they say. I'll try to pick up email a couple times while I'm away, mostly just to help out with the Philippines if needed.

(Just re-reading these rapidly delivered emails makes me tired all over again.)

Going Outside

June is not the best month to take a trip down to the lower forty-eight. But this year it had to be done, so I went Outside on the fifth. It was a whirlwind of a trip, fitting the season. My air itinerary involved Atlanta, Chicago, and Minneapolis for a series of important meetings and visits.

On the fifth I had a full day of traveling, and it ended late at night with me driving out of Atlanta, Georgia, toward the Savannah River Ecology Laboratory (SREL). It was the first time that I'd driven on a freeway for close to two years. Old habits die hard. It was like riding a bicycle.

The next day I drove on to SREL, where I met Travis Glenn and had a tour of the SREL facilities. This was an impressive installation, and there were a lot of diverse research projects going on there. After a good tour of the place, including a look at a monster American alligator, we went onto Par Pond, one of the cooling ponds for the old nuclear reactors. We fished for large-mouthed bass as part of a sampling effort in which the fish are bled and released for a long-term study of the effects of radionuclides on wildlife. The levels of nuclear contamination are low, but studies of organisms under these conditions are critical for an understanding of the long-term effects of low-level environmental nuclear contamination.

The most important meeting of this trip was scheduled for the US Department of Agriculture—Agricultural Research Service's (USDA-ARS) Southeast Poultry Research Station in Athens, Georgia. We'd been collaborating with these folks for several years on disease transport in migratory birds (yes, the cloacal work), and it was high time to go down and meet with them to see where we stood and where we needed to go. David Swayne, director of the facility, gave me an excellent tour of the installation. They have a superb Biosafety Level 3 (BL3) facility there to do experimental studies of diseases on poultry. The facility is well planned to allow experimentation with diseases that are lethal to poultry while keeping these diseases completely isolated, not just from the outside world in general, but also from animals (the breeding stock) just a short walk away. They also have excellent sequencing capabilities to determine the genetic makeup of avian diseases from all over the world. It was very interesting to meet with people whose focus is the diseases that birds carry. Since beginning to work with this group, I've found it fascinating to come at a problem from both sides—in this case host and disease—at the same time. It was great to have the chance to sit down face to face with them and get to understand the project better.

From Athens I had to make a fast drive to Atlanta to catch my flight to Chicago for the annual meeting of the Association of Systematics Collections. I'd never attended the meeting of this group before (even though I was a member), but this year was a very important one from the perspective of databases. It remains unclear just how the data associated with collections and all of the information we work so hard to obtain as researchers will be made available over the Internet. All agree on some data; few agree on all. Finding an acceptable middle ground is challenging. My attempts to moderate some discussion on these issues, and their immediacy in our own collections, made it appropriate to be in Chicago in mid-June.

I arrived there at around sunset and went straight to the meeting's hotel, where I was to be rooming with Doug Causey, who was flying in to attend the meeting from field work he was conducting in Costa Rica. The next morning, Doug and I were out on the streets at a little after 7:00 a.m., walking and gawking our way to the Sears Tower, where the meeting was to be held. It was the Hour of the Marching Zombies. I was amazed at the non-expressions, the stone faces of the throngs of people marching quietly in to work. I was alarmed at their cheerlessness and by the thought of what hour they'd probably had to begin their day to be walking so somberly into downtown Chicago at 7:00 on a fine spring morning.

The night before, as we'd compared notes about what we'd just been up to, Doug had said something to the effect that "You know, compared with other people we lead pretty interesting lives." Joan Beck of the USDA-ARS had said something very similar in an email earlier this year. When it's your life, you don't really notice that what you do every day tends to be outside the norm. But when your nose is rubbed in it repeatedly, you begin to think that it might actually be true. And here I was confronted with legions of people whose faces clearly said it was not their first choice to be here on a fine spring morning. Slaves to the Dilbertian lifestyle may never have been so concentrated. I was equally struck by their silent, zombie-like masses when I found myself out among them on a Friday afternoon. Friday! And during the Blues Festival! You've never seen so many people with flat brainwaves. Work done. Going home . . .

To my surprise and delight, a lost White-throated Sparrow was singing its heart out on a tiny patch of green at a street corner in downtown Chicago that spring morning. But for all of the ears nearby, I think that the song was nearly squandered. The meeting was a success, though, and I learned a lot. But, alas, the hotel room's "intimacy kit" was never opened, leading Doug and me to promise that we'd try to do better next time.

In spite of getting to visit with a lot of great people on this too-hasty trip, a couple of events reminded me of how really poor service can be. The first occurred on my long journey to Atlanta from Fairbanks. On a Northwest flight from Minneapolis to Atlanta, I was very hungry and tired, and I was glad when they served a sandwich snack. The first bite was great. But as I lifted the sandwich to take my second bite, I saw that my first had really been the second: a much smaller bite than mine had already been taken from some sliced turkey that hung a surprising distance out of the bread. How delightful—a sandwich that satisfies two. I cut off the pre-sampled part and finished the rest, too tired and hungry to complain. But I have to say that the savoriness had taken a serious decline.

In Atlanta I found a substandard Thrifty car rental agency. They didn't have the midsize that had been reserved for me, so they gave me a compact that what was supposed to be given at a 15 percent discount. It was only 10 percent on the receipt, but I didn't notice that until much later. The more immediate problem was that the car wasn't in the lot where it was supposed to be. The clerk was conscientious, and went and found the vehicle. But it only had half a tank of gas, and I was of course expected to return it full. And long after a knuckle-biting drive to get it back to the off-site agency in time to make it to the airport on their shuttle, I found that the jerks had already charged me for picking it up at the airport! And of course I was in too much of a hurry to carefully examine the receipt until I was long gone. I'll be avoiding Thrifty and whoever caters for Northwest (now Delta) for a long, long time.

Ugamak and Amak

Right before I left to go Outside, Vernon Byrd of the Alaska Maritime National Wildlife Refuge emailed me to ask about where exactly we'd most like to obtain some cormorants from the eastern Aleutians. Among the possible sites was Amak Island, which hadn't been on the vessel's schedule when I'd last looked. It was an incredible and long-awaited opportunity to get ashore at Amak and collect specimens of the endemic subspecies of Song Sparrow (*Melospiza melodia amaka*), probably not really different from *sanaka*, but needing closer investigation. I thought about it for all of an hour or so before calling and arranging a ticket to Dutch Harbor. I was just lucky

I would be back in time to go. I had two whole days to transition between whirlwinds: to talk with Bob Dickerman and James Maley about their Attu trip and be sure all was set for their Ketchikan trip; to talk with Christy Pruett and Andy Johnson about their North Slope trip; and to go through a colossal amount of mind-numbing budget balancing before I got to go out again. The bureaucrat who had the bright idea to have the Alaska fiscal year end on 30 June should be annually burned in effigy until someone gets bright enough to realize that it's a hell of a stupid idea to end a fiscal year at the busiest time of year. But I temporarily left it all behind.

As seems all too common with end-of-the-line journeys, the flight from Anchorage to Dutch Harbor was delayed for hours. I wouldn't have had to get up at 4:30 a.m. to make it. Heck, I could have gotten up at about noon. But we were in no rush; the boat wasn't due in until the next morning, and it was only a question of how you wanted to spend time waiting. We were just glad they were eventually successful in making some obscure repair, and that we actually got to fly out that day. I say "we" because in the Anchorage airport I joined the Refuge group from Homer going out on the vessel. Vernon Byrd, Dave Roseneau, Arthur Kettle, and John Jamieson from the Refuge, with me, made up the full complement of new people going aboard for this cruise.

Upon arrival in Dutch, I hitched a ride with the Refuge group in a rented truck, and we went to the Grand Aleutian Hotel. There we learned that *Tiglax* would be in by 8:30 p.m. Vern got a room to hold our gear and the Refuge people who would be getting off the boat that evening, and once our junk was stowed we were off: to the AC store for boots and fishing licenses, to the Museum of the Aleutians, and then for a road tour of the island, which Vern, at the wheel, conducted superbly. From the Elbow Room, a bar in Unalaska that seemed to be a famous location for being the source of numerous court cases over fighting; to the development on Amaknak Island that had occurred since Vern had first been there about thirty years ago; to the ideal setting of coastal homes on a sunny evening—we watched one resident put the finishing touches to a whole grilled salmon. Dutch Harbor and Unalaska is a great area to visit.

We slept that night on the vessel, and the next day—a Sunday—we sat around for more than half the day waiting for delivery of the foodstuffs ordered to resupply the vessel. When they finally arrived in early afternoon, all hands hustled the two pallet loads aboard and we got underway.

Bob, the cook, must have put some type of sleeping potion in the food for dinner. I could hardly keep my eyes open after eating. The rocking of the vessel as we steamed for Ugamak and Aiktak islands was the quintessential soporific, and after a couple of hours I abandoned my efforts to stay awake reading, and slept like a rock. Late that night we anchored up between Aiktak and Ugamak islands. The two USFWS technicians stationed on Aiktak for the summer were aboard in the morning talking, doing laundry, and engaging in a mindmeld with the Refuge folks about their seabird work here.

Once Vern, Jeff, Dave, and Arthur completed a perimeter Pigeon Guillemot survey, I was dropped ashore on Ugamak Island to collect specimens. The rocky beach was covered by washed up kelp, making it very slippery. It was like walking on very lumpy wet ice. But this was where the birds were concentrated, so I worked my way along the shore until a sheer cliff stopped further progress. At the same time that I was cursing the practically frictionless surface that the kelp created, I was amazed at how much invertebrate life was present in the washed up mess. It was no wonder that Song Sparrows and Pacific Wrens did so well as residents out here when they had such a rich food source.

I could tell right away that this was an island without foxes. The birds were quite tame, and I was able to collect specimens as an underappreciated land-based predator. It was a good opportunity to learn that we'd finally gotten our reloaded .410 gauge 12-shot ammunition recipe down to a fine, effective point. These reloads were highly effective on Ugamak. Things were different on Amak Island, though, where there were red foxes. Even before I collected a single bird there, three red foxes had paced me on the beach. I couldn't tell whether I had interrupted their beach patrol or if I was just a local curiosity. Maybe I was both. After a good, productive day on Ugamak, I processed birds aboard the vessel, had more of Bob's excellent food (with sleeping potion), had a shower, and hit the rack just as the lilting motion began, indicating our passage into unsheltered waters on our way to Amak.

We anchored up offshore of Amak Island very early the next morning, and when I came out on deck I learned that we were fogged in. The guillemot crew headed out at dawn and had to get directions from the bridge about which direction they had to go to hit the shore. It was calm enough that we couldn't even hear the waves lapping on the rocky shore. This calmness was very welcome, and the fog soon began to lift. Not long thereafter, I was on shore headed from the north side westward along the coast.

It was exciting to be on this island that I'd wanted to get to for so long. And, once the fog burned off, it turned out to be a beautiful day. This island was surprisingly "eastern" in its avifauna. For example, it was a striking Aleutian experience to hear Golden-crowned Sparrows singing. The first *amaka* Song Sparrow was a real treat to obtain. And, no, it didn't look any different from the subspecies *sanaka* on my first impression. Pacific Wrens turned out to be more common than Song Sparrows, which was excellent given their complete absence (from prior experience) on the nearby mainland—so close and yet so far away. After passing the shore party setting traps to catch specimens of the island's endemic vole, I kept on going until I couldn't go any farther. In six or so hours I covered a little more than a third of the island's circumference. It was so nice out that I could feel a serious sunburn coming on.

Back out on the vessel, I had some food and processed birds as fast as I could, then John Jamieson took me out in a skiff to collect ten cormorants (*Phalacrocorax* spp.). I'd forgotten just how hard it was to successfully wing shoot passing birds from a moving boat, and I completely missed more birds than I care to remember (while getting my knees bruised) before getting this unique type of shooting down again enough to bring back a basketful of the large black birds. John was an expert driver, which made it a lot easier. These birds were important to add to the collection for several reasons, and we were very glad to get them. At sunset the local mountains were sticking out above the clouds. The large volcanic peaks of Shishaldin and Pavlof dominated. It was a beautiful end to a beautiful day. We weighed anchor and headed back to Aiktak and environs.

The next day turned out to be every bit as gorgeous as the previous two, and we steamed our way slowly among a series of eastern Aleutian islands, assessing seabird colonies from the high, stable bridge. It was like a glamorous pleasure cruise—the calm, sunny weather was incomparable to the more usual Aleutian winds, clouds, and rain, and the wildlife was thick. As we came up on them, flocks of Whiskered Auklets rose, flapped madly on their stubby wings, then dropped like only slightly guided stones into the sea. At one point, alerted by the deceleration of the ship's engines, I rushed back up to the bridge to see what was up. Fountainous exhalations on the surface marked the presence of whales, and soon we were treated to humpback whale tail flukes saluting us as the animals' tails went airborne prior to their diving to lower depths. Later, smaller poofs of vapor indicated

Dall porpoise, and occasionally these animals came up to the vessel to check us out and goof around briefly beside the boat. On one island we saw of all things a herd of Hereford cattle, about as far from their origin(s) as such animals could get.

Being out on the ocean in such fabulous weather was a wonderful change from airports, crowded airline flights, and poor service. We had a luxury cruise through the eastern Aleutians. Both the weather and the birds were surprisingly cooperative. When things are this good—especially when they can be much, much worse—you don't want the dream to end. But *Tiglax* and our group had busy and nonoverlapping schedules to pursue. Those nasty budgets were still awaiting me, A Midsummer Night's (Bad) Dream . . .

Mashie and Niblick

But everything gets dropped when it's time to head to Chitina for fish. We had gone twice last year and still didn't reach our household limit of thirty fish. All of those hours doing hard work on the nets and conforming to seriously uncomfortable rocks—on top of the long drive each way— had Rose a little less than enthusiastic about going again this year. But there was no arguing with our mutual desire for fresh red salmon, and the king salmon we got last year was a powerful gastronomic memory. As we hovered on the brink of indecision over whether and when to go, the wind changed and the smoke from the two big forest fires on the Tanana River flats to the south of Fairbanks set in to make life less than pleasant. We'd been lucky for days: we had watched the smoke from these two fires as they grew steadily to consume over 100,000 acres of forest. (Eventually they consumed over twice this area. The cause was at first a mystery, but it turned out that both were caused by surveying and cutting on the controversial new power corridor intertie—a development that we were assured would have minimal impact where it crossed the pristine Tanana Flats. Still burning a month later, this initial impact was probably visible from the surface of the moon. And they hadn't put up pylons or wire yet.)

But the winds eventually shifted to send the dense smoke to engulf Fairbanks, and it seemed like a good time to take the long drive to catch fish. Much of last summer had been spent in the gloom of smoke from more distant fires. Enough of that—off we went.

We were getting pretty good at these trips, so packing went fairly quickly. The slowest part remained trying to find things we put away in strange places after we last used them. But nearly everything required for a major expedition was somewhere in our large garage, and eventually we were able to put our hands on it. (It's amazing how many diverse trips have been staged out of this garage.) As we pulled out of the garage to leave, we spotted a nice bull moose right behind us. The first bull that we've seen in our yard wasn't too concerned with our presence, and he allowed us to take several pictures while he stood there munching vegetation. His antlers were still less than three feet across and covered in smooth, unbroken brown velvet. Rose thought he was a good omen for our trip.

We arrived at O'Brien Creek at about 9:00 p.m. and found all of our favorite camping spots already occupied. So we put up the tent in a new spot at the bottom of the hill where the road goes steeply up on its way farther in. The weather was excellent (we had left most of the smoke behind hours before), and there were a lot of fish being cleaned down by the river. Dinner was delicious, and we were soon in bed, trying to get a good night's sleep before the next day's fishing and long drive home. I should have known better than to try camping right beside a road that requires heavy motoring to climb.

Rose had checked out some books on tape for the drive each way. The first was a P. G. Wodehouse book entitled *The Clicking of Cuthbert*, a book from 1922, mostly about golf. Now, I consider golf to be one of the more mundane subjects on the surface of the planet, but Wodehouse had such an excellent sense of humor that I suppose I'd listen to anything he'd written. We were not disappointed, and during our fishing the next day we decided that our dip nets should be named in honor of two of Wodehouse's main inanimate characters, the golf clubs called mashie and niblick (or even mashie niblick in a combination club). Such bizarre names, being repeatedly called upon to dig golfers out of bad situations, seemed, perhaps prefaced by "salmon," to be perfect names for dip nets. Apparently these names are no longer used in golf; when we got home we looked them up and found that they've been replaced by the far less interesting name "number seven iron." Yes, English is becoming a poorer language.

Mashie and Niblick performed beautifully. The fish were running hot—I think hotter than we had ever experienced before. We had a good rock, and we had good nets. In four-and-a-half busy hours, we caught our limit. At different times each of us caught two fish in the net simultaneously. And we also each had a king salmon right up to the surface before they slipped out of the nets. Boy, does that get the adrenalin pumping! We kept our nets in the water as long as possible, trying for that one king salmon allowed and tossing smaller salmon back out of the nets once we knew we'd get our limit. Right at the end, Rose caught three reds in the net at once— amazing! Quite a welcome change from last year, when we'd fished long and hard on two different days and had barely made about ten fish each time. As fast as Rose caught them, I'd give her the other net and take care of the fish, giving them a quick tap on the head with the fish club to stun them into submission, clipping off the tips of the tail fins to mark the fish, as required by the permit, rockhopping it over to the stringers, then putting them onto the lines tied to the shore. We had a hell of a good time.

Sam McCallister was our charter boat captain again this year, and he picked us up at about 2:00 p.m. So by midafternoon we were happily gutting and icing down our catch back at O'Brien Creek. It was a gorgeous day out—sunny and nearly calm—and things were going so well that the only way it could have gotten better would have been if the fish had cleaned themselves after leaping into the nets. After our six-hour drive, we arrived home at a reasonable hour (11:00) and rolled into bed very tired. The next morning it felt good to be sore all over—netting and perching on rocks is hard work! By the end of the day we had spent half a day in the office catching up, filled the freezer with salmon fillets, begun a big cauldron of fish-head soup, and were slurping down sashimi with wasabi sauce as an appetizer before fresh grilled salmon. Wow. A person could get used to this.

Just a couple of days later, with the smoke blowing over Fairbanks thicker than ever, it was hard to relax. It's easy to understand how animals get very nervous under smoky conditions. Where to next? Nothing but "Office" on my calendar for a while. Rats.

Do the Hustle II

Twenty soldiers parachuted out of the back of a large airplane as I drove the last mile to get strapped into the Chair of Torquemada (which my imagination has developed and named after the Grand Inquisitor of the Spanish Inquisition). I do not like starting my day at the dentist. Watching these parachutists blossom like strange aerial feces from the rear of a lumbering plane leaving a trail of dark exhaust fumes cheered me up. And it turned out that the dentist didn't have to use the drill.

This year we were right up to the end of July, and I still hadn't fully recovered from my brief field effort in Belize in March. During that trip my email "In" box (from which too much does not escape) leaped from around 100 messages to almost 700; it was presently hovering just below 400. What's the point? Good question. I am able to rapidly communicate with anyone, and people with brushfire issues are able to communicate similarly with me. But if you don't have a brushfire, my foot won't be there to stomp it. Not a way to accomplish large goals. We had one important field effort cancelled, which enabled me to finish some pressing business and ruthlessly prune my email in box (down to all of 390 messages). Anyone else in favor of going back to the Pony Express? I have yet to solve the problems that email brings together with its advantages.[17]

---

17. Not long after this, out of self defense, I invented my yet-to-be-written killer email app. In response to an incoming message, this program would make appropriate calculations and send a reply something like this: "Thank you for your email. It is number 4,371 in my Inbox, and at current response rates you should receive a reply in two years, seven months, and three days. I look forward to getting back to you then." It would certainly cut down on trivia. But, alas, this app exists only as vaporware in my brain, a sort of sanity balm for stressful days. But I have stopped stressing out about keeping up with my Inbox, which presently tops out at over 22,000 messages.

21
The Long Fall

AT HIGH LATITUDES THERE ARE numerous witty sayings about how much of the year is winter. And there is a lot of truth to these sayings; spring and fall tend to be very short. During spring in Fairbanks we talk about "leaf day," when all the leaves seem to pop out at once. In fall you can miss all the color if you're gone for a couple of days.

This year we'd had a phenomenally protracted fall. Moderate lows, lack of a hard frost, and no winds gave us the most beautiful fall we'd seen since coming up here. It was surreal in many ways. One evening when driving home we saw a lynx by the side of the road. It was the first we'd ever seen, and it was as tame and cooperative as could be, allowing us to back up and park next to it for a better view. We've often had red fox wander through our yard, but it was a particular thrill to see this graceful wild cat less than a mile from home.

They All Fall Down

The idyllic weather here was rudely disturbed first by the drudgery of work and the inability to escape it completely—unlike last year, when Dad came up and we were able to get out moose hunting for several days in a row. But it was entirely shattered by the terrorist acts of 11 September. How does one absorb, cope, and eventually grow with these horrific events? The scale and brutal cruelty of those acts remain very difficult to come to terms with. The scenes burned into our brains were too much like an overly violent movie to be real, but the reality kept us glued to the news and awake for weeks. We'll still be living with the ripple effects of this for decades.

Everyone's mind has burned into it some of those terrible images of fireball crashes, the towers falling down, the Pentagon cratered, and a crash site in Pennsylvania. And the international nature of the victims brought the losses home to too many worldwide. It seemed that everyone knew someone who knew someone—a friend or a relative or even a family member—who was in the Pentagon or in one of the World Trade Center towers. I recall a report that people from some sixty-three countries were among the missing at the World Trade Center. The silent skies following the grounding of US air traffic declared the immediacy and gravity of these events to everyone in the US.

Our president's initial responses were halting and poor. Once his speech writers and handlers began to get a renewed hold on his public persona, things became substantially better. But I hope that the moron who inserted the word "crusade" into the initial diatribe is out of a job. Thank goodness that was yanked in a hurry by someone with more sense. Almost as little thought went into the initial title of "Operation Infinite Justice," which was not hastily enough renamed "Operation Enduring Freedom." One good reason to keep track of history is so that we don't remake some of the boneheaded mistakes of the past. We have no desire to go back to the Crusades. And we have no need to. This isn't about religion. This is about moral decency and basic humanity. And it isn't a black-and-white, normal-hats/turban, we're-good-they're-bad issue, either. As we well know from events perpetrated in the US by Americans, such as McVeigh, Kazinski, Gacy, and Rudolph, zealots and twisted people who care nothing for the lives of others are generated in our culture quite as well as in others.

As a biologist, I'm looking at this and thinking that the sex bias is off the charts. Legally mandated estrogen shots for young males displaying certain behavioral and psychological patterns would solve a lot of these problems. Yes, it might generate some new problems, but I think it would easier to handle the tamer behavioral outcomes.

Despite the fact that the weapons used in the hijackings were legal to bring aboard domestic flights, we saw a ferocious tightening of many other aspects of security. Increased safety is a universal desire, and there are many improvements that can be implemented. But it will be all too easy to go overboard and sacrifice some of the very liberties we have taken for granted as United Statesians in our zeal to feel safe. Plastic butter knives and eyebrow tweezers are not credible weapons. Finding the balance between the maintenance of civil liberties and the maintenance of safety will be a long-running challenge.

Maybe it's just me, but targeting an international group of civilians with death to make a point seems phenomenally stupid—a guaranteed way to elicit such a giant backlash that your point would get withered up and blown away. Before 11 September, I would have thought that someone intelligent enough to be a functional member of society and fly jets would think similarly. Not anymore.

If you turn it around, one can see a certain David and Goliath quality to the suicide bombing of the USS Cole. That expression of outrage was directed more along traditional lines of societal disagreement. Even the Pentagon assault—although it, too, included a high proportion of civilians—could be viewed as a military engagement. But the World Trade Center attack crosses all lines. It is more—a lot more—than just the scale of the loss of life. More people are killed each year on US highways (presently averaging around 43,000 per year). And I think it's also a lot more than the movielike cataclysm of seeing big buildings blowing up and falling down.

Perhaps what is so disturbing about the World Trade Center attack is that it rocked the very foundations of our concept of civilization. It caused us to wonder about things we have not had to wonder about before. Like safety, yes, a legitimate concern of everyone. But I think it goes beyond that. After all, it is still safer to work in a highrise office complex or get into an airplane than it is to get into your car. (Although the fact that someone else is driving the airplane probably has a considerable psychological effect). I think that somewhere deep down it causes us to wonder about the point of it all—of all of our work to collectively build the culture and society of humankind into something better, something that has somehow been improved by our presence, and all that we bring to our jobs, avocations, and lives through our experience, training, education, and hard work.

If our most complex societal constructs can be eliminated by the acts of a few societal insects, then what is the point of our efforts? Well, there is a point, and we can console ourselves that although we humans do some really stupid things, and there are many things that we can do to clean up our act, we also do some really neat things. It's an exciting time in human history to be alive, despite our remaining faults. Human resiliency will enable us to grow mental scar tissue and carry on. And the manufacture and deployment of terrorist insecticide is a growth industry.

The ongoing anthrax scare had me mystified, though. Perhaps it's the biologist in me again, but until this bacterium is introduced in such a way as to jeopardize the lives of thousands, I personally scoff at the ineptitude of those using this feeble means to sow terror. But clearly I'm in the minority. Vice President Cheney was being secretly squirreled away like a stash of precious nuts. For all of its real and supposed faults, the US Postal Service is a pretty damned reliable service, and everyone gets mail. That seems to be an effective way of sowing fear, despite the vanishingly small risk to the average citizen. The people perpetrating this terrorist act must have been from outside our culture, though, because they pissed off the wrong people. Whether earned or not, the phrase "go postal" suggests that the USPS has among its employees some tough people, and now they have something upon which to focus some legitimate rage. I say we turn them loose on terrorists, too.

Short Moose and Caribou Hunts

No, I wasn't hunting short moose or short caribou. I went after regular-sized ones. But I could only go for a short time—too busy at the office with piles of work. I just had to get away one day, so I took a short trip to go moose hunting. I couldn't get far away in just a day trip, so I decided to take a drive down the Elliott Highway toward Minto, where I hadn't been before. It was very good to get out and walk through the woods, even if I didn't find much moose sign. One memorable find was the mother of all used spruce-cone piles—a massive concentration of husked and eaten spruce cone bracts that had to be the work of generations of red squirrels. One chattered at me while I stopped and took a picture of the legacy of its ancestors.

About a week later, after taking most of my nose off at the grindstone, I got proposals submitted and decided that it was high time to get out and enjoy a little bit more of Alaska. The morning after I'd gotten things submitted, I headed out for the McComb Plateau. There was a permit-only hunt there on a walk-in basis—motor vehicle restrictions were on through the whole season. I'd packed up a couple of days of food and water the night before, and I was ready for some entertaining time in some scenic country.

But after driving down there, I found a sign saying that the hunt had been closed by emergency order. What a drag. I sat there thinking about it for all of two minutes before continuing on down the road. I'd gotten a permit for another hunt down in the Mt. Fairplay area, and I hadn't been there before, either.

It was a longer drive, but it is always fun to see new country. On the Taylor Highway you pass up and over a fair amount of open tundra, and you can use binoculars to glass the slopes. By the end of the day, I must have glassed several hundred square miles, both what was visible from the road and a lot on the back sides of the hills, which I accessed after hiking up and over the top of the wooded hills that most of the road wound through. On the back sides of these hills, I found remote and silent country, and I walked around up there for hours, enjoying open spaces and some incredible weather. There was no trace of humans on the landscape or in the air during this time, accentuating the remoteness of the country pierced by this winding dirt road with so little traffic on it (all invisible from the back side). There wasn't any sign of recent caribou, either, but I did pick up an old piece of a shed antler. After too much time cooped up in the office, this was a very therapeutic day.

As I walked the miles down off the mountain, clouds moved in as evening approached, and a light rain began just as I made it back to the truck. I'd intended to spend the night on the tundra back up at higher elevations, but I knew from a lot of work that there weren't caribou around, and I didn't feel like camping in the rain to relearn this same fact in the wet morning. So I drove straight on back, arriving late at night well refreshed from a long day away from it all.

Barrow

Fall ended for me when I stepped off the plane onto the runway in Barrow. The snow cover was complete, and it was cold and windy. It was 10 October. Apparently it had already been winter here for a month. At times it is hard to believe the climatic variability in Alaska. This was one of those times.

Deb Rocque and I had decided in a few short hours to take advantage of Alaska Airlines' web special airfares, which coincided perfectly with an email from Robert Suydam that the Ross's Gulls were in at Barrow. We hadn't collected specimens in Barrow since I'd been in Alaska, and I wanted to get some Ross's Gulls and a look at the Arctic Ocean and Barrow, Alaska. Deb was really interested in going, too, and she needed a break from studying for her PhD comprehensive exams. We were about the only two in the lab who could get away right then. We couldn't be up for long, but our timing was excellent.

Robert picked us up at the airport on a Wednesday morning, dressed for the cold, dripping some blood onto the floor tiles, and smelling of oily sea mammal. He had just come from the bowhead whale butchering site on the ocean beach, where he, Craig George, and others had been taking data and samples while much of the community was butchering the animal. It was a large male, over fifty feet long. One of the testes weighed 310 pounds! This whale had been taken the day before and towed in by twenty-one boats to arrive just before dark on the evening before our arrival. The butchering had begun immediately and went on all night.

We wanted to get out and see this rare phenomenon (rare for those who don't live in Barrow) before trying for gulls. We picked up our rental car, met important people, got our junk stowed in the Arctic Research Facility (ARF), and then got a permit for our bird collecting from the Ukpeagvik

Iñupiat Corporation. Then, after a quick change into long underwear and field gear, we headed out loaded for gulls and for taking pictures.

The Arctic Ocean was a beautiful sight to see. There was still a lead a couple of miles wide open between the shore and the pack ice, with both young and old floes bobbing about between. Cleaned bowhead whale skulls from past kills were erected at several points along the beach, and several major buildings around town also had whale skulls erected in front of them. Out of town, not far beyond the old Naval Arctic Research Laboratory complex, we found a lot of people out butchering a massive whale hauled up onto the beach.

The bowhead whale is a filter-feeding cetacean that lives at high latitudes. In summer, the Pacific Ocean population migrates north into the Beaufort and Chukchi seas, and in winter individuals may go as far south as 45° N in the Pacific Ocean. These animals have truly massive heads—about 33–40 percent of the total body length is head. Along each side of the upper jaw, which is long and narrow, there are rows of hundreds of thin baleen plates (about 300 on each side). These plates are long, thin, tapering, black, very flexible appendages that these animals have instead of teeth. They are used for filter feeding. In the bowhead, the baleen plates can be over ten feet long—the longest of any whale. This individual had one great row of them still exposed before being removed in the butchering process.

As a substance, baleen is like very heavy fingernail or stiff, flexible plastic. The plates have a fairly sharp outer edge, and the inner edge has heavy, hairlike fraying. These plates could be thought of as sort of long, tapering, flexible sword blades with hairy inside edges. They are packed together in dense rows along both sides of the upper jaw, with the sharp edges pointed outward and angled somewhat forward. To feed, the whale swims through concentrations of zooplankton near the ocean surface with its mouth wide open. The baleen plates hang straight downward and allow water and food to pass through into the mouth. When it has a mouthful of food (and I'm guessing that a lot of water passes through and out the back sides of the mouth while the animal gets a good mouthful of food), it closes its mouth (in the process of which the baleen folds upward and back), and the gigantic tongue forces the remaining water out while the small zooplankton get trapped in the mat of fibers created by the tightly packed hairy inside edges of the baleen plates. Gulp. I can't imagine how much food stays caught up in the hairy mat until the next open-mouth feeding once again runs water through the plates with the direction of the hairs. I also can't imagine what the inside of such a mouth would feel like. (Or maybe I know already from those fuzzy-mouthed mornings.)

During the height of the commercial whaling era, baleen was a valuable product of the whale fishery; among other things, it was used for buggy whips and corsets. Now it's sold as novelty and art for about ten dollars or more per foot. So the row we found still exposed was pieced up shortly thereafter in the butchering process. You can find baleen with and without artistic etchings on the walls of many Alaska homes, hotels, and gift shops.

Historically, both traditional and commercial whaling made extensive use of the thick blubber, and bowhead whales yielded more per animal than other whales. Now, however, most of the blubber is discarded, because it is no longer commercially saleable, and it is no longer needed for lighting and cooking by the natives. The meat, though, is very important, and, surprisingly, so is the skin and outermost inch or so of the blubber. This is muktuk, and it is eaten both raw and cooked.

I was surprised at the consistency of the skin. I expected it to be thick and heavy, but found it instead to be remarkably thin and soft. Not so soft as to make it very chewable, however. Dan Gibson had said it was like chewing a chunk of eraser soaked in oil. Either it was just this big old animal, or Dan uses much harder erasers than I do. It was serious work to chew a piece of this animal's muktuk. The oil is rather savory, though, having a not unpleasant flavor and a good mouth feel. Later I microwaved up a piece of the meat that we didn't need for a genetic sample. It is a rich meat with a strong flavor. It was somewhat tough, too, but the gamey taste wasn't bad.

One of the coolest things we learned in Barrow was that these giants of the sea can live for a very long time. At the museum in Barrow there is a display of old harpoon heads recovered from modern whale kills—points from previous encounters with humans from which the animals had escaped. Several of these points are ancient stone heads, last used a century or more ago by native hunters! This evidence suggests that these whales may be the longest-lived of all mammals. As more data are gathered, we are apparently seeing corroboration of what the stone points imply—that these animals may take upwards of twenty years to reach sexual maturity, and that they can live for amazingly long periods of time.

The Iñupiat of Barrow are justifiably proud of their whaling heritage, and they seem to be excellent custodians of the resource. They work closely with the International Whaling Commission, and they established their own whale management commission when early census work by outsiders disagreed with their own impressions of abundance. And they were right—there were more animals than the international community had estimated. They also employ their own biologists, who are producing some really interesting data on whale biology.

The inventions of kerosene, plastics, and electric lights greatly reduced the value of whale hunting early in the last century. But whale oil and meat had other commercial uses, like margarine, soap, and dog food, and commercial whaling was a big industry until the 1970s, when whale populations were driven to such low levels that commercial exploitation was no longer profitable and public outcry achieved internationally meaningful conservation legislation. As a consequence, whale populations are rebounding worldwide, and we will probably see an increasing push for a resumption of limited commercial whaling from countries like Japan, Russia, and Norway. In the meantime, the limited levels of traditional whaling conducted by tribes like the Iñupiat clearly can hold an important culture together.

We enjoyed having the chance to walk around all of the butchering activity and talk to some of the folks there. They were extremely friendly and happy to answer stupid questions from tourists like us. We gawked and took pictures until our hands got too cold. Then we stood around parts of the carcass (like the incredibly giant tongue!), talking with some of the guys butchering until a flock of about sixty to seventy Ross's Gulls flew casually by low overhead. That brought our minds back to business, so off we went.

Ross's Gull is a true denizen of the North. It breeds primarily in arctic and subarctic Siberia, but some breeding presence has also been recorded in the Canadian subarctic and in Greenland. After breeding, unlike most other high-latitude birds, it heads north into the Arctic Ocean, where it spends the fall moving along coasts and among pack and drift ice. Its winter range is unknown, but is most likely to be at sea in the Pacific Ocean south of pack ice. Barrow, Alaska, is one of the few places on the planet one can easily get to where this bird can be predictably found. It is present here in autumn just prior to freezup. They'd shown up in the hundreds on the weekend prior to our arrival, which had prompted Robert Suydam's email.

Figure 21.1. Bowhead whale (Balaena mysticetus) *tongue, with Deb Rocque and her tongue for scale, Barrow, Alaska.*

And here we were seeing them up close and personal. I'd seen skins before, and had even had the chance to prepare a specimen that had been found dead outside the species' normal range. Perhaps their most endearing characteristic is a rosy pink hue in the body feathers that would ordinarily be white on most other gull species. During the breeding season this captivating pink hue is quite striking. In the first-year birds that we were mostly seeing here, it is very faint and delicate compared with breeding-season adults. This gorgeous hue is perhaps the most ephemeral feather coloration I know of. Trays of older specimens show little trace of it, because it seems to fade rather quickly with time, even in specimens kept in the dark. As a consequence, field guides usually portray the species as being much, much whiter than it actually is in life, because the specimens they used for models were faded.

We parked our rental car on the shore of the beach at the end of the road and sat and waited awhile to see what the gulls were doing. Smaller groups of Ross's Gulls came occasionally down the shoreline, but very few came over land any real distance. One thing we thought was a little odd was that there was a lot of traffic at the end of the road. The road doesn't go anywhere; it just stops there at the base of Point Barrow, and there's nothing much but a lot of desolate open space between there and the North Pole. But a lot of people came down to the end, stopped for a little while, turned around, and then went back toward town. After a little bit we decided to walk the shoreline and get away from this traffic in our search for gulls.

We were lucky enough to get a couple of birds right away. It was great to see these elegant little gulls and to get a couple of them in the hand. After putting these in the trunk of the car to cool, we got serious about heading northward up the beach toward the point. The wind was blowing moderately well, and the wind chill was down around -15° to -20° F. Although Deb had been raised in Maine, she had never experienced this kind of cold and wind before. For me, it was very familiar—like a January day in southern Minnesota. Walking against the wind was a little challenging, and you'd gradually pick up a cold ache in the forehead. Deb said that she'd rather eat two gallons of ice cream to get a cold headache like that.

The gulls were all flying against the wind, almost straight north. So we walked a fair amount of time facing backwards watching out for them. Few came over land, though, and we learned on a couple of them that if you didn't drop them straightaway they'd use their last couple of wingbeats and the wind to get out to water. It wasn't swimming weather, and besides, we'd neglected to bring our swimsuits, so we pushed slowly on thinking we'd pick up these birds on the way back after they'd had a chance to drift back to shore. But that wasn't to be. The nasty Glaucous Gulls didn't miss a trick.

They were on these couple of floating birds in no time at all, dragging them out farther and farther away from our shore-based antics while tearing them to pieces and swallowing them. It was very frustrating. So we worked hard to get birds over land and took only sure shots. Nobody likes to lose a shot bird—especially such a beautiful bird, and especially to have it eaten in front of you by a real avian pig while you stand cursing helplessly on shore.

Years ago, when collecting gulls in western Alaska, I learned that other gulls in a flock would come in to investigate what was going on with a shot gull because the sudden dropping of the shot animal was equivalent in their experience to a feeding movement. So a rapidly dropping gull is a good lure to other gulls, and I have used dead gulls and terns since then by tossing them up into the air to bring in others. I'd thought about this before leaving Fairbanks, and had intended to bring some white handkerchiefs to toss, but couldn't find any while packing. So on this day, when we saw gulls approaching, we ran farther inland and kicked at dirt to draw their eyes. Ross's Gulls are a curious bird, and this worked enough for us to bag a couple more. But their numbers dwindled as the wind picked up. And soon we were close enough to the strange mass on the horizon to tell through binoculars that it was the famous bone pile—the dumping ground for butchered whale carcasses out on the point. Bones, guts, and waste parts were hauled out there to keep polar bears away from town. We didn't want to get any closer to possible bears, so we headed back. Conditions deteriorated, and the gulls pretty much dried up, so we quit for the day and went back to the lab to process the birds we had gotten.

That night, in a largely empty bunkhouse, Deb and I each had a whole bunk room to ourselves. When I put sheets on the bed and pillow, the heavy smell of rancid whale wafted up, and as I lay in bed reading it didn't seem to grow any less. And each time I awoke in the night to the bunkhouse's small noises, that funky aroma hit me anew. The next morning Deb remarked about it, too, so it must have been in the sheets. We asked later about how it could have happened, and Robert guessed that it was a transfer across laundry loads caused by whale oil residue sticking in the washing machine and dryer. It was a new smell to us, but anyone familiar with marine mammal smells in general would know its category instantly. It's a smell you can get used to fairly quickly, despite its gaminess, and for weeks after our trip I smelled it every day when I pulled on my gloves, because I hadn't gotten around to washing them.

The next morning the wind was still blowing quite strongly, and we sat in the car at the end of the road from dawn until noon without seeing a single Ross's Gull—and very few Glaucous Gulls, either. This was very disappointing. Given the conditions, it was very nice to have a heated, Ford Taurus gull blind in which to sit on the shore of the Arctic Ocean. Just another day at the beach. For much of the time we listened to the radio broadcast in Iñupiat, which was filled with the gutturals of the native language. It was fascinating to listen to, even though we had no idea what they were talking about. What was fascinating was to listen to such a totally foreign language being occasionally interspersed with "six o'clock" or "October fifteenth."

But no gulls—damn! And I was going stir crazy sitting in the car. Eventually we decided to brave the elements and at least walk up the beach again to find no gulls. So we marched north against the driving wind. We didn't have to turn around very often for gulls, but we did so often to save our face flesh from getting frozen. Early in our march a guy driving an Arctic Tours four-wheel-drive van pulled up to see what we were up to. He was surprised to see a couple of white people carrying guns and heading out to the point. We hadn't intended to go all the way out, but he told us that he'd spent some time out there today and that there were no signs of bears. So we marched all the way out, being passed once at a distance by a very large forklift carrying some of the most recent whale out to the bone pile.

Eventually we made it out to the cold point, where the bones and recent remains of many whales were piled. It was an eerie place. In the tearing wind, Glaucous Gulls and windblown snow covered most of the pile. Only the recently dropped pieces remained fully exposed. We cut some pieces off for genetic samples for the museum and got a good dose of whale odor on hands and gloves. There was no sign of polar bears, although we had heard at the whale carcass the day before that two had been sighted out here earlier in the week. We kicked around for a little while before heading back south—*with* the wind for a welcome change. No gulls of interest passed us the whole time. But another forklift went by with a pile of remnant whale parts. This guy was serious. It's tough to drive a big front-end load over rough country, because you can't see when to go slowly so you don't lose your load due to excessive rocking. This guy decided he could go faster by driving the several miles *backwards*. I'll bet he didn't get his neck uncrimped for weeks!

Upon our return, we spent some time back in the heated Ford Taurus gull blind before giving it up and heading back toward town for some hot tea and a break. Along the way we found the butchering activity completely finished and Glaucous Gulls all over the remains, feeding intensively on the soft whale fat. I remarked to Deb how elegant these ice gulls really were when you stopped to think about it. The Glaucous Gulls were quite at home in the frigid conditions, elegantly gliding along against the cold wind and daintily alighting on whale parts to tear away at this bounty of late-season food. I was particularly captivated by the delicate variegated patterns in the plumage of the birds of the year. We'd decided that since we hadn't gotten any Ross's Gulls we'd take a couple of Glaucous instead. I lined up a couple of adults and took two with one shot. When Deb ran over to pick them up, one of them horked up a big wad of smelly spooge onto her sleeve. She still hasn't let me forget that I called them "elegant." And we took two more before sunset that day, after waiting more fruitless hours for the vanished Ross's Gulls.

On the next day, our last in Barrow, we began again at dawn at the end of the road in our heated Ford Taurus gull bind with the local, guttural-filled Iñupiat news playing away. But conditions had not improved very much. We saw gulls, but they were all out at a distance over the water. After awhile we decided to try various points along the shore to see whether they came closer to land anywhere. After driving around, we eventually found a gravel pit on the edge of the sea where Glaucous Gulls would nick the coast and use a bluff there for a little slope soaring as they beat their way north against the wind. And it wasn't more than half an hour or so before we saw a couple of Ross's Gulls doing the same. They weren't coming by very frequently, but they were here, and we spent the rest of the day there in our heated gull blind, waiting for Ross's Gulls to pass close enough to warrant our leaping out and trying frantically to lure them in.

At last, on this final day, we were properly prepared with decoys. I had loaded up a couple of white socks and a white bag with dirt, and when gulls came close enough to try it out, Deb and I would leap out of the car and start throwing socks in the air like crazy. Surprisingly, it worked. Several times we lured birds in from up to a quarter of a mile at sea. We didn't get more than a couple of shots, but it was progress. We got a couple of birds and a good lesson in how to work things next time. Every once in awhile someone drove by and stopped nearby to look out over the ocean. The few who saw us leap out of our car in the strong wind and start madly throwing dirt-filled socks into the air must have thought they'd been invaded by insane people. But we had a good time and saw some neat things, and we got a few of these elegant gulls of the far north.

Figure 21.2. Cabin and whimsical baleen palm trees on the shore of the Arctic Ocean, Barrow, Alaska.

The next morning as we left at dawn, we saw that the pack ice had crept in and was right up to the shore in places. At the airport we ran into some real post-terrorism blundering on the part of good-hearted people trying to keep our skies safe. Long after our locked Action Packers had been checked, we were asked if we had any firearms, which of course we did—dismantled and locked in our checked baggage, as they are supposed to be. They had to go get them off of the airplane so we could put the signed pieces of paper in them that assured anyone who cared to read that we had unloaded them, that they were locked in hard-sided cases, etc. Well, when they got our baggage off, they didn't like the fact that the shotguns were locked in with boots, underwear, books, and toothbrushes—despite being broken down completely into pieces (and unloaded, as our signed pieces of paper said). And they wanted to take every item out and inspect it. Gloves on, this is what they proceeded to do. Strange. There had been no problem with this whatsoever on the flight out of Fairbanks (or on any other flight for years).

We wanted to get on this flight, so we sought a solution to their statement that we weren't going to be leaving with things like this. We wound up hurriedly emptying Deb's already mostly empty Action Packer (from the inspection) into my pack and a cardboard box and then packing all the pieces of the two guns into this one Action Packer so they'd ride alone. They did let me wrap the pieces in a towel so they wouldn't be banging together in that big, empty box. After hastily locking the boxes and running tape around just about everything standing still, we chucked it all onto the forklift standing by and sent it off back to the cargo hold. And we made the flight. In all, it wasn't any worse than many border crossings I've been through, but making such a fuss over something that makes no difference to passenger safety in the name of passenger safety gives a strong message about just how far we have to go to intelligently fight terror in the skies.

Hurricane Iris

I called home on the night before we left Barrow. The most important message was one relayed from Andy Johnson in Belize: Study site wiped out; want to come home. Yikes. I'd followed the damned storm online until the night I left the museum, and my last impression was that it was likely to go north of Toledo District, where our study site is and where Andy had been merrily engaged in banding birds since I left him there in August. Well, no doubt to the relief of Belize City, which lies in the north of the country, the hurricane made landfall in the south.

We went straight to the museum upon landing in Fairbanks, and there I learned more details from an email Andy had sent before trying to call. He had spent the night of the hurricane in a room at Peter Aleman's small hotel in Big Falls, together with many of the community's members. The whole thing lasted just one and a quarter hours—with sustained winds of 145 mph and gusts estimated to 200 mph. Wow. In Andy's words, "2030 the wind was howling like I hope to never see again. By 2145 it was over. Dawn revealed a war zone. Big Falls lost ¾ of its roofs and probably ½ its houses; everybody suffered some damage."

I was not able to get through to Andy, but I spent the day assembling more information about the hurricane and conditions in southern Belize. The US news was alphabetically stalled between Afghanistan and anthrax. This Belizean plight, a natural disaster of great moment and a humanitarian need if ever there was one, had been lost on page sixty-three in the classifieds, so to speak. It was difficult to find cogent information even on the web.

Peter Dunham, at Cleveland State University, answered the telephone on the first ring. On this Saturday afternoon after the hurricane, I suppose every person with people in southern Belize was trying to do whatever was possible from a distance to determine what the situation was and how to help. Peter is a saint, and he was hard at work doing what he could from a distance. Years ago, Peter did his PhD in archaeology, working on a project in southern Belize. He runs the camp we've used there on Don Owen-Lewis's farm. It was Peter's desire for biological inventory work in the Maya Mountains that got the two of us connected in 1997. And, although I admit my interests got stalled in the fruitful lowlands, Peter's been a gracious host to our endeavors in the district. And so has Don Owen-Lewis.

Peter relayed to me what news he knew, and I was able to get some from the web. The British Army had described that southern Belize looked as though a giant lawnmower had gone over it. The majestic rainforest of southern Belize was gone—snapped off at about thirty feet or less and ripped to shreds. From the human perspective, 72 percent of homes in Toledo District had had their roofs blown off. The electronic images that Peter forwarded and those on the web revealed a lot of damage.

But, surprisingly, there had been very little loss of human life. The rapid passage of the hurricane and the lack of deluges of rain had probably prevented more deaths. Most of the fatalities were visiting Americans, who were advised by their dive captain to weather out the storm aboard the dive vessel tied to a dock. Perhaps among all hurricanes the odds were better that way than being in a land-based shelter at sea level. But in this hurricane, the odds were different; wind and the storm surge capsized the vessel, and those aboard drowned.

On the bright side, the survivors in southern Belize were not cut off from relief efforts. The Southern Highway was open, and there were electricity and phone connections to Toledo District. I tried calling Andy repeatedly throughout the day, but was unable to reach him until nightfall. He had been out with Don, Jimmy, Francisca (Don's daughter and son-in-law), and their family, helping people recover from the storm. Everyone there was all right and working on recovery.

Andy was okay. He had signed his email "Rattled," as I guess everyone was, and the objectives of his research seemed to be wiped away with the forest. Living through such a storm, witnessing such damage, and having one's hard work seemingly snatched away was rough, but he was in good health and mostly still had a place to live (although with his tent pitched in a partially roofed structure there was some repair to do). As long as his health and welfare weren't further jeopardized, I recommended that he take advantage of the situation and wrest something potentially quite good from the havoc. It's psychologically difficult to see your goals blown away, and I'm sure he was wondering how he would get his thesis done now that the data source was destroyed. But we had a lot of pre-hurricane data on that site, and he had just spent almost two months marking that avian community. He was standing in the middle of an amazing opportunity to determine how bird communities respond to such natural devastation.

So I talked about rolling with the punches, making lemonade out of lemons, etc., and Andy was a receptive listener and good field biologist. Many biologists would give a lot to be in Andy's shoes, with such beautiful pre-storm data and the chance to be out right afterward to continue sampling amidst the wreckage. It's hard to change directions at the drop of a hat, but Andy was game for it. He described the study site as "covered in 3-8 feet of trees and debris, you could walk across the plot without touching the ground, it's like an extremely messy clearcut." But it was possible with a hell of a lot of machete work to put the nets back up in the same net lanes (or as close as possible). Fortunately, he had taken the nets down before the storm. Don had described to Andy what he had earlier described to me: that the last time they had a hurricane here the wind hadn't been so bad, but the flooding had been terrific, putting much of the country—including our study site—under water. So Andy and Santos Hun went back out into the toothpick factory and began cutting lanes and stringing nets. Without shade they couldn't have the nets open when the sun was strong, and Andy was eating out of cans like a hobo; but every bird captured was a golden little data point, and through Andy's and Santos's efforts we'd all learn a lot about how birds respond to natural disasters.

But all was certainly not well in Paradise. I remained troubled by what Andy relayed to me of my good friend Don Owen-Lewis's situation. The home he built and raised his family in had been essentially destroyed. This oasis of tranquility and stellar avian diversity in the midst of Paradise—where Don (a British expatriate) had established a farm, raised a family, and made a forty-year history—was largely a fond memory. Andy relayed a little of Don's situation. Of sitting on the remains of the verandah looking out over the suddenly open country. Of moving out. I think the scope of the devastation was brought home to me by a statement made from his verandah by this forty-year resident who knew the country like the back of his hand. "Damn me. I never knew there was a hill there."[18]

The Last Harbinger of Fall

Quite a long time after sending an email that he was on the way, Matt Miller showed up in Fairbanks. Adopting a pattern quite the opposite of the classic "snowbird," Matt had left the University of Arizona in late September and driven over 6,000 miles with a friend to reach Fairbanks just after our first lasting snowfall blanketed the earth. What a ride.

Matt's arrival brought our full complement of students for the academic year into the fold. We were up to six graduate students and three undergraduates in the lab, and things were really cooking.

So, what is it like in Fairbanks at this time of year? On one morning, rushing about trying to get stuff for the lab that I hadn't had time to get the night before, I went into Fred Meyer's, my favorite store. You have to love a store where you can go in and buy paradichlorobenzene and espresso. One-stop shopping. The fact that I found a need to get these things and enjoyed

---

18. We followed up on this effort with further studies of the birds' response to Hurricane Iris, which was really fascinating. Many of our banded birds just hunkered down and remained, despite the loss of their appropriate forest habitat. Those recaptures reminded me of interviews with people who remained on Mount Saint Helens before the volcanic eruption there in 1980—except that so many of our banded birds lived through the ordeal. Don Owen-Lewis had to move away to another property in Big Falls, where he lives today, ready to host visitors to a greatly recovered area in Toledo District, so rich in birds that I labeled it "Paradise" during my first visit in 1997.

being able to do so must be a seasonal thing. I could have gotten fresh whole halibut, too. And with Halloween approaching, we were starting to get a little chill in the air; the first forecasts for double-digit below-zero temperatures had come coolly off the presses. Good skiing was just about here.

22

Your Story Sounds a Little Fishy, Mr. Winker

A King in my Mental Net

AS JUNE RACED BY and the hectic field and office schedules of July approached, I found myself watching the web data on the passage of salmon past the sonar counter near the mouth of the Copper River. As the numbers built, I found myself with a king salmon in my mental net and unable to concentrate on getting mundane work done.

Consequently, Rose and I headed for Chitina on a Thursday afternoon with our dip nets Mashie and Niblick tied to the top of the truck. The drive was good and scenic, with great weather, and we listened to another P. G. Wodehouse book on tape as we raced along:

"My wife's gone to the West Indies," says the main character.

"Oh, Jamaica?" asks the other party.

"No, she went on her own."

What a comic author! Maybe you had to be there.

The road beyond O'Brien Creek had been closed by a landslide that the Alaska Department of Transportation was no longer going to keep clear. This meant that a lot more dipnetters than usual would be relying on the charters, and that a weekend trip would be more competitive than we wanted.

We arrived after nine in the evening, and for the first time in our experience here, there were not people cleaning fish by the creek. This was not a good sign. But we pitched the tent, cooked up a tasty dinner, and went to sleep looking forward to a nice day on the river.

Hermit Thrushes were singing by 3:00 a.m., and the day dawned clear and calm. It was going to be a beautiful day, regardless of what the fish wanted to do. We got in line to go out with Sam McCallister. Roger checked us in and emphasized the situation:

"The fishing's been shitty. Sam wants everyone to know that it's been shitty so nobody complains and whines about wanting to go to another spot. The fishing's shitty everywhere."

The message was clear. The day before, people had fished all day and caught only about three fish per person. That's a lot of work for so few fish. Today looked like it would at least be a very nice one on the river, so off we went in the first boat.

We were on our rock with our nets in the water by 7:35 a.m.—the earliest yet. And we caught a nice big red by 7:45—an auspicious beginning. But the place we were dropped had the biggest, baddest, roiling boil we'd ever worked. And even working very hard, we settled into a slow average of just one fish per hour. The fish varied greatly in size, from the smallest we've gotten to the largest. But at this slow pace we kept them all.

The weather was glorious. It was one hell of a day to be out on the river. So we enjoyed ourselves even though the fishing was slow. There was another Hermit Thrush here, serenading us from the moment of our arrival. One of our last fish was a king salmon of 30–35 pounds. It hit like a load of lead just slouched into the net, and I began hauling it in knowing that something big was in there. As we saw it surface, we were both afraid it would flop out; so Rose slipped her net underneath mine, and together we brought this whopper in. A conk on the head put it into a tractable mood, and after several pictures I got it securely onto a stringer. The adrenalin from this fish was quite a rush. King salmon was going for $10 a pound in Fred Meyer's when we left; this was at least a $200 fish!

Figure 22.1. The author with a king salmon (Oncorhynchus tschawytscha), Chitina, Copper River, Alaska (photo by Rose Meier).

Sam and Roger came and picked us up just before 7:00 p.m., a bit later than usual. Back at O'Brien Creek we gutted the fish quickly—there were only nine—and hit the road. Before leaving, we checked the fluids and filled the radiator, as we had to do before leaving the day before. It was about 8:00 p.m. when we headed out on the 320-mile drive home. We crawled the long way back up out of the Copper River Valley the thirty miles or so back to the main highway and got gas in Glennallen. During this initial hour or so, we had to stop and let the engine cool and add more water. I was mystified about where the water was going. The engine itself had been running hot on long trips for about two years, ever since its first overheating. This initial overheating had caused the heater core to go also, resulting in a loss of heat to the cab in winter. I'd gotten an estimate of what it would cost to repair it, but it was too high. And, besides, I'd already been through one winter with no heat. It seemed easy enough to dress warmly and keep the window open to prevent window frost, and it was only a six-mile drive home (this is a guy thing; Rose and I did not agree on the result of my cost-to-discomfort ratio calculation).

Two hours later we'd finished the Wodehouse tape of *Uncle Dynamite*. In this tale, Reginald "Pongo" Twizzleton, "Barmy" Ickenham, Hermione Bostock, and her father "Mugsy" had worked out their complex and humorous problems, and we were grunting slowly up the long hill north of Paxson. The truck was running rather hot, and at the top of the ascent we decided to pull off, let it cool, and fill it back up with water. I was surprised to find it acting seriously overheated, although the needle had not gone into the overheated zone. I refilled the radiator after the truck had cooled awhile, but then it wouldn't start again. That was a surprise. It just cranked over and over without catching. For some reason, my eye caught a drip coming out of the tailpipe, which was not normal. I caught a drop and looked at it—it was antifreeze green. Uh oh. I quickly pulled the oil dipstick to see whether the whole crankcase was full of water also. It wasn't. So we only had a blown head gasket, not a cracked block. Not that the details mattered; we were stuck here. It was 12:30 a.m.

The sun was just down, Gray-cheeked Thrushes were singing all around us, there were no insects, and an almost-full moon was rising. It was a gorgeous evening. We weren't excited about being stuck on a long and lonely road, but we had our camping gear and a spacious gravel pit all to ourselves. We soon had the tent up, and by 1:00 we were lying down to sleep with the last of the thrushes singing the moon up. It was easy to leave our considerable problems for later because we were so tired.

It got down to about 34° F in the night, but we had been fully prepared for cool weather and so had been perfectly comfortable. The cacophony of bird song that began between 3:00 and 4:00 didn't faze us; only the heat of the sun got us out of the tent at almost 8:00. The light I saw in the distance before we'd gone to bed proved to be the first bit of civilization on the shore of Summit Lake. After striking camp and packing and locking the truck, we set out walking north along the road toward Summit Lake and its alluring nocturnal light. We only had to walk about a mile and a half before arriving at a group of cabins and a home there. But there was a note on the door of the home, saying they'd had to go to town for an emergency, and there was a crazy dog barking wildly inside. So just as we had been congratulating ourselves on how easy it had been to find a phone—while walking up the driveway moments earlier and seeing the phone sign—luck turned a cold shoulder and we were suddenly as lost as we had been when we set out.

As we walked in, we had noticed someone backing up a boat over by a large RV. It almost looked like he was practicing. We decided to ask him whether the owners would be home soon. What a great guy.

"I'm just practicing backing up my boat," he said.

Apparently it was still a new rig, and he wanted to get comfortable with it before taking it to the boat ramp. The owners were probably going to be away for a while, so he offered to take us to a phone. As we went, I asked him how long he'd been in Alaska. He'd first come in 1939, and he'd been stationed on Adak during the war. He'd driven a landing craft on the invasion of Kiska. He had a lot of interesting stories, and I wished we had the chance to hear more of them. This kind gentleman left us off at the Paxson Lodge, and we were soon on the phone with our insurance company, finally using that towing insurance we'd been carrying for years.

It took awhile to arrange towing from Fairbanks, over 180 miles away. Geico doesn't arrange much long-distance towing in Alaska, it seems, and the guy on the phone had a lot of work to do before finally getting things worked out. We eventually got it clear that Ron's Towing and Service from Fairbanks would be coming down in a few hours to get first us, then the truck. We had a great breakfast and then sat out in the sun on the lodge's deck. It was a gorgeous day.

A few hours later, we were in the cab of a loud tow truck headed north through glorious scenery, getting an expensive chauffeured ride back home. Our chauffeur was a great guy named Rich. The poor old truck rolled along behind us. Our trip home by unexpected means took the rest of the day. We fileted fish on Sunday and began eating piles of sashimi and cooking our favorite king-salmon-head soup. We also grilled the smallest one we'd caught—whole, over wood chips. Oh, man, that was good. On Monday night I had a great new snack idea—a sashimi omelet, with cambozola cheese and wasabi. This, too, was delicious. And on Tuesday night we began feasting on the soup as we finished off the sashimi. And so, despite the loss of the truck, we had a fast and savory rebound from the trip.

Niblick Rides Alone

Following July's field work and proposal deadlines, I was eager to get back down to Chitina to get more salmon. Going into the winter with only nine fish from our first trip was not a happy prospect; it meant that we would run out of fish before next year's season.

But we still didn't have a second vehicle, and Rose couldn't take off from work in the middle of the week. The truck had not been repaired yet, so a run to Chitina was problematic. I watched the fishing reports on the web and periodically called on the phone to learn how the fish were running. A huge number had passed the Miles Lake sonar in mid-July, almost 200,000 more than projected. The Alaska Department of Fish and

Game had accordingly set a "bonus fish week" from 29 July through 4 August, allowing each permit holder to get ten more fish. This meant that we'd be able to go back and get thirty-one fish during this week—if only we could figure out a way to do it! Well, we did. Or at least we figured it out so I could go and wrestle some fish home.

Rose's mother, Betty, and her sister Margaret were up for a little more than a week to visit us and attend the Fairbanks Summer Arts Festival. Rose had the brilliant idea to rent a small car while they were here to accommodate our complex schedules. We just decided to keep it for a few extra days, and that gave me the wheels needed to get to Chitina again. I was chomping at the bit to get down while that big slug of fish was still passing through the canyon south of O'Brien Creek, but on Sunday—the first day of bonus fish week—I caught the flu that everyone else in the house had already had. It sure kicked my butt. I couldn't go on Sunday for sure, nor on Monday; I couldn't even work a full day on Monday. On Tuesday I sure didn't feel up to it, but because I had to be back on Thursday I left on Tuesday afternoon.

The little subcompact (a Daewoo Lanos) would never have been sufficient for both Rose and me, but for just one person, all the gear and the coolers fit in reasonably well. The net handle, tied to the top, was almost as long as the little vehicle. I was off—the first trip to Chitina without Rose. Even with another Wodehouse book on tape, it was a long drive.

This little car was fast, though. I made it down in about five-and-a-half hours. I found our favorite campsite occupied, and so I pulled into another we had used in the past. As I stretched my cramped body, I saw Kelly Auer walk by in chest waders. I ran up and hailed her—I was very curious to know how the day's fishing had been. She and Andy Johnson had fished for the afternoon right there at O'Brien Creek, standing in the cold, rushing water and sweeping their nets with the current to catch fish as they swam upstream. They'd arrived in the early afternoon, but only one guide was running and he (Mark Hem, of Hem Charters) was not taking out new customers so late in the day. So they fished right there from shore, and they did pretty well, too. They were finishing cleaning their catch and were headed back to Fairbanks that night. Later I learned that they'd done the whole run—down, fish, and back—in about twenty-three hours. That's too intense for me, although it's a common way to do a Chitina run among Fairbanksans. I pitched my tent and tried to get some sleep before going out the next morning.

Sam McCallister was out for boat repair, leaving just the single boat of Mark Hem on the river to handle the higher-than-usual traffic of this year with the road closed a mile below O'Brien Creek. People began lining up for the charter remarkably early. I got in line before 6:00 and still was only able to make the third boat out. As we all stood there waiting, we watched one particularly good dipnetter working the river right by the creek. By my calculations he would be able to get his limit in about three to four hours. But he sure had to work for them. Sweeping is seriously hard work. I'm not sure my back could handle several hours of it. To sweep, you hold your net out pointed upriver, drop it in, and work it along the bottom with the rapid current until it reaches a point downstream where it's angled too steeply to catch a fish. Then you pull it in, lift it up, and swing it back upriver. The longer the handle, the farther out and deeper you can reach. And from what I've seen, wearing chest waders and leaning out as far as you can go with a twelve-foot net handle produces the highest capture rate. That's hard, wet work. I had no problem waiting for the third boat. Mark began at 7:00 and got people out fast; I was out fishing by 8:30.

It had been my serious concern before leaving Fairbanks that perhaps going on a fishing trip was not the best plan for getting over the flu. And after a poor night's sleep, and as I sat on a rock beside the raging river at 9:00, feeling like five pounds of crap in a one-pound bag, this concern seemed to be justified. But I took three aspirin and kept my net in the water. And ten fish later I felt a *lot* better. Taking three aspirin and catching ten red salmon is my new recommended cure for the flu.

The fish began hitting the net as soon as I put it in the water, and the first three were on the stringer in what seemed like no time. But then things got a little slow for a while. Mark came by in his boat and suggested I try holding the net out away from the rocks a little bit, and that seemed to work for a little while. I was on a well-fissured rock sloping steeply into the rushing, muddy, gray-beige water. This rock projected out from the bank along the edge of a large back eddy, one of the largest and slowest I'd been on. It was a couple of acres of slow water moving along a cliff and steep landslide, with my rock ending at the point where the raging river and this huge eddy met on the upriver side. I tied the net off to a piton someone had hammered into the rock, but I didn't tie myself off because the ensuing tangle would have increased the risk of falling in. I planned to hold onto the net if the unthinkable happened. And, as it got hotter on this clear, blue-sky day, I shed my lifejacket (something I would not ordinarily recommend).

I hadn't fished in this exact type of situation before, and it took awhile to learn just how the fish were swimming in the local currents. There were a lot of fish here, but they were frustratingly difficult to land. I had far more bumps than fish in the net, which meant that they were angling across the back eddy's current and hitting the net from the outside. Also, I saw something I hadn't seen before—I actually saw the fish in the water. This water is so turbid that you can't see into it more than about a millimeter.

But in this large back eddy, some fish were occasionally coming up and lolling on the surface briefly before going back under. So I was seeing the occasional fins, lips, and even eyes on the surface—almost always out of reach of my net, though. I did eventually scoop up one of these volunteers and felt I'd finally outwitted them. But when you're poking your net into water this turbid, you're still basically just trying to reach out and tag fish in the dark.

As I worked the first couple of hours, I finally figured out that the moving front of the interface between the two currents was where the fish seemed to get concentrated (rather than along the steep rock shoreline), and that whirlpools were especially likely to have fish riding them. The latter I first realized from watching where the occasional fins and lips were appearing out of reach farther down the back eddy. Once I had this figured out, I watched for the big surges that set the interface to really roiling and reached out and held my net on the interface as it came rolling in. And when a whirlpool came in reach, I rode that as long as possible. A twelve-foot net handle (an upgrade from our former eight-foot handles) is a useful thing. This technique was lethal for the fish.

The sun hit my little spot, a light breeze kept me reasonably cool, there was a total absence of mosquitoes, and the fish were piling into the net. It doesn't get much better than that. Rose had made an excellent lunch for me, so I even had a good riverside picnic while I continued to fish. It actually looked like I'd be getting close to the limit of thirty salmon. As the day warmed up, the river rose a foot or so, and this caused enough of a change in the local currents that I had fewer roiling interfaces to fish that were within reach of the net. So it got a little slower. But I steadily filled the stringers. One of the last bumps I got was a very heavy one on the edge of a fine whirlpool, and all of a sudden I was hauling in one heck of a heavy load.

It was two reds in the net at once, and two of the largest of the day. Getting those bruisers landed and on the stringer was serious work.

I stopped one fish short of the thirty-one possible on my permit this day (we'd gotten nine on the first trip). Thirty salmon is a lot of fish, and by midafternoon the fishing really slowed down. So when Mark came by in his boat at about 2:00 p.m. and I had thirty fish, I gave him the sign that I was ready to return. It was a gorgeous day, and after loading in my junk and the heavy stringer-loads of fish, we headed upriver to pick up another successful pair of dipnetters before heading back to O'Brien Creek. As we sped along through the spectacular scenery of the canyon, another group flagged the boat and pantomimed that someone there had fallen and gotten injured. Mark put in, and we found an older gentleman with a bloody bandage on his head. He'd fallen backwards onto a rock and dinged himself seriously enough that we had to get him in. He'd pretty much limited out on fish; we carefully piled him and his catch into the boat and went back to the creek. EMTs from Chitina came down and checked him out while he had his fish cleaned. He was okay, but I know his accident reminded a lot of us about just how dangerous this river can be.

Cleaning thirty fish seems to take about twice as long as catching them. Each person who had stood in line for the charter in the morning was coming back in with his or her limit. The gulls along the creek were so stuffed with offal that they were not very interested in the phenomenal load of goodies going down the creek as everyone cleaned fish. I'd never seen so many fish being cleaned along here at one time. A group of six people brought in 200 fish. Rose and I typically just gutted our fish here, washed them well in the creek, then layered them into coolers with ice brought down from Fairbanks. I did this as fast as possible, then hit the road and zoomed back home. Because it had only taken five-and-a-half hours to catch a full limit, I made it back home by 8:30 p.m.—almost four hours earlier than usual. After a shower, I slept like the dead.

Next morning I began to filet these beauties. I finished half of them before going into work, and after work Rose and I finished off the rest. It was a lot of fish. We began eating the piles of sashimi for dinner, and it lasted for four days—even with sashimi, cambozola, and wasabi omelets. You'd think maybe you could get sick of salmon, especially when consuming mass quantities of it at this season. But a week later we were thawing out some of those tasty filets for dinner again.

23

Hootchies on a Slack Tide

IT'S STRANGE HOW ONE of your favorite pastimes can quietly slide into oblivion through neglect, but that's what happened to me with fishing. After stellar fishing for salmon with John Klicka here in Alaska in 1990, I drifted completely away from the sport—knowing that all other fishing pales in comparison to what we experienced then fishing for salmon. Last year Rose and I bought new fishing gear with the intent of getting out and doing some salmon fishing, but our intended trips to do so never materialized.

Thank goodness people come up to knock us out of our ruts. Dad's visit two years earlier finally got me out big game hunting after years of good intentions. This year, my brother Sean, his wife Wanda, and their family (Colin, Emma, and Gannon) came up in late August, and Sean and Colin wanted to do some fishing. This late in the year, there are good silver salmon runs down along the coast, and Rose and I had often talked about wanting to go to Valdez and try some ocean fishing for these beauties. Schedules being what they were, Sean, Colin, and I headed down on a fast trip in midweek. The Valdez Fishing Report on the radio sounded good, and just before Sean, et al., arrived I'd heard that the key to success with the silvers was "hootchies on a slack tide." I had no idea what a hootchie was, but I expected to learn while buying lures just before our departure.

I'd talked with people who had fished in Valdez for pink salmon and silver salmon, and so I was familiar with our options. A half-day charter was a more sure thing, but a lot of people are successful (while the fish are running) when fishing from shore along the Allison Point area over near the oil pipeline terminal. Our last stop before leaving was at Fred Meyer's to buy some food and the secret fishing lures. But there were no "hootchies" to be found, and the salespeople hadn't heard of them. So we bought a selection of Pixies (highly reflective metallic spoons with colored plastic centers) and headed out.

We zoomed straight down and began fishing from shore along Allison Point at about 5:00 p.m. on a Wednesday. There were a lot of people out there along the rocky shore, but hardly anyone was catching anything. Gossip had it that the fishing had been great, then poor, etc.—classic shoreline scuttlebutt. The fishing was always good just before you got there. But it was great to be out standing on a tranquil ocean shoreline in the scenic Valdez Arm of Prince William Sound—despite the smell. A lot of used-up pink salmon were lying about dead or dying; the latter were often wiggling out their last bit of life. After a couple of hours of not catching anything, we went in search of a campsite. We found a great one away from everything and almost empty this late in the season. We pitched the tents and went into town for some dinner.

There was quite a bit of evening activity at the public fish cleaning tables, and we strolled along enjoying the signs of others' success. Mike's Palace was busy, but our wait was well rewarded by their excellent halibut specialty and their lasagna. We didn't finish eating until it was close to dark, so we bagged our plan to do a little evening fishing and instead went back to the campground, hitting the sleeping bags by 10:00 p.m.

We were up next morning at dawn, striking camp and heading straight for the shore. There were very few people fishing yet, and the tide was almost out. Within seconds there were three lures arcing through the still air and plopping into the calm water. It was a gorgeous morning. You could see seven glaciers among the valleys across the bay, and, although it was overcast, not a drop of rain fell. For the first hour this was plenty to keep us entirely tranquil and happy with the long drive down and the whole experience. A young seal came in and poked its head up a few times to check us out. A sea otter moseyed by. Then the fish began to hit. Wow! Having a fish strike and getting one of these big ones into shore was electrifying. We were really having fun. We probably lost as many as we caught, but it was the strike and the fight that was so much fun.

Figure 23.1. Sean Winker with a nice catch of silver salmon (Oncorhynchus kisutch), Valdez, Prince William Sound, Alaska.

After I lost one that I'd dragged half out of the water, Sean went up to the car and got the landing net we'd been too lazy to bring down. That prevented any further losses right in at the water's edge. But some of the ones we lost threw the hook while still out a ways. It took Colin a little while to have Lady Luck shine her torch on him, but he was soon in the lead for putting fish on the stringer. It was just as fun to watch a good fish fight and the occasional leaps out of the water as it was to have one on the line yourself. And out on the water the uncaught fish were leaping, taunting our feeble casting efforts and spurring us on. At the end of two incredible hours, the fishing got very slow—the tide was fully out, and it was like a fish retreat signal. We'd landed ten nice fish among the three of us, making for a pretty heavy load of fresh salmon. Surprisingly, it was after the real action that most people arrived to fish. After gutting our fish by the shore and hauling them iced down in the cooler up the bank to the car, a woman who was headed down to fish with her two children was incredulous that we'd caught these beauties right there at the shore she'd been fishing every day for nine days.

It was clear that we'd been very lucky, catching a short window of perfect fishing. After getting some coffee and a snack in town, we went back out and fished for a couple more hours, but none of us caught another one. We'd checked out the city dock, but found people only catching herring, so we went back out to Allison Point. It was very slow for everyone, except for the occasional accidental hooking of one of the "living dead" pink salmon carcasses floating or barely swimming by. Getting these spoogey things off the hook without touching them was the biggest challenge of the afternoon. But we did have the great scenery, and a Steller's sea lion came by to check us out briefly. Eventually we packed it in and headed back on a fast drive home—in complete agreement that we'd had a great trip. My second fish had been such a great fight that it alone had been worth our two days to me. I'd coaxed it into shore three times, and each time it decided it preferred deeper water, powering out fast with my reel screaming as the drag grudgingly gave out line. That whopper must have been about fifteen pounds, and all three of us subdued it when we finally got it ashore in the net. Helluva trip!

But after returning, we still had a burning question: What's a hootchie? I just had to know, so I looked it up in a Google search. It's a plastic, squidlike lure made by a Canadian company, and it's always trolled.

We'd been very lucky in hitting fish. We learned from more radio listening that the silvers weren't really in yet—they were hanging out deeper than usual at forty- to sixty-foot depths. Only the charters and other people in boats were really getting into them.

We had a final, fitting battle with these fish. The night after we got home, everyone tore into a big plate of sashimi, dipping pieces of these thinly sliced morsels of raw fish into a wasabi and soy sauce mixture while a whole fresh fish was cooking slowly over smoke on the grill.

24

Hey-Ho, Off We Go! Along the Alaska Peninsula!

LAST FALL, JEFF DENTON of the Bureau of Land Management (BLM) approached the University of Alaska Museum with a plan to team up to do biological inventory work on scattered pieces of BLM lands in the southern BLM district of Alaska. The agreement that we hammered out between the two institutions was the first comprehensive cross-disciplinary effort that the museum had engaged in. All of our departments, both the social and natural sciences, participated in the planning process, and beginning in June we collectively began an intensive, blitzkrieg-style survey of BLM lands in southern Alaska.

Our department, Ornithology, was going to be involved in three of the BLM trips—roughly twenty percent of our department's total trips this year. I penciled myself in for one of these trips: the one to survey scattered pieces of land along the Alaska Peninsula. This was a big piece of Alaska that I hadn't seen before, and its relative inaccessibility meant that few specimens had been taken along its length. Our intention to participate in these trips began early in the year with air-safety training—a whole day of education in safe and unsafe practices around aircraft. We thanked our lucky stars that we didn't have to take the more intensive three-day course in helicopter flight that involved a buckled-in dunking in a water tank to practice escape maneuvers (at least that was the rumor of what we could have been in for).

James Maley and I left with Dusty McDonald and Kris Larsen (representing Mammalogy) and Sandra Jennings (representing Entomology) at 10:30 p.m. on 2 July on an all-night drive to Anchorage. We arrived pretty early at BLM headquarters (5:30 a.m.) and so went off to the "Golden Donut" for some coffee and a morsel of sugary sustenance. At least a couple of us were alert enough to make sure we tried something golden, hoping for the specialty of the house. But it was the coffee that made the real difference. At 7:30 we met with Jeff Denton at BLM headquarters and learned that we would leave on a charter from the Anchorage airport at about 9:00. At F.S. Air Service we piled all of our gear onto a large scale and watched as the pile approached and then just barely topped 1,000 pounds. Then we all went in and stood on a scale to get a total mass for the flight so the crew could load enough fuel. And off we went to King Salmon in a Fairchild Metroliner, a rather cigar-shaped, dual-engine, propeller-driven craft. Those of us coming from Fairbanks spent the flight sleeping.

In King Salmon we shifted to a chartered flight with PenAir on a Cessna Caravan, which would take us to the Bear Lake Lodge. We were on the ground for only a short time in King Salmon while the plane was fueled and our baggage transferred. This flight again allowed some snooze time. We landed at Bear Lake Lodge in the early afternoon and met Warren Johnson, his daughter Laurie, son-in-law Shawn Ramsey, and other personnel at the lodge. It was a remarkable establishment on the shores of a large lake not far south of Port Moller. Warren's dad (Don Johnson) had established the lodge here nearly fifty years earlier for guiding hunters. It was still a hunting lodge, and their main claim to fame was Alaska Peninsula brown bears. They managed their take pretty well, too—in the season before our arrival they took out about twenty bears, averaging over ten feet in length. During the summer season, salmon fishermen come in. There was a group of Austrians there when we arrived, and they seemed pretty happy with their fishing.

James and I went out right away to begin surveying the local bird community. We were struck immediately by breeding American Robins—a breeding range extension—and a vagrant Violet-green Swallow, both present on the lodge grounds. We found the densities of birds in the area to be fairly high, reflecting a mosaic of alder thickets, open tundra, streams, sedge marshes, and the lake. While we were out, Mark Hollows, our pilot from Prism, flew in with the Bell 500 helicopter that was to support this leg of our expedition. After a short time on the ground, Mark left with Dusty, Kris, and James to find a good spot to place a small-mammal trapline and to check out some other birds. I already had enough to work on for the rest of the day.

Next day we went out to pull mammal traps and then on down to an area near Cape Lieskof on the north side of the peninsula (not far north of Izembek Lagoon) to begin surveying BLM lands. This was a rapid-fire survey, with little time on the ground in any one place. I'd never worked on such a rapid basis, but it is an excellent way to look over a lot of country and get a shirtsleeve idea of what the birdlife is like. I collected on our first area for a couple of hours before Mark flew in with the next crew. In calculating Mark's maximum allowable flight time (eight hours of flight in a fourteen-hour day), fuel, and personnel, we decided I'd go back to camp with Jeff and the birds I'd obtained, to lessen both the transport load and the prep burden.

We dropped James and Sandra off at an interesting-looking lagoon on the next piece of BLM property up the peninsula, then flew on back to the lodge. Each of these flights provided a bird's-eye view of the landscape and wildlife. Mark generally flew at an altitude of about 250 feet, giving us a good view of the country and the animals that we flew over. On the way down in the morning we saw about eleven bears; most of them were around a beached sea mammal carcass—spaced out away from each other at a few hundred meters, enough to avoid constant interference. Small herds of caribou were more widely spaced along our route. Jeff recorded the localities of each (the GPS worked beautifully while in flight). I was soon back skinning up the morning's proceeds in the bunkhouse.

Late in the afternoon all of the groups came in. James had a good tale to tell about his activities. He'd picked up some good birds, but he was unable to get one of the Green-winged Teal that he'd seen at that lagoon. This was one of the species we really wanted from the peninsula; this area is one where the North American subspecies (*Anas crecca carolinensis*) comes into contact with the possibly valid Aleutian subspecies (*A. c. nimia*) and where the Old World subspecies (*A. c. crecca*) could also occur. But we'd seen scarcely any teal, despite a lot of flight. The number of waterfowl on the many ponds in this area seemed rather low. With the desire of getting some Green-winged Teal from this far down on the peninsula, I went out the next morning with the mammal crew to see whether teal would be more accessible in the morning weather (and wind) of the day after.

We flew out with four passengers—a little crowded in the Bell 500. But I got off early to hunt the lagoon. I was there. The teal were there. We were there. About two-and-a-half hours later, only the teal were there. I missed. They had been all grouped up together, so I only had one chance, and I used both barrels on one bird without getting it. I walked a good piece of the lagoon without putting up any more teal, and began returning along the same route both to facilitate pickup (i.e., so they could spot me in the drizzle) and to see whether I could put up any teal by returning to the favored haunt I'd stumbled upon in the first half hour. But I kept on going and still no helicopter. No teal, either, which was really disappointing. I did see three Sabine's Gulls pass by at too great a distance to collect. It was very interesting to see this species for the first time.

Among James's experiences the day before had been picking up about twenty Japanese glass fishing balls. This lagoon sounded like one of the densest concentrations of these balls that I'd heard of. His tale of these floats was true. In my passage back along the shore, I saw more than I'd ever seen before in one place. They were all over, washed up into the lagoon during previous high tides and tossed ashore among the other debris. These handblown orbs of a rather thick, pale-blue glass are common beach finds in Bering Sea, Alaska; they are deposited after breaking free from the Japanese fishing industry and riding the Pacific current that goes somewhat clockwise from Japan. The most common size (and the size of all of these in this lagoon) is about three inches in diameter. I already had a fair number from various beaches around the eastern Bering Sea, but as I strolled along the grassy and cluttered beach after hunting all of the teal in reach and after the helicopter was due, I began to pick up some of the cleaner balls and drop them into my helmet bag. I carried my helmet in my helmet bag (dangling by a strap from my backpack) so that Mark would be able to pick me up wherever he encountered me.

And as I kept on walking toward the drop-off point, not finding teal and not hearing the helicopter, I kept on picking up balls, passing up the ugly ones or the ones that would require cleaning. Soon my helmet bag was full, so I dumped it into my backpack and kept on going. I was thinking that most of the rest of the group wasn't going to have much beach scrounging opportunity, so I grabbed enough for everyone, still leaving behind as many or more than I took. When I'd walked all the way back to the drop-off point (not in the plan), I had over forty glass balls, and the helicopter was about forty-five minutes past due by my estimation (which admittedly was crude—it's tough to guess how long it takes people to get their work done; heck, I can never do it for my own work).

The helicopter eventually made it with everyone happily aboard. We headed back to camp to allow Mark to refuel. Commuting by helicopter is a visual treat. It would be hard to get tired of cruising along at about 250 feet, with a rapidly changing view of the countryside and the animals upon it. Even though most of us were exhausted during these commutes, the chance to observe something exciting kept the eyes roving, and regularly someone would remark over the radio to look at the animal(s) at x-o'clock. The terrain itself was fun to watch passing by, but it was really neat to see bears, caribou, Sandhill Cranes, Tundra Swans, and the occasional wolf. On this trip I noticed strange tracks on the tidal flats of Port Moller—lots of meandering tracks that went from the shore out into the water—with no animals visible. It was odd. It was common to see occasional bear tracks going out from shore to look for stuff exposed by the low tide. But these mysterious tracks looked like a herd of animals had gone from shore into the ocean—or vice versa. We were just a little too far off to see what had made them, but I was curious. It turned out that on a different shuttle flight Mark and Jeff saw a full herd of caribou bedded down on the tidal flats at low tide. Weird. They must have been trying to escape insects, even though we did not think the insects were at all bad.

With the helicopter refueled, a group of us went off to the Port Heiden area, where James and I hoped we might find the elusive relict population of Marbled Godwit (*Limosa fedoa beringiae*) that was known to breed farther up the Alaska Peninsula. This was our first work headed up the peninsula from the lodge, and we were struck during the flight by an apparently strong decline in animal productivity as we headed in that direction. There were definitely fewer caribou, bear, swans, and cranes—all animals that we were getting used to seeing in abundance from the air. They were all still present, but their numbers seemed lower.

After a brief tour of the area by air, we settled on being dropped in the Reindeer Creek drainage, at a low elevational point in the BLM landholdings in this area. Although the winds were a little strong on the tundra above the small stream-cut valley, down in the floodplain things were hopping. Hermit Thrushes and other species were singing down there, so we got to work with enthusiasm after a quick lunch break in the lee of the cutbank.

We use 12-gauge, side-by-side shotguns for collecting birds in arctic Alaska[19], but we have barrel inserts ("auxiliary barrels") that scale down the type of ammunition that you can use in a barrel that is chambered at the manufacturer for twelve lead balls to the pound ("gauge" refers to the number of lead balls of that diameter that make up a pound, though you would only shoot something of that diameter from such a weapon at large game). I was using 12 gauge in the left (full choke) barrel and .410 dust (12-shot) in the right barrel at the time, standard procedure for museum specimen collecting in open and semi-open habitats. When you are at the right distance to assure a clean death and minimal specimen damage, you use the appropriate barrel. We are good at this, and it is a rapid way to selectively sample an area's avifauna.

After a few hours at this site, we were ready to be moved. When Mark came in with the next group, James, Sandra, and I went down to the mouth of Caribou Creek to see what birds this habitat attracted as it hit the sea. It was a pleasant spot. Although it was in reach of Port Heiden on a dirt track

---

19. As noted earlier, arctic is used here in the sense of Congress and the National Science Foundation, referring to arctic habitats rather than geography north of the Arctic Circle. In Alaska, arctic habitats occur well south of that line.

that brought four-wheelers and pickups to the creek valley, it was still wild Alaska. Bear tracks, for example, were abundant.

Figure 24.1. James Maley crouches beside the recent tracks of an animal that we did not want to meet close up, the brown bear (Ursus arctos), Alaska Peninsula, Alaska. The bear slugs we are required to carry seem rather small (one is standing in front of the track just in front of James).

When James and I made it down to the meeting of the stream and the sea, we encountered one of the coolest things that we saw on the whole trip: pumice. There were countless small pieces of both dark and light pumice along the beach, tossed ashore along the high-tide line. They were pebbles and small rocks, mostly, and surprisingly light for their size. In one area we found dense windrows (or "waverows") of the stuff over a foot deep. In a couple of places there were acres of it, and it felt weird to walk through and over it and to kick it. Heavily deposited pumice is a very strange substrate.

We didn't find any birds we needed that came within range. But a pair of Sabine's Gulls flew by at a distance, and later we saw a small flock of what seemed like Marbled Godwits go by at a distance. This was a species we really wanted to get, but we knew that our opportunity to do so would be improved when we got up to Ugashik Bay, farther up the peninsula. I was pooped, and so sat by the drop-off point, taking notes while James and Sandra continued to collect in the area. I told James that we could use a Bank Swallow (there were dozens nesting in the bluff forming the NE riverbank near the sea), then laughed every time I heard him shoot, knowing how difficult it is to get one on the wing. At one point while writing notes, I looked up to see a Common Raven flying along the bluff of the riverbank. It saw me and our junk and headed over to investigate. I began fumbling for shells of an appropriate size (I was loaded for small birds), but could only get one low-base number 8 into the gun by the time the bird was overhead. Fortunately, that was perfect: with one shot it came down stone cold dead not twenty feet from me. It was one bird that we'd really wanted from the peninsula, and I was relieved that a single shot had done what I was unable to do in the morning with the teal.

Mark came and got us at about 7:00 p.m. The flight back was largely uneventful, but a gorgeous Grumman Albatross airplane passed us, headed for Cold Bay, and the pilot spoke to us over the radio. This pilot (Terry), apparently a chief pilot for Alaska Airlines, was headed with his wife Connie and eleven passengers to Attu Island. He figured that it would be about a 6.5-hour flight the next day. It would have been interesting to speak with them on their return trip. It was about time to change commanders on Attu, and I wondered what this group was headed out to do.

Laurie was good enough to hold dinner for us; it had been a long day. We processed and froze our birds and finally hit the hay, exhausted, at 10:30. The next day promised to be as long or longer. The plan was to send me, James, and Dusty up to survey the two BLM plots of land up near

Ugashik Bay. Our biggest hopes were to get some specimens of the endemic godwit subspecies. Dan Gibson and Brina Kessel had been to Ugashik Bay back in the 1980s to collect a series of these birds. Their series of something like eight birds, taken along the muddy shores of the bay, served as the type series of the taxon that they later described as *Limosa fedoa beringiae*. The Alaska Peninsula population of this species is very isolated. The nearest neighbors are down in the Midwest (Alberta, Saskatchewan, Manitoba, Montana, and the Dakotas). We were very keyed up to get tissues and skeletal material from this population, and we really hoped we could run across some in the short time available.

Getting up to Ugashik Bay from Bear Lake Lodge with a load of people in the helicopter was going to be difficult. It was 120 nautical miles in a straight line. Mark was leery of such a trip fuel-wise. It was additionally complicated by the winds, because a good headwind in either direction would make all the difference between success and failure. He figured that we'd have just ten to fifteen minutes of leeway, which is cutting it a little close. But Mark is a can-do kind of guy. To help make it happen, he first took off the cargo rack—a very helpful piece of equipment on one side of the bird that nevertheless sacrifices several knots of speed. Next, he took a fuel stash up along the route about fifty miles. Those eighteen gallons of Jet A could make all the difference.

We waited awhile for a low fog to lift before beginning the day's flights. Kris Larsen got dropped off on the nearby mountains as soon as it was feasible (on the fuel stash run). Mark came back after topping his fuel tank off at Port Moller (after the fuel stash run), and we lifted off for Ugashik Bay at about 11:30. The flight up was pretty uneventful, but Dusty did see a black wolf. We stopped along the way at Reindeer Creek to pull the mammal traps left there the day before. James and I were perhaps too focused on this, though. James saw what was almost certainly a Marbled Godwit fly by, but he saw it too late to get a shot. We did need to get the traps up and be off, though, so that we could squeeze the Ugashik Bay flight into Mark's legal limit of flight time for the day. We'd planned to leave Ugashik Bay by 4:30 to make this cutoff. Kris and Dusty had set some good traps out; we pulled in a number of northern red-backed voles, packed up the traps and pitfalls, and hit the air again.

The flight time to Ugashik Bay really wasn't too bad from Reindeer Creek. Mark was asking whether we were close, and I was trying to get Paul Fuselier's digital camera to work; Paul was surveying these BLM lands for their wilderness potential and he'd entrusted me to photograph the area because we could only make one trip. As we were figuring out where we were and going down a little (having gained altitude to better see our position), James spoke up and said he'd seen a godwit on a small lake we'd just passed. And so, at about 250 feet going 120 mph, the godwits were found. We turned around, and Mark put us down a little way from the water's edge so as not to scare the birds.

We set off walking across a rather dryish sedge and sphagnum boggy plain or meadow to the lake's shore. James arrived first and spotted a godwit nearby; Dusty and I pulled back and James snuck up to the bird and shot it. It was indeed the much-hoped-for Marbled Godwit. You'd have had a hard time finding happier ornithologists. I continued on down the marge while James took care of his bird, and soon an angry godwit came calling and flying at me. I got this one and barely had time to reload before another came at me. And as I ran to recover it another came in. The densities here were unexpectedly high. We wound up getting quite a few from this lake and surrounding boggy meadow. Then, after a very long, boggy walk back to the helicopter (and figuring out how to work that damned camera—*hold* the button down), we went up again to choose another area to sample—somewhere less boggy and more conducive to setting mammal traps. We took some photographs, selected some higher land within another lake and boggy meadow area (there were thousands of hectares of this habitat), and put down again.

Figure 24.2. The author, Mark Hollows (pilot), and James Maley in Marbled Godwit (Limosa fedoa beringiae) *country, Alaska Peninsula, Alaska (photo by Dusty McDonald).*

We still had to work fast because of our time limit. Dusty began setting traps while James and I went in opposite directions in search of more godwits. I strolled around through a boggy brush zone not finding much of interest, but finally gave that up and headed for a nearby lake where I could hear James shooting up a storm. The walking here was very difficult—it was quite boggy. The surface was as dry as the previous area had been, but it was boggier here, with standing water. But there was a godwit calling off in the distance on the marge of a big lake, so onward I trudged. As I marched steadily toward it, I suddenly noticed too much white from where James had been at the edge of the lake half a mile away. Earlier, as we'd approached that first lake, I'd said that with godwits on the water it was likely that someone was going to have to get naked today. My binoculars told no lies—James was so excited that he'd gotten naked on the tundra. (Seriously, as you've guessed, he'd dropped one in the lake).

The bird I'd been after turned out to be three, and they were shy. I picked up two of them (one with a pleasing wing shot), and the third went over toward James. A good wing shot at half a mile or so is an interesting thing to see. I saw James, clothed once again, lift up and put a bead on the bird, then I watched as the bird dropped, then I heard the report. Then I watched in dismay as he walked about searching for the bird well short of where it had fallen. He eventually figured that out and found it. I began the long slog back to the copter. Pooped out, we all met back there shortly. Despite all his shooting, James had only gotten two birds—the first one had taken eight shots. But this gave us eleven for the day, a stupendous success. We hadn't dared hope to even see any, much less get a good population sample. And both the densities and the increased breeding range of the species that this area represented were excellent discoveries.

Very happy all around, we took off and headed for a smaller piece of BLM land to the northeast not far off. Having made it to our prearranged departure time (4:30), but wanting to finish the job up here, we were just going to photograph this small parcel. Mark felt that we had enough fuel for this additional run, and it went smoothly. But the second we were done he let out a loud "Woohoo!" and spun on a dime to head back (damn, you feel like you're going to fall out when they do that). We made good time going back, stopping to fuel up at the cache he'd left in the morning and making a call to Paul's voice mail in Anchorage. We'd finally gotten the satellite phones to work for getting word to base by relaying messages to Paul's voice mail. It wouldn't have worked well in an emergency, but it kept Jeff informed. Paul had joked earlier about leaving strange messages on a friend's phone, something about "... his 10,000 pounds of halibut nuggets deep fried in motor oil are ready for delivery, we just need a credit card number." We left a message that 10,000 pounds of godwit nuggets were on the way, and that we'd be there by 6:30 p.m. And we were—tired, and packed in with a lot of empty fuel jugs, but very happy.

"Peewee"

An easy way to document successful breeding in an area is to take a nestling or fledgling as a specimen. This has an additional benefit of adding a fleetingly-held plumage to a collection (the downy or juvenal plumages, depending on species) and directing the concordant mortality toward the age class with the lowest survival rate. Taking parent birds during the breeding season can provide evidence of breeding (and better skin and skeletal specimens), but they tend to be in worn plumage and they also often have dependent young. As a collector, you juggle these considerations and collect accordingly. As you might imagine, baby birds are rather high in the cute and helpless ratings, and collecting them for scientific specimens is a bit of a mental hurdle. When confronted with a parent caring for a nestful or brood of young, this is a rather easy hurdle to cross; one less juvenile means a greater likelihood of survival for the remaining brood (which still faces something like an 80 percent mortality rate during the coming year). But, nonetheless, there is some hesitation in taking one of these youngsters as a specimen.

The breeding American Robins at the Bear Lake Lodge were something that we needed to document. Consequently, rather than take an adult—mostly seen carrying food to a bulging nestful of young—I waited until the nestlings were ripe and plucked one out before they fledged. This caused much more of a stir than the taking of local adult birds, perhaps because of the heartlessness of it all. But that's why they pay me the proverbial big bucks. Science can draw a pretty clear line, and that's the business we're in (besides, cats and windows kill a lot more birds than we do).

The next day, a couple of Tree Swallows decided to fledge a little too early. They were helpless, and some of our campmates tried to help the first one back into the nest. Kris named the little tyke "Peewee." But Peewee popped right back out and fell helplessly to the ground. And then a nestmate joined him. The parents were not particularly attentive, and a cold night was approaching, so we plucked one of the two ripe tundra berries rather than take an adult, and our pattern was firmly established. We'd never live it down. Some of our tripmates were horrified, but I have to say that the trip was entirely successful if only for the fact that we added juvenal and downy plumages of several species to the collection that we had not had before. The downy baby Northern Pintail may have been the straw that broke the proverbial camel's back. Running Peewees down on the tundra may be how others remember us forever. But, as a contemporary bumper sticker regarding moose and wolves suggests, 10,000 predators can't be wrong.

Onward, Ho!

We carried 12-gauge slugs on this trip because the density of brown bears was about as high as one could experience in Alaska. But, while we saw a *lot* of bears, nobody had a real encounter. Safety first! Many trails I followed were made by bears and had phenomenal recent bear activity, but I never had an on-the-ground encounter with a bear. Some of these tundra highways were exclusively bear, and you could tell both from the ground and the air which ones these were by the "double shuffle" pattern of two big paw tracks separated by a very narrow strip of vegetation. We saw some awesomely huge bear tracks on the ground. I for one was glad that we only saw the really large bears from the air. And we saw plenty from the air—at one place we saw eleven bears in one area—but nobody wound up being too close to one.

Our run up to Ugashik Bay was our last effort based out of the Bear Lake Lodge. That evening we processed birds until late at night, then slept poorly because the next day was a travel day. That morning we packed up to move up to Cottonwood Cove, a small cove on the north Pacific coast next to the larger and more famous Ursus Cove, coastwise from Lake Iliamna and near the top of the peninsula. It took me two hours to pack; giving away most of the glass balls I'd picked up helped. There was room for all the frozen birds, too. I added them at noon, just before the Cessna Caravan arrived to pick us up. With the short runway and lack of wind (it had dawned a clear blue, perfectly calm day—extraordinary), we had to shuttle everybody over to Port Moller in three groups to get the whole group and our baggage off from the longer runway there.

I went with the first group to check out the rumored "Eskimo Curlews" that had been reported there as recently as the day before. Such reports are not uncommon in late summer, because people don't know what young Whimbrels look like. After helping to load the Cessna with plywood for the lodge, Dusty and I walked on down toward town to see if we could see these birds. Off the runway the road itself was heavily tracked up by bears. A young male had left the runway area in a hurry as we landed. It was neat to walk a road where there were scores of bear tracks and no human footprints. (In fact, it was fun to put rare human tracks over common bear tracks in many of the places we walked.) But by the time we reached the Port Moller dump all I knew about the rumored birds were that their tracks were the right size for Whimbrels and too small for Bristle-thighed Curlews, a bird less likely to be here now.

The flight to Iliamna was interrupted only by a refueling stop in King Salmon. At Iliamna we found James comfortably seated in the airport lounge with his shotgun leaning against the wall. James had gone with Mark in the helicopter to Iliamna, stopping along the way at Ugashik Bay to pick up the small-mammal traps left there the day before. He'd gotten two more godwits during their stop! Apparently when arriving at Iliamna he'd just walked into the airport lounge with the gun on his shoulder (he had no gun case; we had all his bags). A trooper had eventually noticed and confronted him about it, but it was probably just a formality because the governor of Oklahoma was there at the time. People are sensible about these things in the bush; the shotgun was still assembled and leaning against the wall.

We began shuttling out of Iliamna in a DeHavilland Beaver—a classic (if loud) old bush plane, probably forty years old if it was a day. George, the pilot, took us up to a drop-off strip east of Pedro Bay. From there, an A-star helicopter came to pick us up for the short hop across the mountain to Cottonwood Cove on the coast of Cook Inlet. Both of these flights were pleasant, because the weather and the scenery were excellent. Tim was the pilot of the helicopter, and he was our chauffeur for the next several days.

Steve Morris and Al Batten met us at the landing site near Steve's lodge on Cottonwood Bay. We threw our gear into wheelbarrows and took it to the small lodge nearby. Steve showed us how to use the propane-heated tent shower, where to find cool drinks in the stream, and how to get to the Conex and shed over by the airstrip. Our "lab" in the shed attached to the Conex was about a five-minute walk from the lodge. We spent some confusion and energy getting things sorted out after dumping our sleeping gear—putting most of our junk down in the Conex and shed. Cass was serving as the cook for our stay, taking vacation time from her real job in the health services to get out to camp for some of the summer. She had some great spaghetti ready for us for dinner.

This lodge was a bit more rustic than Bear Lake Lodge, but then it hasn't been there for fifty years. The next morning dawned clear and gorgeous, and we were ready to begin sampling the mountains nearby.

Bungmasters

The A-Star consumes about one barrel of fuel per hour. Unfortunately, Tim's bung wrench had been stolen on his last job. We had to attack the fuel dump with poor tools and determination. That first barrel was quite a challenge to open, but with a hammer and a large screwdriver we beat it into submission. Before we began the flights on our first day, Tim looked at Kris and said, "Debung that barrel." Debung. What a verb. We latched onto that one, and the bird and mammal crews acquired a nickname at the same time that we became expert at removing bungs from new barrels.

Fly and March

When we'd gotten fueled up, off we went. Tim took us up high, we got oriented over Lake Iliamna, then we headed for some of the highest vegetated country. It was a gorgeous day, and we soared over and around the high peaks as we searched for good places on BLM lands to sample. We decided to split into two groups so that we could cover more country. I got dropped first in some rather sterile-looking habitat at tree line; Dusty, Kris, and James went off to look for something even higher that would be more suitable for lemmings.

There were no surprises for me where I was dropped, but I had four hours to get acquainted with these birds. The insects were incredible—black flies, their brown relatives, and mosquitoes. It had been ten years since I'd seen insects this bad (in Newfoundland and Nova Scotia); I put on bug dope and tried to keep the buggers out of my eyes as I walked. I worked the windward slopes to further keep the insects at bay, and I went down in elevation for the first two hours. Interestingly, the only Gray-cheeked Thrushes I heard were lower down than the uppermost Hermit Thrushes; normally one would expect them to be reversed, given their habitat preferences.

The damned alders were very thick, and I had to cross a lot of patches of them, both going down and then circling back up. I had to hustle to get back to the drop-off point on time and arrived sweating like a horse only to have to cool down in a cool breeze for half an hour. I waited on top of a rock promontory for the helicopter's return. As I waggled a leafy branch in front of my face to keep the buggers off, I ate lunch, wrote notes, and contemplated lichen salad flavored with Hermit Thrush song.

Tim came and got me, then we went over to pick up James, Dusty, and Kris in a big boulder bowl at a slightly higher elevation. James had picked up a White-tailed Ptarmigan there, a really good specimen to have. We processed birds back at camp until Jeff and the other BLM guys came in. They said they'd seen a pair of Surfbirds at a high point, a species we really wanted. So we loaded up again and went back up to the high country. We were a little pooped, but the chance to get Surfbirds and perhaps some more White-tailed Ptarmigan was not to be passed up.

The really high country there was quite sterile. James and I separated and worked the area carefully. We had four hours up there, so we were able to cover some ground. I headed for a lovely, shallow, bluish lake that had a boulder spill and some snow fields around it. I hoped I'd find some ptarmigan there, and I did. We found no Surfbirds, though. Back at the pickup point, Kris described seeing a ptarmigan with little yellow chicks. This seemed unlikely; I had found some White-tailed chicks and they were not yellow. Kris was adamant, though, so we looked around for them. When we did find a family, the chicks were not yellow, and we gave Kris a bit of a hard time about that. It troubled him that his color description had been so far off. Then we heard the helicopter coming and had to hustle back to the pickup point. As we rushed for the copter, what should we flush but a Rock Ptarmigan and her little yellow chicks! We worked quickly together to grab two of them, then boarded the copter. Kris was exultant; his color vision was not screwed up. It was very interesting to find Rock and White-tailed ptarmigan breeding in the same place (syntopically); there had been no discernible differences in elevation or habitat where we had just found these two ptarmigan families. We were the last group in, and we were pooped, but it had been a great day.

The next day some weather blew in. We weren't going to get much done in the high country. Nevertheless, it was important to get back up there and pull some of the mammalogists' traps—they had all their Museum Specials up high. Tim went up and poked along the low country beneath the cloud ceiling to determine whether we'd be able to get to either of the sites set the day before. Probably because the land had been warmed up by the sun the day before, the ceiling lifted a little in our first inland valley. Tim was able to drop us just at cloud level in the boulder basin where the boys had been yesterday. Tim went and sat down at a lower elevation so he wouldn't get socked in while we pulled traps. The birds were very slow, so when the four of us had the traps pulled we called for "Mother Bird" on the radio. Tim responded that the "Mother Ship" was on its way and then came and got us.

He dropped us in Ursus Cove to sample low country. It was raining by then, and we holed up briefly to take off our flight gear in a convenient hunter's shack before heading out to work the coast there. Tim returned shortly with the botanists. The coast there has some structure, and I was hoping we might find some Song Sparrows. We didn't. I'm beginning to suspect that they only occur in this western region where there are extensive kelp beds, which create sufficient beach debris and insect life that food is available to these birds year-round. Except for a few areas with massive wood pileups, there is little for a Song Sparrow to feed on along these beaches or intertidal zones.

The rain became heavy. I ducked into a thick patch of alders to see if a Hermit Thrush would play with me, but it didn't want to. As long as I was out of the weather in there, I dialed up Rose on the satellite phone to leave a message that I was fine. Then I donned full raingear and went back out into the wind and rain to return along the shore to the drop-off point. Tim came in to pick folks up shortly thereafter, and soon everyone was processing specimens and writing notes back at the Conex and lodge. We actually got a little down time with the poor weather, which was welcome.

Fortunately, it dawned almost perfectly clear the next day, which was to be our final full day of the survey on the peninsula. James and I weren't sure where it would be best for us to go, so we let the mammalogists and botanists go out first while we looked over maps and talked with the BLM folks, who had seen pretty much the whole area in their aerial surveys for wilderness potential. We finally decided to go over to the Bruin Bay area and that coast down there.

Figure 24.3. Bruin Bay area, south side of the Alaska Peninsula, Alaska.

The cliffs there are conglomerate and too friable to support many cliff-nesting seabirds. Tim dropped us off on the northeast corner of the bay on the seaward side, where there was a good conjunction of habitat types, including rocky tidal flats, alder thickets, dense wood debris thrown up along the wrack line, and some of the local conglomerate cliffs. We added a number of seabird species to the area's bird list and had some glorious weather to work in, but we collected few birds of note. The most important were a pair of Black Oystercatchers, which we skinned up when we returned to camp in midafternoon. The gas-operated freezer there was too small and slow to deal effectively with large birds, so we salted the skins for finishing later back in the lab. We completed our work just before 7:00 p.m. Cass let us grill up the oystercatcher breast fillets, which we butterflied and seasoned well with salt and pepper. They were pretty good—like salty diving duck. Everyone enjoyed a small piece or two. (We often get funny looks when we cook up meat from the specimens we prepare, but it seems like such a waste to just throw it away.) It was a gorgeous evening, and everyone was in a pretty good mood as we wound down from the day and the trip.

The next morning we were up early and packing to begin the long trip home. The most difficult part was packing everything up to take up the same amount of space as it had on the way in, even though we were adding frozen and prepared birds. But we get good at that, being rough in outward-bound packing and scientific about it when returning. Tim began shuttling us to Pile Bay on Lake Iliamna by 9:00, and we were all there waiting for George of Iliamna Air Taxi to come and fetch us in his Beaver by 10:30. The glorious weather held throughout this four-flight travel day. Tim brought us out of camp in the A-Star; George took us into Pedro Bay in his Beaver; a Pilatus Porter got us from Pedro Bay to Anchorage in jig time; then we had to wait. James and I took a taxi from Iliamna Air Service's hangar to the main terminal, then were put onto a standby list because we got in rather early. Because we were standby passengers, all our bags had to be x-rayed and checked. I was glad that the woman had me remove my film before that occurred.

We had to stand by while our guns and ammunition were hand checked. Then we both drew special security inspection when we went to sit at the gate where our first possible flight would leave from. That was fun—boots off and all[20]. Imagine our delight when they changed the gate from which this flight would leave, and we had to go to the other concourse and through security again. Again we drew the especially thorough check, boots and all. Having not bathed or changed clothes in four or five days, this couldn't have been fun for anyone involved. But we weren't able to get on that flight, of course, so we had to go back to the A-concourse, from

---

20. This was before Richard Reid, the infamous shoe bomber, made unshod passenger screening mandatory in the US.

which the next possible flight would depart. And, you guessed it, we got the special check again at security, boots off and all. Amazing. But to our delight, our names were called at the last minute for this next flight—yet because we were standby passengers we had to go through the special check *again*—boots off and everything, one more time. Exasperating.

As I walked down the ramp to the plane, an old song kept going through my head, with the words slightly changed: *"Going through security, they held me for so long; They finally gave me back my boots, and I was gone . . ."* Paul Fuselier had said that the best answer to this new security was probably just to wear sandals and a robe and open up for inspection when asked. He's right.

On the long journey home, and since returning, I kept thinking about the vastness of the country we'd been through. Flying over and working in such stupendously massive country humbles with a giant impersonality any serious ambitions to survey its biodiversity, making mere human endeavors seem puny. It's comforting to be back in familiar surroundings and feel like we really did learn a lot about so much of that big region. But there is so much yet to do.

25

Crazy Horse and the Caniboots

LAST FALL, AS I WENT into the second winter without heat in my truck, Rose said she wasn't going to ride with me anymore. Later in the season, with the temperatures around -25° F and my window down to keep the interior from frosting up, Old Man Winter reached in and tweaked me on the nose with a somewhat painful touch of frostbite. Wind will get you when you're not careful, and, also, as it turns out, when you're too cheap to put $500 more into an old truck to get the heat fixed. What can I say? We live close to work, so I don't have to drive far. But when I couldn't get up the driveway again on the warm winter days, it was the last straw: I promised Rose that we'd have a new truck before next winter. The fact that my old truck had lasted so long had delayed this need for a long time; it had been about eight years since I'd bought it.

Researching, searching, finding, and buying vehicles is a time-consuming process, and here in Fairbanks it can be a frustrating one as well. Four-wheel-drive pickups are popular here, and their resale value is surprisingly high. We're also at the end of the road, so the stock of used vehicles is rather small compared with larger metropolitan areas. The work of finding my next truck began well before the snow melted, but time was passing with no luck. And then came June, when the death of my old truck's engine made the matter a bit more pressing. I had to create a solution, because the best things appearing in the newspaper and on the lots in town were not what I really wanted. It wasn't just that what I wanted was a bit of a moving target, either.

Briefly, what happened was the replacement of a 1990 Mazda B2200 with a 2003 Ford F250. Oh, we'd had our sights set on something more like the old, small truck (except with four-wheel drive), but decent used ones at decent prices just weren't showing up, and, new, they cost about as much as a full-sized pickup. The strange thing was, the gas mileage didn't differ too much, either. This was an eye opener.

If you're going to pay about the same amount for a small truck or a big one, it seemed like the big one would be the way to go, especially because it opens up the possibility of having a camper, too. And that possibility was one we'd discussed with interest on numerous occasions while putting up a tent late at night in horizontal rain. And having the wall of that tent slapping you in the face all night, cold and wet, would tend to reinforce the image; so that, over a bleary-eyed and groggy breakfast in light rain at the approach of a gloomy dawn, the subject seemed to come up again, naturally. Personally, although not getting excited about the bad sleep that seems inherent about short-term, tent-based camping, I thought campers were a sort of thing to look forward to in retirement. But one doesn't buy a truck very often, and if getting a big one cost about the same as a small one—*and* put campers into pre-retirement reach—well, we'd be stupid not to set ourselves up properly. At least that's the reasoning we used to switch the search image to a full-sized pickup.

That search became more intense when the old truck engine died, but the used-truck market in all sizes was quite poor in Fairbanks. I was getting some good bike riding in for a couple of months there. Things were not much better in Anchorage, either, I learned as my search expanded to their newspaper and Internet sites. Part of the problem was that the camper reasoning also dictated what type of full-sized pickup we would need. To keep the camper world open, you really need a three-quarter-ton pickup, and these are less common. Oddly enough, another part of the problem was the obscene resale value on these vehicles up here. We were seeing trucks two and three years old that were priced and selling for more than new trucks! Wacky! I think this must be sustained by people who don't want to ride their bikes while waiting for the right vehicle to come up. The last part of the problem was that pickup fashions here do not run to my taste. Short beds, ten cylinders, automatic transmissions, and diesel engines were four undesired features that seemed to occur in combinations of never fewer than two.

Well, this thinking and the coming winter had me really doing my homework, and it became apparent that the solution was to buy the vehicle I wanted new. I'd never bought a new vehicle before, so this was a major step. After reading all the reviews and checking out the appropriate web sites, I built the vehicle I wanted electronically and, with a click of the mouse, solicited quotes from several dealers. A couple of weeks later (some dealers don't treat electronic customers seriously and need a little push to come up with a quote), I ordered a brand new, 2003 Ford F250 Super Duty, extended cab, four-wheel drive pickup. Then I rode my bike for a bit more while I waited for this truck to be built and shipped to Alaska. (Actually, Rose let me ride with her often enough that bike riding was not onerous; I never had to ride in the rain, for example).

A new, full-sized, three-quarter-ton, extended-cab, four-wheel-drive pickup in dark green is a rather large beast. I took a few long walks around it at the dealer's, trying to take it all in before climbing aboard. Double the cylinders and about double the size of my old truck, it seemed very big. But by the time I drove it home from Anchorage, it seemed to be just the right size. My first new vehicle cost more than my first four vehicles combined.

At something like 260 hp, it probably has more power than those first four combined, too.

In my constant newspaper search for used vehicles, a pattern difficult to give up even with the new truck in the driveway, I naturally kept up with the camper market at the same time. I'd also done some Internet homework on these beauties and so knew a little about them. One thing I noticed was that as fall approached, prices plummeted as rental companies and dealerships tried to unload their stock for the winter. It was a good time to be a camper shopper, and we had set ourselves up properly in the truck department. We hadn't thought we'd bite so quickly, but our reasoning was that if we were going to buy one anyway, we might as well get one as soon as we could find one we liked at a good price. That way we could begin the enjoyment of being camper owners as soon as possible. This seemed like a particularly good idea as we saw the unanticipated fall sale prices drop some very nice campers into our price range.

Johnny Cash's song about the automobile factory worker who brings out auto parts in his lunchbox over the years to build himself a free car has, in the end, his skeptical wife looking the contraption over and saying, "Honey, take me for a spin."

Anyway, it's a catchy line, whether you like Johnny Cash or not. Rose's first spin in the new truck was across town to look at campers. Much to our surprise, we found one we liked that very day. A week later we went back and looked again at an upgrade because the one we wanted had been boxed in for a short-bed pickup. We still liked it.

It's almost magic when a good, honest, and knowledgeable salesperson works with you to learn what you want and then continues to work with you to find a way to get there. It was an unexpected pleasure to work with such people as we went through the process of buying a truck and then a camper. And it didn't take too long to get used to driving a behemoth around with a big camper on its back.

Back in the late 1960s, when Dad purchased "The Farm," I remember as a little kid getting to ride my first horse, an animal named Comanche. This somehow became the name of my first pickup. Then, when I replaced that with a more recent model of the same small Mazda, Comanche II trotted me around until last June at Summit Lake. To Rose on her first spin in the large green monster, it seemed just crazy to have leapt from one of the smallest of trucks to one of the largest, and, when I asked her what she thought it should be named, Crazy Horse popped out almost instantly. I was just getting used to Crazy Horse by itself when we dropped Turtle the camper onto the back. Now it's *really* big! The cars coming toward me now seemed to scuttle off to the sides of the road (and I don't drive down the middle—honest!). Crazy Horse and Turtle needed to get out on the road and get broken in and get the kinks worked out. Fortunately, I desperately needed a break from the office. I'd just finished my annual report, and in going over the whole year day by day, I learned that I had *not* worked on just nine days thus far in the year. Going out to see some of Alaska in late fall seemed just the ticket—I'd been too busy to get out hunting even once thus far.

Caniboots

When Sean and family were up earlier in the fall, young Emma had returned from the Large Animal Research Station (LARS) much impressed with the caribou. She told Rose and me all about the "caniboots," putting a new term into our vocabulary. I'd tried to get close to some caniboots last year, but had had no success. Unfortunately, Rose couldn't get time off work just now, and she really doesn't care for hunting anyway, so I talked

James Maley into coming along for a run up to the North Slope. James had been up earlier in the season but had found it too wet to get the requisite five miles off of the Dalton Highway to shoot an animal with a rifle and then drag it all the way back out. The restrictions are pretty tight on using firearms to hunt along the Haul Road. Dusty McDonald had been on late fall hunts up there many times, and he told us in detail how we should do it.

So early on a Friday morning in October, we headed up the Haul Road; Crazy Horse was fully gassed, and Turtle was stocked for a winter camping experience that none of us had had before. The drive was smooth and easy. There was a little late road construction going on at one point, but otherwise there was not much on the road. I think we saw more Spruce Grouse than vehicles.

The one stop for construction proved very entertaining. As we pulled up to the flagman, a Gray Jay landed on the hood of the truck. I asked the guy whether he had them trained to eat out of his hand, and he answered yes—that another guy had left a bunch of Pop Tarts behind and the jays had quickly learned to land on his hand as he doled them out. So in about ten seconds James and I had our hands out the windows with corn chips in them, and about five seconds later we each had a Gray Jay working us for free handouts. They'd perch, look, take our offerings with a little bill-to-chip "clack," then fly off to stash the morsel somewhere clever before returning for the next piece. It was good fun. Every road construction stop should have trained Gray Jays to keep the public entertained. I wonder if federal highway dollars could be extended to cover this program. Curious to see how brave the birds were, James pulled his handout into the cab once he had his bird returning; and, sure enough, after hesitating for a moment on the side mirror, it flew right in and perched on his hand. Something about the odd surroundings spooked it, though, and it tried to exit out the windshield; so James had to grab it and toss it out the window. But it wasn't very traumatized, because after preening for a minute it was back on James's hand outside the window, enjoying a special treat of dried fruit.

This was the closest we came to any animals on this trip. It was a good thing that foreknowledge of this did not spoil our simple, childish glee. We zoomed on, and Crazy Horse logged its 1,000th mile just north of Atigun Pass. We arrived and "pitched camp" (read "unlocked the camper door and turned on the furnace!") well before dark. Raring to go, James put on his boots and skis and headed off over the hill to do some scouting so we'd be prepared to leave in the right direction before dawn the next day. I had to find my socks and long underwear. With a whole camper for a suitcase and little time to pack, a lot of stuff gets put in weird new places. I skied off about half an hour behind James.

Figure 25.1. Caribou hunting camp in the Brooks Range, Alaska.

There was a group of four hunters from Wisconsin in the camp. They had been here for two days and had seen no caribou. We had been surprised to see none near the road north of Atigun. There were no tracks, either. And skiing up over the low hills, we saw very little to be optimistic about, animal-wise. It was very nice to be out skiing in the foothills of the Brooks Range, though.

As darkness settled in, James and I readied our equipment and had a hot dinner in the warm camper. I still couldn't get over the fact that we were living in the lap of luxury in the back of a truck. We laughed about it, being newcomers to such cushy camp life, and we pulled the curtains in an effort to perhaps evoke a little less envy in the poor buggers out there in tents. In the afternoon and night, three more vehicles pulled in to join the hunt for the weekend.

Next morning came very early. I think I looked at my watch every fifteen minutes after 4:00 a.m., even though we knew the sun wouldn't rise until about 9:30. We got up for real at 6:00 and cooked breakfast (on a gas stove in the back of a truck in a heated camper—still difficult to believe) before throwing too much gear into our packs and lashing everything to our sleds (packs, rifles, and skis or snowshoes, depending on the traction strategy needed). Then we hooked up and began mushing up over the hill in the predawn darkness.

It was a glorious morning. The sky was beginning to lighten up in the east, the stars were out, and the last tattered remnants of northern lights were doing a little sky dance in the cold, calm night. It was big and quiet on the trail. James had put his skis on right away and was able to get up the first hill. I had put on my snowshoes and had my skis strapped to the sled; from last night's scouting I knew I needed the enhanced traction to make it up with the sled, and this strategy worked well. I changed to skis when the uphill portion was behind us, and after that we both moved quickly. When it was light enough to shoot, two hours into our journey, we were at the requisite five miles off the road, looking over a lot of barren country.

We made a great big loop, stopping at every vantage point to carefully look over and glass the surrounding country for any sign of caribou. But we didn't stop for long. It was about 0° F by our estimation, with temperatures perhaps as low as -10° F in the low spots. And in those low spots there was enough of a breeze from cold air flowing down off of the mountains to really put a chill on you if you didn't keep moving. We wound up covering more distance than any previous track-setter had gone, but to no avail: there were neither caribou nor fresh tracks. Signs of past successes could be found, but nothing from within the past couple of days. We finally turned around at a point where we crossed just one set of tracks that had gone farther out— and we could see the gut pile at the end of that trail that told us why.

This was big, quiet, gorgeous country, and we both enjoyed getting out and seeing it in winter. We had seen just a few people during the day, several miles away. The ski back continued to be fun, but we were dragging a little as we topped out on the last hill and looked down to the camp area below. The final run was a long, fast downhill adventure with it being an open question of whether the sled would overtake you as both you and it raced downward in gravity-assisted speed. I was surprised that neither James nor I fell, and that neither of us got tangled up or stopped by our sleds. This last slope greatly eased the return, and we reached Crazy Horse and Turtle six hours after setting out.

With the camper heated up and some hot soup on the table, we talked over our options and decided that the absence of caribou in the area was unlikely to be solved by the passage of the rest of the day and a night, and that six hours of hard skiing a second day in a row might be a little rough given growing stiffness in a few places. If the caribou had been there, we would have been raring to go out again (though we agreed we would pack less junk on the sleds), but, without them, just going out for more hard skiing would be masochistic. So we drove home.

It was a good choice. Several days later we knew more. We had both remarked that we had surprisingly little stiffness from the day's skiing, but a second day would have changed that a lot. And James learned that the herd had passed through the Brooks Range and was now on the south side of the mountains out of reach of the Haul Road. So further searching on our part to the north would likely have been fruitless. But I've got a future appointment with the caniboots. We're just not sure when or where the meeting will be held.

I finished up this account a week later, as October came to a close. A couple of nights before (at 3:30 a.m.) we had a magnitude 6.7 earthquake. It was really cool, and, I learned later, the largest earthquake in the interior in ninety years. There was no major damage, but during its forty-five seconds I knew it was the largest one I'd been through, and if we had tall buildings in the region it might have proven catastrophic.

26
"Winker! Traveler's Diarrhea!"

CLASSIC. I COULDN'T BELIEVE he'd just yelled it out to the waiting throng. I smiled and had a hard time not laughing out loud as I stepped up to the counter at the pharmacy to pick up my "just in case" Cipro prescription. I could feel everyone's eyes on me, looking for signs of such a disgusting ailment. But there were no brown stains on my pants, nor a mincing step, nor any stomach clutching. I was just an ordinary guy getting two things done at once and preparing for another trip.

This came near the end of a particularly grueling period at the office. Somehow I was able to get five proposals submitted over a six-week period. This was unprecedented in my experience, and something I hope never to accomplish again. The plan had been only three (or perhaps four if one request came through), but plans can get changed when you work as part of a group. No matter; I was so exhausted by the end that I had to scrape myself off the floor to get away on this long-anticipated trip. At the time, I figured I'd much rather have traveler's diarrhea for two weeks than go through all that proposal writing, but I hoped that the products would prove to be fundamentally different. Although the two would be equally exhausting, I still held out hope that the verbal flow would be a little more productive over the long haul.

But western Alaska's migratory birds were long gone to their tropical winter homes, and I needed to get out and follow them there. We had two groups out in the Neotropics to sample migrants there (in Belize and Panama), but nobody yet in Southeast Asia this season. I hadn't been there in two years, so it was my turn. Also, Rose and I hadn't had a real vacation together in three years, so we decided to link one to this trip and see something new for both of us. Thus, a month or so before the now-infamous terrorist bombing, we bought tickets to Bali.

When work is grinding you down to a wet pulp, a planned vacation is like a life preserver dangling ever closer to your reach. The bombing in Bali caused the deaths of almost 200 people, the result of some human scum deciding that killing innocent civilians is a good way to further a demented agenda. As a serious, life-or-death matter, this event caused a lot of people to change their travel plans. And this makes perfect sense. Why go somewhere unsafe when the rest of the world will be more welcoming? Well, hopefully this event would catalyze the Indonesian government into decisive action to eradicate this problem from within their borders. The economic consequences of letting things go so far were sure hitting hard in Bali. Skipping right to the bottom line, Bali is a wonderful place to visit and I would recommend to everyone to go there. We didn't change our travel plans. In our view we stood about the same chance of experiencing a life or death mishap on icy roads here at home. If anything, an event like this bombing is likely to make most places safer in a sort of clearing-after-the-storm manner. I just hope they can prevent future storms.

Singapore

Flying to Southeast Asia makes for a long trip. We left Fairbanks at 1:00 a.m., and I think we spent about twenty hours in the air. I know I didn't sleep for much of that time. We went from Fairbanks to Seattle to Tokyo to Singapore. After the ten-hour Boeing 747 ride to Tokyo we just stood for forty-five minutes, waiting to board the next six-and-a-half-hour flight on another 747. As we waited and our muscles adjusted to a happily upright position, exotic destinations were announced in flawless Oriental English.

In Singapore, Navjot Sodhi was kind enough to pick us up at the airport at about 1:00 a.m. Navjot is our collaborator in Singapore, and we wouldn't be working there without him. It was great to see him again after two years, and we looked forward to picking up where we left off. We gabbed for a couple hours before we all felt too tired to continue, and Navjot left us in good quarters at the National University of Singapore until Monday morning. Rose and I got some much-desired sleep before venturing out on Sunday morning. We found some great food (rotis), then went off to Jurong Bird Park for most of the day. I'd been there before, but Rose hadn't, and the park's birds are captivating enough to warrant repeat visits. We spent even longer there than Tom Braile and I had two years ago, slowly going through all the exhibits.

The bird park was crowded, but it was not difficult to find places without many people where you could watch the many different birds on exhibit. Our favorites were the penguins and the large, mixed-species aviaries. The penguins are in a large, glassed-in, refrigerated area where you can watch them swim right up against the glass (they are marvelously agile in underwater "flight"), and the outdoor aviaries are just packed with a myriad of birds, most of which show little fear of humans. One thing that we both enjoyed much more than we thought we would was participating in the feeding of the birds at one of the aviary feeding stations. At first we were going to avoid the spectacle and the small crowd of a dozen or so people, but then we noticed that they were allowing and even encouraging audience participation. For one dollar (Singapore dollars were exchanged at about 1.7 to the US dollar) you could buy a small cupful of mealworms. With some of these spread on your outstretched hand, individuals of a species of African starling would hop right up and feed from your palm. But the really cool thing was feeding the bee-eaters (*Merops* spp.). When we threw a handful of mealworms up into the air, bee-eaters from the surrounding branches and vines would swoop in and pick them right out of the air. If we only threw up five to seven, they got them all. It was amazing. Any that they missed went to the starlings on the ground. I was impressed with the speed and agility of the aerial insectivores; Rose was impressed with how hot the starlings' feet felt.

The next day we spent the morning with Navjot, catching up on gossip and making sure things were smooth for the later, work portion of my trip. Navjot showed us some pictures of his recent research trip to Sarawak— truly a wild-looking place to be doing bird research. Then Rose and I went off to the airport, headed for a week of vacation on Bali. The Singapore airport is amazingly spacious and accommodating. It seemed more like a mall and restaurant complex than an airport; the lines to check bags, get boarding passes, and for security were fast and painless, and the whole airport seemed underpopulated. This seems to be an airport built for a capacity not yet realized. Nice change! Our Singapore Airlines flight to Bali was two-and-a-half hours long. They served beer and wine with the meal, and—reminiscent of pre-terrorism days—they served the meal with metal cutlery. With an episode of Mr. Bean on the movie screen and extremely courteous and attentive flight attendants, we were happy travelers.

Bali

In Denpasar we cleared Customs and Immigration with ease, but then we picked up a couple of obnoxious porters who stuck like glue until we got aboard a taxi for Ubud. The exchange rate here was 8,700 rupiah per US dollar—a weird calculation to have to perform in your head when considering prices. In this new (to us) currency, we paid $115,000 for the hour-long cab ride up to Ubud, and after just five minutes on the road I considered it a hell of a deal. Not only do they drive on the "wrong side" from a US perspective, but their roads are very narrow and often crowded. Cars, trucks, and a million motorbikes jostle for position in a freewheeling manner that makes one inexperienced with this traffic very nervous. The sheer numbers of motorbikes were amazing. And someone must have made a helmet law, because it was rare on this cab ride to see anyone without one. The variety of helmets was amazing, too, with people wearing everything from genuine motorcycle or bicycle helmets to hardhats and those rather soft, plastic, thin, one-layered, head huggers that would do nothing for your head in an accident. I even saw one teenage guy wearing a shellacked basket upside-down on his head. It was truly bizarre.

Our driver was good, and he kept pace well with the crowd. We never really got out of urban development, but the road narrowed to absurd levels—with everyone continuing to do their jockeying. I had no ambition to rent either a car or a motorbike here! It took some poking around before our driver found the place in Ubud where we were staying, but he dropped us off an hour or so before dark. We dropped our junk in a wonderful room with a polished stone verandah and a gorgeous carved and painted wooden door, then we went out to see a bit of town before it got dark. In a quick inspection we found Ubud to be a bustling but not crowded town with a lot to see. It was underpopulated with tourists despite a clear capacity for housing, feeding, and entertaining more. We had an excellent evening snack before returning home after dark in a light rain. (Bringing our folding umbrellas turned out to be one of our best packing ideas—from Singapore on.)

Bali is at 8° S, and so it has more daylight than Singapore in this summer-in-the-southern-hemisphere season. Coming out of Alaska during the short-day winter season, we noticed stuff like this. But the night can be loud with creatures—dogs, chickens, frogs, and geckos—and it is tough to sleep past dawn (6:00), so we didn't stay out late partying (as if we had to change our ways!). On nights with rain it could get particularly loud, and we named some of our loud nocturnal companions "Donkey Toad" and "Screaming Gecko Boy."

One thing that struck me about Bali was that the Balinese culture runs deep, and despite catering to tourists they retain very close ties to their culture and religion (mostly Balinese Hinduism). As casual visitors we didn't see a crass capitulation to the tourist dollar, but instead we seemed to be welcomed into the lives of ordinary people as part of the environment and their celebration of life. This was quite different from other places where I've skittered quickly across the tourist-oriented areas of countries like Mexico, spots where it is possible to spend a whole vacation and never bump into any culture whatsoever, other than the sterile atmosphere of "we're here to collect your tourist dollar while you fritter away time in air-conditioned comfort on a beach." We usually avoid such places; here, it was hard to find any.

The only solicitation that we experienced came from underemployed providers of transportation. This was almost ceaseless. They were hungry for business, and in walking along the street we were obviously in need of conveyance. "Transport?," "Taksi?," and just hand motions of driving (hands steering a wheel moving back and forth) with raised eyebrows were all too common. We got good at shaking our heads and giving a polite, "No."

The Balinese are exquisite artisans and craftsmen. Virtually everything they do has some artistic expression or flourish, and the product of this deeply ingrained expression is just wonderful to see exhibited everywhere. From the stone carvings of the temples to the ephemeral daily offerings at these same temples, beauty and pride of work are ubiquitous. Western culture has imparted some of its own concepts of beauty (and propriety) on Bali. The paintings did nothing for me, but expressing one's artistic self in paints on canvas was apparently a Western introduction. The masks and intricate carvings in wood and stone were most impressive to me, and I began to learn the names of some of my favorite subjects—Garuda (king of the birds and Vishnu's steed), Barong (a mythical beast, sort of a friendly, hairy beast to people and a bad dude toward evil), Rangda (the hairy witch), and Chiluluk (ferocious-looking dude). Rose enjoyed the intricate weavings (ikats), and there were a lot of all of these things to see; the many shops of Ubud were a constant source of interest. There is a phenomenal diversity of arts and crafts for sale in this town, and we really enjoyed looking, although relatively little could cross

Figure 26.1. Dance masks of various mythical creatures on sale, Bali, Indonesia.

our mental acquisition threshold, with both of us simultaneously applying the want-to-buy and we-can-carry-this-home filters.

When you look at the great diversity of artistic output here, you find a small percentage that celebrates sexuality in a manner more open than we're used to in Western society. Flying monkeys with massive erections are one strange manifestation; wooden floor models of three-foot erections are another. Historic depictions of Balinese women with bare breasts harken back to an earlier, *National Geographic* sort of era; this seems to be one place where Western concepts of morality have had a major influence in life, but not so much in art.

A combination of religion and art is manifested in elaborate ceremonial dances, costumes, and masks. We were happy to see that many of the various masks used in the dances were for sale in some of the shops, and from what we could tell they had not downgraded them for tourist sales; they were wearable and functional. We attended one of the dances on a clear night in front of a temple, and we were captivated by the strange-sounding gamelan music and the very ritualized dances. Without knowing the story, it was tough to get involved with the whole event. The music is so unfamiliar and so foreign (i.e., non-Western) that you can't get caught up in the tune, as you can with opera, and there was this guy droning in a whiny singsong voice sort of singing along and apparently telling the story. But the dancing and costumes were quite captivating, being so elaborate and ritualized, and we watched the hour-and-a-half show with total attention. I really enjoyed the snapping Barong, danced by two people. As we left the show to walk home, we were amused by one of the young women dancers still in her very elaborate costume putting off in front of us on her motor scooter.

Don't Blow on a Monkey

The Monkey Forest of Ubud is a beat-up primary forest tract with a large troupe of small, greedy, crab-eating macaques. We did not buy bananas to feed them, so they pretty much left us alone. Such was not the case with others who had food. We visited two of the temples in the Monkey Forest on our first visit. The main one was okay, but the second one—used for cremating the dead—was awesome in its statuary. The two statues flanking the main gate of this second temple were particularly hideous—magnificent monsters with long tongues out, over (on one) a full child's body, and (on the other) over just a head. Gruesome in the extreme!

Figure 26.2. A carved stone statue of Rangda, evil demon-queen of Balinese mythology, eater of children and leader of an army of evil witches. Bali, Indonesia.

Accidentally, we had timed our visit to coincide with the celebration of Kuningan, one of the more important annual festivals. As a consequence, everyone was in the mood for festivities, and we saw a lot of activity in the streets—dancing, music, and costumes. On the big day, we went back down to the large temple in the

Monkey Forest to observe some of the festival from that perspective. We found the entry to the forest to be packed with parked motorbikes and with a few latecomers streaming in toward the main temple. All were dressed in their very best shirts and sarongs, and the women carried large, covered baskets of food on their heads. Kuningan comes at the end of the ten-day Galungan, when all of the gods come down to earth for the festivities. Galungan celebrates the death of the tyrant Mayadenawa, and on this last of the festival days (Kuningan) everybody comes out to celebrate and thank and say goodbye to the gods. The temples are heavily laden with food offerings—stacks of fruits on plates are to be found on the many small home and roadside temples. (It's a feast day for the temple rats, too!) It is this holiday that has all of the penjor out along the streets as well—long bamboo poles sticking up from the sidewalks and arching out over the roads with little woven decorations and offerings to the gods.

We hadn't packed along or picked up any sarongs, a required piece of apparel to enter a temple, so we couldn't go inside to watch more closely, but we enjoyed hanging around outside, watching people and the ever-present monkeys. The latter were carefully going through the small banana leaf offering trays to be sure there wasn't a grain of rice left somewhere. Their bickering and goofing around was fun to watch. In standing next to a small statue, on top of which a young monkey was perched, I learned not to blow on a monkey (it bared its fangs at me), and Rose learned not to stand too close to one (it jumped on her).

There was an elegant exodus from the Monkey Forest temple at the close of the morning ceremony, and we followed the procession of basket-carrying women and burden-free men out to the motorbike lot and watched everyone pile happily aboard and head home.

We go to the Country

By coincidence, on Thanksgiving (our holiday, not theirs) we hired a car and driver for the day to go for a drive through the countryside and up into the mountains. Daewa was our very capable driver, and he showed us a lot of interior Bali.

Our first stop was to watch people planting rice in flooded paddies. They were extremely good. They had floating flats of rice seedlings that they would skim along behind them with their legs or feet while, bent low, with their hands they would rapidly boom, boom, boom, boom plant four seedlings in a fast row before backing up for the next row. One hand held a bunch of seedlings; the other took one and rammed it home. Their rows were regular in all dimensions, with experience rather than measurement. Daewa, our driver, just stopped in the road and talked with us about it all as we watched and took a few pictures. The traffic figured its way around us in the remaining lane. The roads here are so narrow, and there's no shoulder, so there's no option but to stop in the middle of the road. It probably seemed odd only to us.

A stop at a butterfly farm was only mildly entertaining, but it didn't delay us long in getting farther up into the mountains and to the temple of Batukaru, situated in a forest. The temple was nearly deserted, so we didn't feel too goofy renting the requisite sarongs and sashes, putting them on, and going into the enclosed, open-air interior and poking around and looking at the temples and statuary. Our way back to the main road was along winding back roads through mountainous country, and we enjoyed seeing the terraced rice paddies along the way. In one valley where they were harvesting rice, we stopped again and were able to take some pictures and watch the harvest progress. A little farther on, there were several ladies out picking different varieties of rice, decapitating the stalks and tying just the heads together. They seemed very happy with our interest in their work, and Daewa showed us one plot nearby where black rice was growing. This is a special variety used for a delectable dish everyone here seems to relish—black rice pudding. Winding along these roads through the terraced valleys was one of the most memorable aspects of the whole trip.

Higher up in the mountains, past the lakes Bratan, Buyan, and Tamblingan, which were enshrouded in clouds and only partly visible at the time, Daewa showed us the forest agriculture of the high country. Up there they grow coffee, cocoa, hydrangea, and cloves. The last are full-sized trees, and the forest in many areas is made up entirely of this crop. It was really great to see this plant, the produce of which played such an important role in world history in the seventeenth century, when foreign nations, especially the Portuguese, Dutch, and English, battled among themselves and the people of the East Indies to profit from the spice trade. Cloves are native to the Spice Islands, or the nearby Moluccas. For over a century the Dutch monopolized the spice trade of what is largely Indonesia through the Dutch East India Company. They had one of their regional headquarters at Batavia (now Jakarta) on Java, the island right next to Bali. It seems likely that cloves were brought to Bali early in this period of economic globalization.

The clove is a rather unprepossessing spice when you shake it out of a jar into the palm of your hand; it looks like a very small mace and has a distinct smell. It is a dried flower bud, and its oil was once deemed to be particularly useful. For example, dentists used it up until the early part of the twentieth century as a local anesthetic; if you had a cavity, you would numb the tooth with cotton wool soaked in a treatment of clove oil for a full ten days before the dentist drilled out and filled the affected area. These days, I think the only time I see cloves is with cooked ham.

The mountainous roads were quite steep and twisty. There is no way you could have roads like this in a land of winter snow or full-sized vehicles. Here a regular Jeep is a large vehicle, and their cargo vehicles tend to be quite small. My Ford F250 pickup would be a monster that everyone would have to scramble to the side for. We turned around in the town of Munduk and stopped at a couple of places to take pictures of this interesting high-country agriculture.

Daewa seemed puzzled but accepting of our interest in the agriculture of the region rather than in any particular destination (what can you do with a couple of farm children?). But he reserved one of the best places for last. This was the Puru Ulun Danu temple at Bedugul on Lake Bratan. This temple was tall and slender, with an eleven-tiered roof system. It was situated on a small island in the lake, although the lake's level was so low that it was landbound when we were there. Large statues of frogs sat at the base of the corners of the temple, facing outward to greet visitors.

Daewa drove us back to Ubud in a pouring rain—our luck had fortunately held all day. Along the way, as we drove through one village, we saw a large pig being carried along the sidewalk, hanging upside-down from a stout bamboo pole, all four of its feet tied together over the pole (the animal hanging crosswise) and its mouth tied shut. As we drove by, looking, Daewa laughed and said "sate" (pronounced "sa-tay"). Then he explained that this pig was surely on its way to be butchered the next day for the big feast of Kuningan coming up on Saturday, just two days away, and that pork sate was a very popular feast-day dish.

Urban Cleanliness

One day, as we walked along the street in the nearby town of Mas, we saw a very unusual thing. The sidewalks there are often a series of tiled concrete planks laid crosswise over the top of a concrete channel that handles urban runoff. If they weren't so often in disrepair (broken, missing, or gap-spaced), you might not know there was water rushing along beneath your feet. But often there are also grates in the sidewalk, so you can see the graywater stream below (or a drying substrate if it hasn't been raining hard in the past few hours). Along the main drag in Mas, we saw some rather large grates that could be opened up on hinges. At one of these, opened, a woman was down in the channel, calf-deep, washing clothes. She soaped them up

and scraped and beat them on the sidewalk itself, which was at her abdomen level. Then she'd disappear below as she bent to rinse the garments. This was very odd from our perspective, and we wondered just how our laundry was being done at the same time. On our last morning, as Daewa drove us to Denpasar and the airport, we saw a similar washing event taking place along the main road, only this time it was a baby that was getting soaped up.

Figure 26.3. Beautiful handmade basket cages housing fighting cocks, Bali, Indonesia.

Food

We found the food on this trip to be fantastic. This would be a trip worth taking if only to eat—a gastrointestinal tour, so to speak.

Every day brought wonderful food, no matter where we were. Each morning, breakfast was brought to us on our verandah, an addicting spread of choices that included fresh fruit, coconut-banana crepes, French toast, muesli, and yogurt. With fruit juice, coffee, and time, this quickly became a very relaxing way to begin the day. We read, wrote notes, and watched the wildlife in the garden around us. Spotted Doves, Olive-backed Sunbirds, and Scaly-breasted Munias were the common birds. One morning we watched a long, thin, green tree snake leap through the vegetation and catch a small lizard.

The day before Daewa took us out to see the countryside, we pre-ordered the smoked duck dinner at the Casa Luna Restaurant. This duck takes six hours to cook, which is why it must be ordered the day before. So at the end of our day out, we had this exquisite dinner for Thanksgiving. It consisted of one delicious, moistly cooked and smoky duck that had baked in coconut bark over smoldering coconut coals for six hours. Inside the duck was a pile of really great spices, which, with the juices, went very well with the yellow rice. The accompanying vegetables were equally savory, and this was a special dinner to remember. English not being a native language here (but being very commonly and well spoken), we saw some very creative spellings on signs and menus. One that we particularly enjoyed seeing at one small restaurant was "smock duck," and this is probably how we'll now remember this dish (although we experienced the misspelling and the actual food at different restaurants).

The orange juice in Bali was the only thing I didn't like. For some reason it tasted like burnt motor oil had been added. But why drink something as plebeian as orange juice when really exotic fruit juices abound? In retrospect I should have taken better notes on the foods we had; a food tour would be both phenomenal and affordable. Seafood paella, curried chicken, Balinese sate, and rijstafel are some of the dinners that will stay in my mind for a long time, and returning to sample them again is on my list of things to do.

It's a Monkey Scorcher!

Equatorial heat is something that the northern *corpus* takes some time to get adjusted to. We'd begun to acclimatize before leaving Alaska by taking regular saunas, and this does help, but while we were in Bali slowing down in the middle of the day and cooling off felt very good. Air conditioning seemed rather rare there, and at least in this season, when the rains were beginning, it didn't seem needed. But ceiling fans felt good, and each day for a light lunch we tried to find a place with good air circulation. And although it took a couple of days to get into the habit, we found that trudging home to our hotel and taking a swim in the pool was just what the doctor ordered. It was on one of these trudges that Rose coined the phrase, "It's a monkey scorcher!"

Actually, when we got back to Singapore, we found that Bali had been cooler. Perhaps it's the urban concentration of concrete and asphalt, but air conditioning was a necessity for us in Singapore. With a great vacation behind us, Rose went back to Alaska and I stayed on to do some bird work in Singapore. Jet lag really clubbed me on my return to the dark; we were under four hours of possible sunlight. And, with temperatures well below zero, hot weather was a distant memory. It did feel good to get back out on skis, though. Good health all the way through that extensive traveling meant, among other things, that I wouldn't need to go get a just-in-case prescription for Cipro next time.

27

King Me!

FOR TWO YEARS, ROSE and I intended to go fishing with hook and line for king salmon, but for various reasons we were unable to get to it. Having the gear had sure helped out the previous year when Sean, Colin, and I went down to Valdez for silver salmon, but it still hadn't been used for the fish it was meant for. This year's success at Chitina had, to our surprise, not included a king salmon—one of our favorite eating fish—so the incentive was there to finally get off and wet a line for this pinnacle of Alaska fishing.

I'd been grinding away on two proposals simultaneously and finding that it was not going well during business hours due to something just short of a million interruptions per day. This left me putting in long hours on evenings and weekends during the most magnificent summer I think we'd seen since we came to Fairbanks.

"Enough!" I cried.

Why not put in a good "proposal Saturday" and go fishing on Sunday and Monday? This put the temporal struggle in proper perspective: invest your time where it could be most effective. So, yahoo!, after a particularly productive office Saturday, we headed out on Sunday morning in Crazy Horse and Turtle to check out some of the Chulitna and Susitna river tributaries for king salmon.

The weather was dreamlike. The temperature was perfect despite clear skies and sun, and where we were fishing there were no biting insects. Rose sat for a couple of hours and was content to enjoy the afternoon and watch me repeatedly cast and reel in my lure. It was fruitless, but eminently therapeutic. Hermit Thrushes sang beautifully from the opposite bank, and as it got later another of my favorite birds began its wild song from the dense riverine second growth beside our fishing spot: the Gray-cheeked Thrush. Bonaparte's Gulls were feeding at the mouth of the creek. They swam about with necks oddly craned to search the water ahead of themselves. For such a gorgeous little gull, their voices are quite hideous. But songs from the thrushes, a Northern Waterthrush, and a Fox Sparrow polished the evening's symphony. Ahhh. The fish roiled; my lure came in fish-less; and all was well with the world.

After a delicious dinner, which Rose whipped up in the Turtle Commissary, I enabled a fish killer. We had gear for two, and, although Rose had expressed little enthusiasm for hook-and-line fishing, no one could debate the therapeutic qualities of standing on a bank of such an evening and wetting a line. Less than a minute of casting lessons produced mastery not only of the art of not catching fish, but of looking good and having a good time doing it, too. We called it a night at 10:00; the sun was still beaming on us and the birds were still singing, but the fish were not interested in our presentation.

I was out early the next morning, trying again, and Rose soon followed. As they had the night before, the occasional splashes of fish kept taunting us. But after several hours of fishing in both evening and morning, and not hooking anything, we decided to try another spot. We'd watched one fisherman catch a small king (a "jack") the night before, but neither we nor anyone else had any luck here while we were present. Watching someone catch a nice fish can keep you going for hours, though. Another fisherman said he had spent several days farther down the Susitna, and although they'd seen a lot of kings jumping and rolling, they hadn't hooked any. Seeing kings jump sounded like fun, and we wanted to check out more of these drainages anyway, so after a tasty breakfast we drove south.

The weather was still idyllic. Things were more crowded down around the good access points, and it took a little effort to find a place to park, but we were soon walking down a trail to the Susitna River. A half-mile walk brought us to a steep bank at the river's edge. There were a lot of people farther upriver, fishing in what seemed to us to be crowded conditions, so we hung back and decided to fish the edge of a backwater of the main river, a good 100 meters from others. Right away we saw kings jumping, so we decided this was as good a place as any to toss out a lure.

It was beautiful here. Denali beamed down on our tranquility, we would cast and reel, and, again, all was well with the world. If you're going to not catch fish, this was certainly one of the nicest spots to do it. Therapy continued. We plooped our lures into the somewhat turbid Susitna current and nonchalantly reeled them in. Until all of a sudden Rose was nearly pulled in. I leaped over, worried that she actually would be pulled in, hoping I might help her before she let go of the rod. She was very happy to turn it over to me. I checked the drag and let the fish run, telling Rose that this was the fun part.

"No. I just like casting," she said.

I suppose that when you go from a fishing novice to having a big monster trying to pull you into a fast-moving and turbid river, some of the fun might depart. I was in ecstasy. I'd caught all of Alaska's salmon species except this one on hook and line, and in my experience there is simply no better fishing.

But catching the others is a big step short of hooking into a king. This was one strong fish. I kept looking at my watch, wondering just how long this fight would last, and I switched arms to keep them both loose. The fish used the current well, saving a lot of its strength for its second long run out. I was sure after ten minutes that we'd get this one landed; after fifteen minutes I was even more sure. But suddenly something gave. After a twenty-minute fight, the hook came free of the fish and our paths once again assumed separate courses. During the fight, it had leapt repeatedly from the water, an amazing spectacle. What a rush. Later I realized that I'd been more hooked than the fish.

With elevated adrenalin levels, we both went back to casting and reeling, and this time it was my turn to get a hit. I set the hook and settled in for a good fight. The monster ran. After losing the last fish, I set the drag lighter and let it go. And go it went. Slowly, inexorably, the line just kept going out. Occasionally the fish would leap or roll, and I was amazed at how much line I had on my reel. This was a good one—probably 35 pounds—and stronger than the last. And it still kept going out. Finally I had to tighten up the drag so I wouldn't run out of line. The fish was getting tired, and I was able to retrieve some line, but then it ran again. Finally I had to tighten the drag up even more as I saw that there were only a few meters of line left on the reel. Tink-tink-tink, tink-tink-tink, the fish was still taking line. The stress was high. Then, in a sudden, sickly moment, the line went totally slack. The fish was off. An adrenalin-pumping five-minute fight left me with nothing but a lot of line to reel in. When I got it all back, I examined the end. It looked like the line had broken right at the knot. I'd tied on the steel leader just a couple of hours before, so I knew the line and knot were good, strong, and nick-free. We'd just exceeded its tolerance.

I tied on a new leader and put on a new lure as fast as I could. Actually, this was slower than I would have liked, because I needed to change a treble hook to a single hook to meet the fishing regulations for this drainage.

In the meantime, Rose was playing with fish. One king leaped repeatedly out of the water coming straight for her. If we'd had a landing net we could have scooped it right up, it came so close. It was fun to watch all the animal activity around us as we continued to cast and reel, cast and reel. To our surprise, a seal kept poking its head up and checking out everything. Although I imagine it would be hard to find a better spot to hunt salmon, we were probably eighty to a hundred miles from the ocean, and I was amazed to see this animal here. It was probably a harbor seal. An Arctic Tern came in several times and used a log projecting from shore as a hunting perch. I had never seen this bird hunt from a perch before. Nor had I seen one so without fear of humans. It concentrated on its fishing while Rose fished beside it, frequently plooping her lure on a short cast right below it; it paid no attention whatsoever. When it saw an appropriate fish, it dove in, snatched it up, and headed off to its nest across the river.

Although we had several more heart-stopping strikes, we didn't hook well into another fish, and eventually we had to head home. This was the last day you could keep a king here (according to the regulations), and we had to be at work the next morning. Despite not landing one of these champion fish, we had an awesome time trying, and we couldn't wait to try it again.

28

Russia

FOR YEARS I HAD SUBMITTED proposals to various funding sources to do field work in Russia, yet every time they were declined. This was annoying, because Alaska shares so many bird species with Russia. And, if the Eurasian H5N1 strain of avian influenza were to come to North America, it would most likely come from Russia into Alaska. But for some reason, bird collecting, genetics, and avian influenza weren't charming reviewers or funding agencies. Nevertheless, the opportunity to go to Russia and do some fieldwork finally arose rather unexpectedly through our broad network of avian influenza collaboration and correspondence.

Out of the blue, and quite independently of any previous proposals, Alexander (Sasha) Shestopalov of Novosibirsk's world famous State Research Center of Virology and Biotechnology (VECTOR) began to write to me and to David Swayne. David is a well-known virologist and the person who had done so much to give our group here a leg up in avian influenza (AI) research in the late 1990s. He is director of the USDA-ARS Southeast Poultry Research Laboratory in Athens, Georgia, and we'd been collaborating on AI since 1998. Due to email spam and unreliable spam filters, my message stream to and from Russia was not very dependable, but David struck up a good correspondence with Sasha, and he copied me on their dialogue. Email is a wonderful thing and a curse; I am just glad Sasha struck up a three-way correspondence, given the software glitches on my end.

At the time, there was not much I could do to advance a collaboration, but enough interest was evident that more than a year later my telephone rang and Michael Callahan, MD, was asking whether we'd be interested in going to Russia for some collaborative AI work. Michael was from Massachusetts General Hospital in Boston and, as Biodefense Program Leader of CIMIT (Center for Integration of Medicine & Innovative Technology), he was working closely with the Russians to develop an influenza surveillance network centered in Siberia. David Swayne had told Michael that he himself was overcommitted, but that his collaborators in Alaska were eager to go. It was true. Michael was working with the US State Department, and they had funding to help former Soviet scientists do productive, non-military research, but it required US collaboration. Enough said—I was soon on a conference call with Sasha Shestopalov, Irene Lerman (serving as a very knowledgeable interpreter), and Michael. We set up a trip for June and then began a lot of detail-juggling to make it work. As time went by, it seemed that something else needed to be done daily to get everything in place on time. Sasha and his colleagues had an impressive AI surveillance presence across Russia, but it was a little lean in the east, where more birds are involved in movements between Asia and Alaska, so we moved things a little in that direction by planning a trip to the Aldan River in Yakutia (Sakha Republic).

Getting a visa to visit Russia was more complex than any other country I'd visited, but I imagine that many visitors to the US experience similar difficulties. The visa application was the beginning of that complexity. It included a detailed listing (with dates) of all the foreign travel I'd done in the past ten years. That took me more than a day to reconstruct. The rather long form, once it was filled out, went to the Russian embassy in Washington DC with the original, formal invitation for me to come (which had been couriered to me via DHL), and with my passport. The latter was returned to me just days before my departure with a Russian visa permanently attached to one of the pages. And I was off.

We live pretty close to Russia, so you might think that a trip there wouldn't be that big a deal. But it is. There are effectively no "proper" commercial flights going west from Alaska into Russia—at least none I could take on this trip (the Fly America Act requires that government-funded flights take a US-based carrier when one is available). So I had to go the long way: Fairbanks-Minneapolis-Amsterdam-Frankfurt-Novosibirsk. More than twenty-one hours of transit time. But I had a four-hour layover in Minneapolis, and this provided a rare opportunity to get together with family. Mom, Dad, and nephew Sam picked me up and we went out to eat for a couple hours of much-needed catching up. Many hours later, farther along and very, very tired of sitting, I had to pick up my baggage in Frankfurt and transfer it over to Siberian Airlines (S⁷ Airlines).

I had had very little time to begin studying any Russian, and on this trip English diminished rapidly the farther I got from home. Unlike my more frequent trips southward, I didn't have such a convenient western European language as Spanish to jump to. During the flight I boned up on the thirty-three-character Cyrillic alphabet. It's a steep uphill battle to have to learn to read the letters before being able to even begin deciphering the strange new words. My progress was poor, as any of the Russians I met will confirm.

Coming on the end of a long series of flights, the last six-and-a-half-hour flight was positively unpleasant; I must have been the only passenger on this overnight flight (my second already on this trip) who even contemplated sleeping. And the seats could not have been more uncomfortable if they had been made of lumpy plywood. Perhaps that was why, to my surprise, over half the passengers clapped and cheered upon our landing. But I digress; one does not travel more than halfway around the world without something to complain about. Oh, but there was more. It took about two more hours to deplane, ride to the terminal in an overcrowded old bus, clear immigration, get luggage, and clear customs. It was all unbelievably slow, which was a real surprise to me. But upon finally emerging from this circus, there was Sasha right outside to pick me up! That sure made a huge difference. And he speaks English—which was also great, because my Russian is nonexistent.

Sasha drove me to the hotel where I would be staying before we left for Yakutia. Named the Golden Valley Hotel, it was nearly an hour's drive from the airport. We drove through a rather flat, northern agricultural landscape: tame woods of few tree species, some Holstein cows, and a lot of fields that looked like they were planted in cereals. I didn't see any large concentrations of buildings, which surprised me, because Novosibirsk was supposed to have about a million people. The roads certainly didn't suggest it, but it turned out that was because we were headed to Akademgorodok, or Academician City—a Soviet-era university town, lovely with its tree-lined avenues separating the buildings. I had the impression that here people seemed to drive and walk among the trees.

After Sasha dropped me off, I took a shower and three hours of much-needed sleep. For lunch I went to the hotel restaurant. The menu was in Russian, so I hauled out my phrase book, but to little avail. The waitress took pity on me and brought an English menu, with Russian in small type. I wish I'd had one of these to study earlier. It seemed sort of funny, though, because all of the music playing on the sound system had English lyrics. After lunch I spent about an hour and a half outside watching people go by before meeting with Sasha and his postgraduate student, Vasiliy. Given my observations of light clothing, pale skin, and seemingly carefree attitudes, I was not surprised to learn that this was the first day of real summer weather in Akademgorodok this year. Everyone was out enjoying it. We had beer and chips at an outdoor beer garden for our first formal meeting. That sure beat a conference room.

The next day Vasiliy gave me a tour of Akademgorodok and the surrounding area. The campus buildings were not architectural showpieces, but the rather heavily forested campus seemed like a very pleasant place. We did a drive-by of the Vector Institute itself, turning around at the border of the neighboring military lands. From there we went on to the botanical gardens, which overlook the dammed portion of the River Ob; the grounds there were very pleasant. We didn't walk around very much. It was hot (~85° F), and Vasiliy, ever the medical professional, was not eager for us to be exposed to ticks and the encephalitis that they apparently carry there. On our drive back, he pointed out the private residences of the academic elite, nestled nicely into the edges of the botanical gardens. During the afternoon and that evening at dinner, I learned that scientists are presently earning very low salaries and that it is difficult to obtain funding. Apparently many scientists who have remained active as scientists augment their poor salaries with other employment and private enterprise. In the 1990s a lot of them left for business; there was no entrepreneurial caste (or at least an insufficient one) after the fall of the Soviet Union, and a lot of clever people had opportunities in a new business sector. As a consequence, many now commuted from Akademgorodok to Novosibirsk for other jobs. We had dinner at a nearby traditionally themed restaurant. I had rabbit and prunes cooked in a pot with potatoes and vegetables (tasty!), and we listened to what Sasha described as popular 1980s-era Soviet music sung by an enthusiastic gentleman. With cold beer and good conversation, it was a very pleasant evening.

The next day we were scheduled to leave for Yakutsk on yet another overnight flight. Earlier in the day, I had the chance while everyone else was getting ready to go to watch people near a small park and a shopping area. I noticed that the women seemed very fashion-conscious and well dressed, while there were practically no well-dressed men. This is strikingly different from Latin America, where the displays are more symmetrical. There also seems to be an astonishing amount of smoking here.

From Akademgorodok we went to Novosibirsk to pick up Alexander (Sasha) Yurlov, an ornithologist and long-time friend and collaborator of Sasha Shestopalov. The latter's son Michael drove us there and to the domestic airport, which is beside the international one. At the airport the security was thorough, and the officials wouldn't let me bring aboard any of my alcohol for specimen preservation, even as checked baggage. It was a critical component for tissue preservation. We are not allowed to bring any specimens into the US from countries in which the Asian H5N1 has occurred without them first being treated in an officially approved manner to kill any possible virus. Alcohol at a concentration greater than 70 percent is effectively the only acceptable method for our genetic samples (and this was isopropanol—not drinkable). Leaving that behind was difficult, but at least I got to keep my machete, which they also didn't like to have aboard, although it, too, was in checked baggage (I use it to cut mist net lanes and have flown all over the world with it). This sort of scrutiny and creative interpretation of the regulations is not limited to Russia. In my experience domestic flights can sometimes enable staff and officials to take little power trips. It is we minions who suffer needlessly. But I began to see that, in Russia, you don't question authority.

Yakutsk

We checked in behind a group of small-statured men of a nationality I didn't recognize, and unfortunately we spent most of the night in their proximity. They smoked every second they were allowed, spoke very loudly, and clearly had a longstanding aversion to practices or products that mitigate body odor. It positively made the eyes sting. It was a long night.

But all was well on the other end: Nikolai Germogenov of the Institute of Biological Problems of the Cryolithozone (permafrost) met us at the airport when we arrived at 6:00 a.m. An ornithologist, Nikolai is also an assistant or deputy director of the Institute, and he was our host in Yakutia. Nikolai had his own driver, and it soon became clear to me that such a professional would be really useful here. I saw practically no street signs, and there were certain habits of drivers and pedestrians that only experience could anticipate and deal with. I found myself quickly completely lost. At the Institute we met with Nikolai's group (I am not sure I caught all of their names, but they included Inga, Masha, and Viktor), a lively and good-natured group with high morale. I really liked a map of bird band recoveries that they had on the office wall. It showed the sources of all the banded birds that had been recovered in Yakutia, illustrating quite well the connectivity of the region to the rest of the world through migratory birds. This was why we had come, but a picture like this is worth a thousand words.

We sat around drinking tea and coffee and talking. After a couple of hours, Inga and Masha took me with the driver to get locally registered, apparently a requirement of foreigners. As we went about this rather frustrating business, Inga and Masha pointed out the highlights and lowlights of town as we drove through it. So we had a good time despite being irritated by first finding that the check-in place had moved, then having a hard time getting the attention of a clearly uninterested official when we found where it had moved to. When she finally did deign to communicate with us it was only to tell us that we'd done something wrong and to send us on our way. I'm still not sure what we were supposed to do, but filling out a form and getting it stamped was what was needed to fix it. It is a disadvantage to come on trips like this from a culture that despises needless rigmarole and paperwork. It is a great advantage to be lucky enough to be able to work with folks who are used to it and able to make the system work. And, being honest and turning the lens around, I imagine that visitors to the US often feel similarly.

Activity in the office continued as folks worked to get this trip to the Aldan River off the ground. After a late lunch, Sasha bought tickets for our flight to Ust Maya, and back at the office we had a chance to speak more with Nikolai and meet the Institute's director. At our hotel that evening we met in Sasha's room at 10:00 for a late dinner of pickles, sausage, bread, and vodka. One of the topics we spoke about was the low salaries for scientists and how one might save for retirement. It is a mess here. Both Sashas were planning for their eventual retirements, and neither trusted investment funds. Apartment owning and renting seems to be the direction they are headed.

Breakfast the next morning in the hotel was a cucumber, tomato, and fresh dill salad, with eggs, bread, fried-pork sausage, and coffee. Before we packed and left, I had time to try to decipher the posted sheet on "Actions in the Event of a Fire." There were nine numbered instructions in Russian and English, and I noted that article 3.4 was "Lead management a stewing fire before a partial fire arrival." Much of the rest was as turgid, so it didn't help me learn any Russian.

There is a definite change in the people of Yakutsk as compared with those of Novosibirsk. In Yakutsk there is much more of an Asian and Native influence in peoples' ancestry. It seemed a bit more conservative, too. For example, there was less fashion-consciousness evident (though still quite a bit). There were also a lot of good-looking buildings and new construction around. Parts of the town were still poor, and there were some bad roads, but there was an air of industriousness and good cheer evident. The Sashas told me that the region is rich in diamonds and coal. An astonishingly ugly feature here was the above-ground insulated piping that ran among the buildings. Apparently in Soviet times buildings were connected to a centralized heating system run by the distribution of hot water. I could see big plants churning out smoke, so I guessed they were generating heat and electricity. Maybe elsewhere these pipes could be buried, but in a city built on permafrost, that's not readily done. The permafrost here was quite evident in the sloping and uneven nature of many of the buildings, too. The old wooden ones especially were decidedly unlevel and undulating.

Our flight was leaving at 4:00 p.m., and we spent the morning and early afternoon back at the Institute. Masha, Inga, and Nikolai were doing the initial paperwork for a specimen export, and other business and talking was getting done, too. Masha and Inga also put together a nice tea of bread, sausage, coffee, and tea for everyone in the early afternoon, which we pecked away at for a couple of hours before going to the airport.

There were no carts or porters at Russian airports, which seemed like a crazily overlooked capitalist opportunity to me—until I realized that I just had more junk than most. Russians have a 20 kilogram limit and seem to be able to stick to it. It is tough to pack light when doing field work, but I need to improve on this because there was a lot of gear-hauling to do. Our total pile now included a big packet of gooseberries (or some *Rubus* species), which had been growing happily until that morning and then uprooted to transplant to Ust Maya at someone's request. We lugged our stuff through two security checks to the waiting area, where we waited about an hour and a half before lugging it all once more out onto the apron to wait for a bus to take us to the airplane. There we waited about another hour before lugging our gear over and loading it ourselves. This was a smaller, twin-engine plane. The seats were hideously uncomfortable, but I consoled myself on the hour-long flight by calculating that at least I was now about halfway through the total amount of flying required on this long trip. Flying to me is by now the antonym of comfort.

Aldan River

Things moved quickly once we'd unloaded the plane ourselves. Alexander (another Sasha) the boat guy was there to meet us after we hauled our gear about 200 meters to the airport access gate. We were hustled right off to the riverbank, stopping only to give Alexander's wife the gooseberries. The three of us took a leak in the large airport outhouse. It was about 7:00 p.m., and Alexander told us to put on some warm clothes, which we did before we piled our gear and ourselves into his boat. The warm clothes were welcome later.

Soon we were scooting along upriver, bounce, bounce, bouncing along at a steady pace. At about 8:30, Alexander stopped the boat at a good clear spot and we had a boat picnic that he produced from his bag. The first course was a shot of vodka all around. I think perhaps the second one was, too, although by then we had the sausage and bread cut up and were eating that, too. As we neared the end of the sausage and bread, we also neared the end of the small bottle of vodka. Then out came the English Breakfast tea and cookies. As we ate, the moon was rising and the sun was angling slowly near the horizon. It was beautiful. On we went as it slowly got dark.

It was after 11:00 when we arrived at our destination, the small town of Tumul, a village of Evenk people. Here we were met by Lev Vartapetov, an ornithologist from Novosibirsk, and another guy who had a van. We threw our stuff into the van and, led by Lev, we walked up into the village to our house. It was an old house, very sloped in floor and walls. We dropped our carried gear and went into a neighboring house for dinner. A native woman and her husband were our hosts here, and it was she who laid on a large dinner. I was more tired than hungry but snacked and had several vodka shots with the boys until I just had to get some sleep. To bed at 1:00 a.m. for me; I did not see what time it was when the others came in.

Nikolai and his family are natives, Evenk people, and the town of Tumul is in a preserve of some type for these people. They are noted hunters and fishermen, but they also herd cattle and horses (eating both). The only other livestock I saw were goats. No pigs or chickens or ducks. Apparently the traditional lifestyle was not too popular, however, for the town was shrinking in population; there were many empty houses. Nikolai spoke nothing of his native tongue. He bore about three feet of scar tissue where apparently a vein in his leg was removed to replace the plumbing around his heart. I hoped that the internal work was more graceful than the external— the scarring was brutal. He had the operation in Moscow.

We got up at 6:00 and got ready to go into the field. After a good breakfast, we got off at about 8:00. There were extensive lowlands nearby that were now grasslands and shallow wetlands. They seemed to remain treeless due to seasonal flooding. Sasha Yurlov carried the shotgun, and he soon exhibited his expert marksmanship by dropping a quick series of birds, including the lovely Little Gull, which was a new species for me. By 9:00 we had a mixed series of birds and were taking a short rest while unjamming the gun. On the way back, gun serviceable again, Yurlov picked up a few passerines, and we returned at noon with a small pile of birds to process. On our way back we encountered one of the village natives carrying a two-bladed paddle (one on each end) and a horse-tail mosquito swatter. The mosquitoes were at medium, so repellent was warranted. After swabbing the birds, we had lunch, then I set to like a madman peeling birds, mostly skeletonizing them because of shot damage and blood. It would have been wonderful to get such nice birds back to the lab frozen, but that's not possible anymore, and Number 4 shot in duck loads really tears up smaller birds. We did not have smaller loads. The boys went for an evening stroll while I finished up the day's birds and wrote some notes.

Figure 28.1. Alexander Yurlov, Alexander Shestopalov, Lev Vartapetov, and a native Evenk gentleman, Tumul, Yakutia, Russia.

Next morning we got out at 5:45 and Lev showed us the area's birds. Seeing Tree Pipits and Pin-tailed Snipe singing and displaying was great, and these were but two of many new birds for me. The Black Woodpecker made a good show, and two *Botaurus* bitterns were giving a deep, booming song from the marshes. Unlike the American Bittern, this species—the Eurasian Bittern—has just one note in its song. At breakfast we made a plan that had us going in different directions. I set out mist nets, and the Sashas (all three) went off in the boat to shoot some waterbirds. Capture rates were low, fitting my impression of bird densities here. Lev had told us that the diversity here was excellent (it had 56 percent of all the species in Yakutia occurring in it), but singing males were thin on the ground. After running my three nets all afternoon, I had just three birds to show for the effort. Fortunately we had a gun, and the Sashas had made good use of it, so when they returned I had my work cut out for me. After the birds had been swabbed for disease screening, I skinned and skeletonized like crazy for the rest of the day, stopping just briefly for dinner at 10:00, when I put three birds under the house on the permafrost to keep them cool for the next morning. Sasha the boatman returned with some fish and four more birds, including Mew Gulls, a desired species. We numbered, weighed, and swabbed the birds, and I added them to the ones under the house and crawled tiredly into bed at 12:30.

The next day's plan was similar, and I was up and opening nets by 6:30. Lev was on a local island doing a bird survey, and the Sashas went out in the boat to a nearby lake. For breakfast we had cold fish, and for lunch we had some big, white, flaky chunks that were like pike, in addition to some fried bony little buggers that took a lot of delicate work to eat. They seem to be common in the river. I plowed through the pile of birds left from yesterday, going out to check nets periodically for a break. I only caught one bird in them all day, though, and some cattle and horses went through two of the nets. It was hot, and the mosquito densities were problematic in the thick vegetation where I had my nets; I stopped and put on my raincoat before going in, despite the heat. We had to beat them off of us upon returning to prevent a bunch from riding inside the house with us. The house was a cool place to work during the day, and the permafrost cellar was a nice feature, too. After lunch at 2:30, I had just finished all the birds on hand when the boys returned from their excursion to the lake with more birds to process. There were not very many, though, so I was able to get through almost all of them before the end of the day. Lev returned with tales of very little sleep, lots of mosquitoes, and getting up at 3:30 a.m. to do his bird surveys.

And so it went, similarly, for our last field day there. In the morning when I was up and preparing birds early, the older lady of the house plopped some gruel in front of me, said a few words, and left. The whole family was going into town in the boat, I learned later when the boys got up and joined me. Netting was slow again, and when I returned I found that the guys were still at home—apparently they'd forgotten to ask our host for more shotgun shells before he left, and they did not want to go out with just six. So I took the gun out on my next net check with the six shells and, using four, brought back three Black-headed Gulls. They were clean, so I spent the rest of the day preparing them as salted skins and partial skeletons. In between, I checked and finally pulled the nets. I wasn't catching anything, and it was our last day there.

After tea, the Sashas and I went for a walk to the observation tower, taking the gun and our now renewed stock of ammunition. There was a nice breeze at the tower, keeping the mosquitoes at bay, and we sat and watched and chatted until I was lured out to try for one of the many Pin-tailed Snipe displaying overhead. They have a communal display, with as many as five and six individuals flying together "peenting" vocally, then diving and whooshing one by one (on these dives they make noise with their outer tail feathers). I took three shots in vain before passing the gun to Sasha Yurlov so he could give it a try. He passed it back to me five fruitless shots later. We let the birds go for a while before the displays tempted me back. After a fair wait, I took one last shot, and bingo! We brought back just the one bird for nine shots. From the tower I was struck again by how much this area looked like Alaska. All that was missing were mountains in any direction. Back home I took a quick (cold) bath in the river, then we had supper and some vodka after swabbing our one bird. I was whipped, so I put the bird under the house to skin it early in the morning.

Up early, I found that the bird stashed under the house had attracted a small visitor that had chewed off part of the head. I was irked that I hadn't secured it better, but as I prepared it I hoped I could make a decent skin out of this little gem by turning that side of the head down. We began packing before breakfast for our return travel, and it wasn't long thereafter that we finished. A little cabin cleanup finished the job, and then we waited a bit for Sasha the boatman. After lunch, we headed out. I thought I'd understood that the plane left at 4:00 p.m., and so was a little surprised when after just an hour on the river we pulled the boat up to a house on the riverbank. We were heartily greeted and brought into the kitchen, where we were served piles of snacks: sausage, ham, fresh eggs, sturgeon (salted), and pickles. This we ate with multiple shots of vodka each from Sasha the boatman's 1.5 liter bottle, which we'd half consumed only an hour or two earlier while having a lunchtime snack at our host Nikolai's house.

This brief stop on the river was interesting in the opportunity to taste sturgeon (very oily and too salty) and to watch the Sashas suck down raw eggs. Apparently this is a country delicacy they do not get very often. Stuffed and feeling no pain, we hit the river again at 2:30 p.m. Nobody was nervous about the time, so I decided it wouldn't help if I was, and two hours later we were still banging along. It was a beautiful trip, but my rear end was glad to finally get out when we arrived at 5:00 p.m. It is a good three- to five-hour trip. The plane left Yakutsk at 4:00—or it was supposed to have done so. It left there late. So, after dumping our gear in the terminal, we returned to the boat to drink tea, eat rolls filled with meat and rice, and wait. But when the plane came in from Yakutsk and we went with our baggage to go through security, a lady reamed us out good for being late. Not only was the security station closed, but they had also oversold the flight. I'm not sure how it worked, but after quite a bit of running around on the parts of Sasha the boatman and Sasha Shestopalov, they fired up the x-ray machine again and let us through—after about a forty-five-minute wait. Sasha Shestopalov was quite relieved, because apparently the next flight out was in three days. (In winter there is just one flight per week to Ust Maya, while in summer there are two.) The flight was packed; I am not sure how they squeezed us on.

Back in Yakutsk, Sasha the driver was there to pick us up. We went straight to the Institute and, though it was well after 8:00, into the middle of a birthday party for Nikolai. Although tired, we joined right in, eating and drinking again. Some business was done, too. Inga came in with a final export permit, and Shestopalov and Yurlov ("the Sashas") learned more about possible fieldwork in Chukotka (my first choice of places to work in Russia because of its close links with Alaska). We stayed up too late, but because we were leaving early in the morning to return to Novosibirsk it was our last chance to talk with these folks. We were lucky they were even available this late in the evening. When the party broke up, Sasha the driver took us to our hotel, where we wasted no time in getting to bed.

Going to bed after midnight with an alarm set for 5:00 a.m. and a big soccer match being watched in the adjoining room did not make for a restful night's sleep. Later in the morning, after a little tea in the Sashas' room (tea, vodka, and the occasional beer seem to be the only way these folks get their fluids), Sasha the driver arrived and we were off to the airport. To my surprise, Nikolai accompanied us.

The airport was a zoo, as it had been before. There were two security checks—one to get into the airport and the next to check in. This time Sasha Y. had a good idea for how to orient my machete so that it wouldn't set off security hackles, and it worked. We went through fairly smoothly this time. Only one of Sasha S.'s souvenir rocks set off the security people. After this it was what was now becoming normal to me: sit in a waiting room until called, show your boarding pass to get outside, then board an old bus (this time it was a bus-cab pulled by a semi tractor), then take a bumpy drive to the proper plane in the long double row of planes down the line, then make a crowded rush to the stairs, then show your boarding pass again, then shuffle aboard to cram yourself into a hopelessly small seat. Oh, the joys of being a tall human.

We made it back to Novosibirsk without incident, and Sasha S. had a driver waiting for us. The baggage shuffle was not too heinous, and, soon enough, first Sasha Y. and I were sequentially dropped off at our respective places with an agreement to meet for dinner at 8:00. I tossed my junk into my room at the Golden Valley and went to see if the Internet room was open. It was, and I spent two hours catching up on emails. Our avian influenza manuscript had been rejected at *Science*, but the reviews were fairly positive and it seemed like a close thing. (This paper was later rejected at *Nature*, I am guessing because they had already commissioned a reporting piece on AI, but I am not sure; our paper was eventually published in *Emerging Infectious Diseases*.)

There is a shopping center close to the hotel, and I found a grocery store there where I was able to pick up some bread, sausage, cheese, and beer, which made a good late lunch back in my room. After that, I found that the cash machine in the lobby would only give me 9,000 rubles, which was not going to cover what I owed Sasha S. for our Yakutia venture, which he had paid for with cash along the way. This was a little worrisome, but as a backup there was a conveniently located bank in the lobby where I could exchange US cash the next day. I wrote notes until meeting Sasha S. at 8:00 for dinner. We went to the beer garden and had a beer and shashlik—a shish kebab of grilled beef with onion. Very tasty.

Chany Lake, Novosibirsk Region

The next morning it was up early to head to Chany Lake, where Sasha Y. was the head of the field research station. I had the remains of the previous day's lunch for breakfast and tried the cash machine again. This time it only gave me 3,000 rubles. This was a disappointing problem. At the bank I was able to exchange most of my US cash (minus the two worn fifty-dollar bills they would not take). This was only a partial solution, though, and this money bottleneck was getting to be much more than just annoying. I was able to get into the Internet room and dash off an email to Rose to see if she could figure out why this cash machine limit was occurring. Sasha S. had carried me thus far on his cash, but I needed to pay him back and had counted on cash machines to make that possible; this frustrating limit issue was problematic. It would be a nice thing if someone had stolen your card and gotten access to your account, but it was a decidedly awkward thing when being only intermittently able to access a machine while traveling.

Sasha S. had an important engagement with folks from Moscow so would not be going to Chany Lake with us. Anna, a member of Sasha's lab group, and a driver came to pick me up just after lunch. I hadn't understood that S. would not be coming to see us off, so I was carrying too much cash—but with no recourse. We went first to Yurlov's office in Novosibirsk. He is in the Russian Academy of Sciences, Siberian Branch, Institute of Systematics and Ecology of Animals, which is located in an impressive building. He had some work to get done before we could leave, so one of his group, Olga, kept me entertained with tea, talk, and a tour of the small zoological museum and a nearby church.

Upon our return from the church, we found that Yurlov had spoken with Sasha Shestopalov and apparently they needed the Yakutia export permit and a sample of the birds I was going to export to be returned to Yakutsk. I was able to dig out a complete Black-headed Gull, and Y. went back in to arrange to send it. It was Friday. I was to leave the next Wednesday. Nikolai was in Yakutsk. This was going to be interesting.

We didn't get out of Novosibirsk until after 5:00 p.m. There were a lot of little things to do before we could leave. During the execution of these things, I learned that it was a seven- to eight-hour drive. Ugh. But I was granted the front passenger seat so I could see the country, and it was important for the birds. Northern Lapwings and Black-tailed Godwits were neat to see, as were many other species seen for the first time. But the roads were bad and the ride uncomfortable, so our stop to eat at a small place off of a gas station at about 8:00 p.m. was welcome. Back on the road, we eventually drove into a major lightning storm, and it rained like hell. This caused the last 25 kilometers or so of dirt road to get just as greasy as could be, and even with four-wheel drive we just poked along, sliding all over and trying not to go into the ditch.

The last gas station available hadn't been pumping (power outage?), and this had a bearing on the next day. But in the meantime, midnight came and went with us still sliding slowly along. We didn't reach the station until

Figure 28.2. Stopping for gas in the country west of Novosibirsk, Siberia, Russia.

1:30 a.m. The power was out, but by flashlight we unpacked what we needed and settled in for the night. The accommodations were quite comfortable.

Up at 7:00, I went for a morning stroll to see the area. I saw a lot, including a Short-eared Owl with a very large vole of some sort. Bird densities there were much higher than they were at Tumul, so when I had the chance to talk to Yurlov just before 9:00, I asked whether I could collect some. He said to put nets up anywhere I liked, so I took my one remaining good net and set it nearby. I am always cautious about collecting at field stations because you need to respect researchers who may be banding or observing birds, but here the banding had ended years ago. By the time a big breakfast was ready (Anna did not want help), I had some notes taken and three birds in hand. I set to skinning those after breakfast and took three more before closing and taking down the net. Anatoly, our driver, had had to go back out for gas for the boats, and we expected him back at about

3:00. I skinned up the day's catch with this schedule in mind. We were going to go out to one of the islands in the lake and spend two nights there.

We got loaded and headed off in the boat at about 5:30 p.m. There were four of us—Anna, Alyona, Yurlov, and me—and we headed across the smaller, southern part of Chany Lake to the northern neck that connects it with the larger, northern part. The lake is big and shallow, and it has a lot of islands on it. We detoured a little to see the Great White Pelicans. This is as far east as the species gets, and it occasionally breeds there. We saw about sixty of the majestic birds. From there we turned and went to the island where Yurlov had a bird camp. Three hours after setting out, we pulled up and met Masha, Yura, and Alexei. We set up our tents beside theirs and sat down for a light dinner and too much vodka. We stayed up talking and drinking until well after midnight.

I woke up at 6:00 to set a mist net, and then put up one of the damaged ones and began repairing it. The camp folks had kept some Carrion Crows for me, and I set to preparing those. They have a crow control program there to keep gull reproduction numbers up. After breakfast and tea, the group headed out in a boat to a Mew Gull nesting colony on a nearby island. I hunkered down over my Action Packer, using this convenient plastic traveling box as a table, and skinned birds all day. The nets were producing slowly, but they were high-quality birds. When the crew came back from their first colony, they brought six dead chicks. Apparently the chicks were starving this year because there had not been a mayfly hatch. Only two of these were fresh enough to skin (although I took tissues on the other four), and one had a full stomach, so I am not sure what was killing them.

The day was hot, but it passed quickly. The gang returned from their second colony after 8:00 p.m.; we had a light dinner, and I skipped the vodka and was in bed by 11:00. The next day was only a partial field day, because our job was going to be done at midday and we were going to head back to the station. I had the nets open by 6:30 and strolled down the island for an hour before checking them. It was delightful to watch Stonechats singing and carrying food, and a nice breeze kept the mosquitoes off. Awhile later, after breakfast and tea, I was skinning a lovely Icterine Warbler as the group headed off to band their last colony of gulls.

I had everything prepared and my stuff packed when they returned, and once we'd packed up the rest of the camp we set off for the station at noon in two very full boats. The breeze that had kept the mosquitoes off had built up some good waves on the windward side of the island, so our first hour was grueling—bumpy and wet with spray. We waited in the lee of another island for the other, somewhat slower boat, and transferred a bunch of weight from theirs to ours. We continued poking along, and eventually we made the dock at camp at 4:30 p.m. "Many hands make light work" soon had the boats emptied and our mountain of gear hauled to the landward end of the 120-meter dock. It was quite hot, and we were all sunburned. Anatoly brought a vehicle, and everything was soon stowed where it needed to be. I grabbed soap and a towel and headed back down to the end of the dock. It was so long because it cuts through a very wide belt of *Phragmites*, ending at a clear, slow-flowing channel that was just a short boat ride to the edge of open water. A very refreshing bath felt wonderful, and I spent the rest of the evening working on import permit paperwork, notes, and repacking things for our scheduled departure for Novosibirsk the next morning.

I got up early the next day to use the oven to bake the specimens. A requirement of importing specimens from H5N1 countries is that they be treated using a method that the USDA approved. In this case, back at home I'd tested baking salted skins at 60° C for thirty minutes, and it was all right. So that's what I did here (though I melted some plastic and bird feathers where they accidentally touched a heating element in the oven). The skeletons and tissues were immersed in strong ethanol (greater than 90 percent), and that was another accepted treatment (though not one that works for study skins).

The continental climate in Novosibirsk may be more extreme than in Fairbanks. The summer days there can be very hot. It must have been about 90° F when we departed the island, which is a rarity back home. From talking with Vasiliy, it sounded like they have more protracted cold spells than we do, too, but the lows may not be as extreme. One neat thing I saw in common use at Chany Lake and in Yakutia were outdoor hand and face washing units: a small bucket of sorts on the side of a post with a valve stem poking out of the bottom. The valve is seated by gravity, and pushing up the stem from below the vessel releases a small amount of water for washing. These were also in some homes that lacked running water.

It was a long, hot drive back to Novosibirsk. We left at 7:30 a.m. and drove fast, stopping only for gas and to take a brief look at the village of Suzdalka, where an important outbreak of the highly pathogenic H5N1 avian influenza virus had occurred the year before. I was back at the Golden Valley Hotel desk, checking back in at 4:00 with two things on my mind: banking and email. The cash machine was able to spit out 9,000 rubles for me, which was a huge relief—I would be able to pay back Sasha Shestopalov. I was also able to get on email to let folks know I was all right and leaving to return the next day. Sasha had met me in the lobby upon our arrival, and we'd arranged to meet at 7:00 for dinner. Nikolai was also here, and he was also scheduled to fly to Moscow the next day and would be able help me if any difficulties arose with the specimen export. Sasha passed me both the

Figure 28.3. The village of Suzdalka, situated on the shore of a lake, was the site of an outbreak of the highly pathogenic avian influenza virus H5N1 in July 2005. Novosibirsk region, Siberia, Russia.

export permit and the letter from him to accompany it, so my earlier bout of paperwork was useful. After cleaning up, I made a second copy and soon enough we had a pleasant dinner—both Sashas, Nikolai, and me.

I was in bed by 10:00 with my alarms set for 3:00 a.m., and shortly after that Sasha S. was in the lot to take us to the airport. At check-in I once again found my lack of Russian to be an impediment. It was easy enough to pay my excess baggage fee (which was much less than it had been on the way in, back in Amsterdam), but I was utterly unable to get the large woman behind the counter to check my bags all the way through to Fairbanks. They were checked only to Amsterdam, where a short, one-hour layover was unlikely to enable me to retrieve them and re-check them before boarding my Northwest flight to Minneapolis. And, indeed, in Amsterdam I did not find my bags and I missed that flight. I arranged with the KLM desk to get onto another flight, and I was fortunate enough to get out on the next one on standby. When I arrived in Minneapolis I called Mom and she came to pick me up to spend the night at home. The woman at KLM had gotten me this far, and I had another flight out the next afternoon. So I had a pleasant, unexpected visit with family before making the remaining part of the journey home—completely uneventful, thank goodness. However, I was very worried about the specimens in the lost bags and wondered whether this critical aspect of the trip had been for nothing. That worry steadily grew, but my bags showed up four days later at the Fairbanks airport, with the specimens intact.

Afterword and
Acknowledgments

Being only the second curator of Birds at the University of Alaska Museum since the collection's inception in the 1950s has placed me at a scientific and geographic frontier that few others in the developed world can experience. This book touches on some of the observations and adventures I've experienced while living in Alaska and studying birds. It is important to note that these experiences and achievements did not happen in isolation, but rather through the help and generosity of many people.

This book is dedicated most especially to my wife, Rose Meier, who had to put up with me whether we were together or apart, here or traveling. It's also dedicated to the many other people who've been great companions along the way; I hope you are able to look fondly back on some of the times we've spent together doing interesting things. And, of course, there have been many, especially my mother and father, brothers and sisters, and close friends (some of whom appear in these stories), whose unfailing interest in what's going on up here in Alaska has kept me writing to tell them. The late David Parmelee and his indefatigable wife, Jean, provided an important introduction to high-latitude ecosystems. Daniel Gibson and Brina Kessel created an incomparable base of Alaska ornithology and made my own transition to a high-latitude ornithologist much easier. It is an honor to carry their work forward. And then there are the birds. They've provided much of the stimulus for my career, and more than a few have lost their lives during the course of these events. The questions these specimens are answering are dealt with in the scientific literature.

AFTERWORD AND ACKNOWLEDGMENTS

Daniel Gibson, Rose Meier, and Kate Ankofski kindly read the entire manuscript, and their suggestions were invaluable. Any errors remaining are my own. I also thank the staff of Mill City Press for their expert assistance in the publishing process.

Those supporting the science that drives these endeavors also deserve recognition. Most are faithfully recorded in each scientific paper's acknowledgments section, but it is important to me to thank them on a personal note here. I would also be remiss if I did not point out that the University of Alaska administration has had a strong and unwavering commitment to collections-based biology, a shining example among state universities in this regard. This commitment began with Aldona Jonaitis, former director of the University of Alaska Museum, and continued during the time covered in this book among many (now former) administrators, from deans of the College of Science, Engineering, and Mathematics (now the College of Natural Science and Mathematics), including David Woodall and Joan Braddock, right up the administrative hierarchy, through Provost Paul Reichardt, Chancellors Joan Wadlow and Marshall Lind, and President Mark Hamilton. Thanks to all for your support. These stories are not to be expected from an academic scientist, but the platform of a research collection can at times provide a springboard for more excitement and less ordinariness than expected.

My students and postdocs have also been an integral part of this collective endeavor, and whether we worked together in the field, the lab, the collection, or in the processes of generating proposals, reports, theses, and scientific publications, their interest and dedication have been tremendously important to our achievements in the Department of Ornithology at the museum. Those present during the times that these tales occurred were Anna-Marie Benson, Christin Pruett, Kevin McCracken, Garth Spellman,

Deborah Rocque, Olga Butorina, Jacqueline Weicker, Matthew Miller, Andrew Johnson, James Maley, David Shaw, Thomas Braile, Michael Lelevier, and Carrie Topp.

Much of Alaska is under federal management, and our work in the state has been supported by many good people in many of the federal agencies, including Vernon Byrd, Jeff Williams, the late Kevin Bell, and all of the excellent personnel of the Alaska Maritime National Wildlife Refuge, Jeff Denton (Bureau of Land Management), and the ever-changing but ever-enthusiastic personnel of the US Coast Guard. The permit-granting authorities of the US Fish and Wildlife Service in Anchorage, of the Alaska Department of Fish and Game in Juneau, and those in Canada, Mexico, Singapore, Belize, Russia, and other countries have also been supportive.

Many national and international colleagues, friends, collaborators, and supporters have been equally important. Patricia Escalante of the Colleccion Nacional de Aves (CNAV) of the Universidad Nacional Autónoma de México (UNAM) has been an invaluable colleague and friend, as has Jorge Vega, of the Estación de Biología Chamela, also of UNAM. Don Owen-Lewis, his daughter and son-in-law Francisca and Jimmie Bardalez, and their wonderful family have provided companionship and a home away from home in Toledo District, Belize. The late Navjot Sodhi of the National University of Singapore provided a rare and wonderful hospitality above and beyond the call for a collaborator. And Alexander Shestopalov of the Vector Institute in Novosibirsk has also been a gracious and generous host.

The many foundations, agencies, and individuals that have provided funding to support our group's work with birds deserve special recognition: the US National Science Foundation, the US Department of Agriculture, the University of Alaska Museum, the National Geographic Society, the W. Alton Jones Foundation, the Coastal Marine Institute of Minerals

Management Services (US Department of the Interior), the Civilian Research and Development Foundation (US Department of State; through the good work of Michael Callahan and Irene Lerman), Brina Kessel, David and Alexandra Sonneborn, Robert Dickerman, the Friends of Ornithology, and an anonymous donor.

The scientific products of our efforts have appeared and continue to appear in a variety of ways, some widely seen and some less visible. The bird collection itself probably falls in the latter category. It is a long-lasting research resource that documents the diversity and distribution of birds at particular times and places. The collection is used by scientists from all over the world in a wide variety of studies. We use parts of it for in-house research, and it is also used in student education and training. There is no internal funding for this work; grants, contracts, volunteers, and donations provide the majority of our support. Consider joining the Friends of Ornithology (www.friendsofornithology.org), a group of generous contributors who have made a great difference over the years, particularly in the research endeavors of our students. The bird collection and the scientific products generated from it can be found here: www.universityofalaskamuseumbirds.org.

You may be interested to know when these events occurred. The dates were as follows: Chapters 1–4 (June–July 1998), 5 (September 1997), 6 (September 1998), 7 (December 1998), 8 (January–February 2000), 9 (March 1999), 10 and 11 (June–July 1999), 12 (September 1999), 13 and 14 (November–December 1999), 15 (March–April 2000), 16 and 17 (May–July 2000), 18 (September 2000), 19 (November–December 2000), 20 (May–July 2001), 21 (September–October 2001), 22–25 (June–October 2002), 26 (November–December 2002), 27 (June 2003), and 28 (June 2006).

The English common names of bird species have been given as capitalized proper nouns because they have been formalized as such by professional societies. This has not yet occurred broadly in other taxonomic groups, so non-avian species were not capitalized. Scientific names are given in the Appendix.

Collecting bird specimens for science is sometimes controversial, even though it remains an important way to study birds and the world they live in. Rest assured that when we engage in these activities, we are not damaging the world's bird populations, which are renewable resources. We engage in responsible sampling under a barrage of permits. A single parking lot or communications tower or ten cat owners will probably do more lasting damage to birds than I will in my whole career (and we do salvage birds that die from other causes for scientific collections whenever practicable). Also, these other causes of avian mortality are not dedicated to the study, teaching, management, and conservation of birds. An understanding of direct and indirect human impacts on bird mortality and how avian population biology is insignificantly impacted by scientific collecting enables this important work in the natural sciences to continue. The bottom line is that it is not at all incongruous to collect birds for science on one hand and to be a conservation biologist on the other; in fact the two are quite well tied together and have been for over a century. If you are interested in learning more about collecting bird specimens for science, I list below some of the relevant peer-reviewed literature. Thanks for reading this far. I hope you enjoyed the book.

Remsen, J. V., Jr. "The importance of continued collecting of bird specimens to ornithology and bird conservation." *Bird Conservation International* 5 (1995): 177–212.

Stoeckle, M. and K. Winker. "A global snapshot of avian tissue collections: State of the enterprise." *Auk* 126 (2009): 684–687.

Suarez, A. V., and N. D. Tsutsui. "The value of museum collections for research and society." *BioScience* 54 (2004): 66–74.

Winker, K. "The crumbling infrastructure of biodiversity: the avian example." *Conservation Biology* 10 (1996): 703–707.

Winker, K. "Obtaining, preserving, and preparing bird specimens." *Journal of Field Ornithology* 71 (2000): 250–297.

Winker, K. "Natural history museums in a post-biodiversity era." *BioScience* 54 (2004): 455–459.

Winker, K. "Bird collections: Development and use of a scientific resource." *Auk* 122 (2005): 966–971.

Winker, K., J. M. Reed, P. Escalante, R. A. Askins, C. Cicero, G. E. Hough, and J. Bates. "The importance, effects, and ethics of bird collecting." *Auk* 127 (2010): 690–695.

Appendix — Scientific Names of Organisms in the Text

Plants

eelgrass (*Zostera marina*)

highbush cranberry (*Viburnum edule*)

Sitka spruce (*Picea sitchensis*)

Arthropods

Mexican pink tarantula
(*Brachypelmides klaasi*)

tarantula hawk wasp (family Pompilidae)

Fish

Arctic char (*Salvelinus alpinus*)

Dolly Varden (*Salvelinus malma*)

king salmon (*Oncorhynchus tshawytscha*)

largemouth bass (*Micropterus salmoides*)

Pacific halibut (*Hippoglossus stenolepis*)

pink salmon (*Oncorhynchus gorbuscha*)

red salmon (*Oncorhynchus nerka*)

silver salmon (*Oncorhynchus kisutch*)

Reptiles

American alligator
(*Alligator mississippiensis*)

gila monster (*Heloderma suspectum*)

Mammals

arctic fox (*Alopex lagopus*)

arctic ground squirrel
(*Spermophilus parryii*)

beaver (*Castor canadensis*)

black bear (*Ursus americanus*)

bowhead whale (*Balaena mysticetus*)

caribou (*Rangifer tarandus*)

crab-eating macaque (*Macaca fascicularis*)

Dall porpoise (*Phocoenoides dalli*)

Dall sheep (*Ovis dalli*)

gray whale (*Eschrichtius robustus*)

grizzly bear (*Ursus arctos*)

harbor seal (*Phoca vitulina*)

humpback whale
(*Megaptera novaeangliae*)

killer whale (*Orcinus orca*)

lynx (*Felis lynx*)

mantled howler monkey
(*Alouatta palliata*)

Mexican agouti (*Dasyprocta mexicana*)

muskox (*Ovibos moschatus*)

northern fur seal (*Callorhinus ursinus*)

northern red-backed vole (*Myodes rutilus*)

polar bear (*Ursus maritimus*)

porcupine (*Erethizon dorsatum*)

red squirrel (*Tamiasciurus hudsonicus*)

red fox (*Vulpes fulva*)

sea otter (*Enhydra lutris*)

sitka deer (*Odocoileus hemionus sitkensis*)

snowshoe hare (*Lepus americanus*)

St. Matthew Island vole
(*Microtus abbreviatus*)

Steller's sea lion (*Eumetopias jubatus*)

tapir (*Tapirus bairdii*)

timber wolf (*Canis lupus*)

Birds – Alphabetic Order

Aleutian Tern (*Onychoprion aleuticus*)

American Golden-Plover
(*Pluvialis dominica*)

American Pygmy Kingfisher
(*Chloroceryle aenea*)

American Bittern (*Botaurus lentiginosus*)

American Dipper (*Cinclus mexicanus*)

American Robin (*Turdus migratorius*)

Ancient Murrelet
(*Synthliboramphus antiquus*)

Arctic Tern (*Sterna paradisaea*)

Arctic Warbler (*Phylloscopus borealis*)

Bald Eagle (*Haliaeetus leucocephalus*)

Bank Swallow (*Riparia riparia*)

Bar-tailed Godwit (*Limosa lapponica*)

Bare-faced Antthrush
(*Gymnocichla nudiceps*)

Black Oystercatcher
(*Haematopus bachmani*)

Black Woodpecker (*Dryocopus martius*)

Black-backed Wagtail
(*Motacilla alba lugens*)

Black-bellied Plover (*Pluvialis squatarola*)

Black-faced Antthrush
(*Formicarius analis*)

Black-headed Gull
(*Chroicocephalus ridibundus*)

Black-tailed Godwit (*Limosa limosa*)

Bluethroat (*Luscinia svecica*)

Bonaparte's Gull
(*Chroicocephalus philadelphia*)

Brambling (*Fringilla montifringilla*)

Brant (*Branta bernicla*)

Bristle-thighed Curlew
(*Numenius tahitiensis*)

Cackling Goose (*Branta hutchinsii*)

Canada Goose (*Branta canadensis*)

Carrion Crow (*Corvus corone*)

chickadees (*Poecile* spp.)

Common Murre (*Uria aalge*)

Common Pochard (*Aythya ferina*)

Common Redpoll (*Acanthis flammea*)

Common Raven (*Corvus corax*)

Crested Caracara (*Caracara cheriway*)

Dusky Grouse (*Dendragapus fuliginosus*)

Eastern Yellow Wagtail
(*Motacilla tschutschensis*)

Emperor Goose (*Chen canagica*)

Eurasian Bittern (*Botaurus stellaris*)

Eurasian Bullfinch (*Pyrrhula pyrrhula*)

Fox Sparrow (*Passerella iliaca*)

Glaucous Gull (*Larus hyperboreus*)

Glaucous-winged Gull (*Larus glaucescens*)

Golden Vireo (*Vireo hypochryseus*)

Golden-crowned Sparrow
(*Zonotrichia atricapilla*)

Gray Catbird (*Dumetella carolinensis*)

Gray Jay (*Perisoreus canadensis*)

Gray Wagtail (*Motacilla cinerea*)

Gray-cheeked Thrush (*Catharus minimus*)

Gray-crowned Rosy Finch
(*Leucosticte tephrocotis*)

Gray-tailed Tattler (*Tringa incana*)

Great White Pelican
(*Pelecanus onocrotalus*)

Great Curassow (*Crax rubra*)

Greater White-fronted Goose
(*Anser albifrons*)

Green-winged Teal (*Anas crecca*)

Gyrfalcon (*Falco rusticolus*)

Hammond's Flycatcher
(*Empidonax hammondii*)

Hawfinch (*Coccothraustes coccothraustes*)

Hermit Thrush (*Catharus guttatus*)

Herring Gull (*Larus argentatus*)

Hoary Redpoll (*Acanthis hornemanni*)

Hooded Warbler (*Setophaga citrina*)

Horned Guan (*Oreophasis derbianus*)

House Crow (*Corvus splendens*)

Icterine Warbler (*Hippolais icterina*)

Ivory-billed Woodcreeper
(*Xiphorhynchus flavigaster*)

Kentucky Warbler (*Geothlypis formosa*)

King Vulture (*Sarcoramphus papa*)

Lapland Longspur (*Calcarius lapponicus*)

Little Gull (*Hydrocoloeus minutus*)

Long-toed Stint (*Calidris subminuta*)

Long-tailed Jaeger
(*Stercorarius longicaudus*)

Long-billed Hermit
(*Phaethornis longirostris*)

Mallard (*Anas platyrhynchos*)

Marbled Godwit (*Limosa fedoa*)

Mew Gull (*Larus canus*)

Northern Wheatear (*Oenanthe oenanthe*)

Northern Lapwing (*Vanellus vanellus*)

Northern Waterthrush
(*Parkesia noveboracensis*)

Northern Goshawk (*Accipiter gentilis*)

Northern Pintail (*Anas acuta*)

Ocellated Turkey (*Meleagris ocellata*)

Ochre-bellied Flycatcher
(*Mionectes oleagineus*)

Olive-backed Pipit (*Anthus hodgsoni*)

Olive-backed Euphonia
(*Euphonia gouldi*)

Olive-backed Sunbird
(*Nectarinia jugularis*)

Orange-breasted Bunting
(*Passerina leclancherii*)

Orchard Oriole (*Icterus spurius*)

Pacific Golden-Plover (*Pluvialis fulva*)

Pacific Wren (*Troglodytes pacificus*)

Pale-billed Woodpecker
(*Campephilus guatemalensis*)

Pechora Pipit (*Anthus gustavi*)

Pelagic Cormorant
(*Phalacrocorax pelagicus*)

Peregrine Falcon (*Falco peregrinus*)

Pigeon Guillemot (*Cepphus columba*)

Pin-tailed Snipe (*Gallinago stenurus*)

Plain Chachalaca (*Ortalis vetula*)

Red-necked Phalarope
(*Phalaropus lobatus*)

Red-throated Pipit (*Anthus cervinus*)

Red Crossbill (*Loxia curvirostra*)

Red Knot (*Calidris canutus*)

Red-breasted Chat (*Granatellus venustus*)

Red-breasted Merganser
(*Mergus serrator*)

Red-capped Manakin (*Pipra mentalis*)

Resplendent Quetzal
(*Pharomachrus mocinno*)

Rock Ptarmigan (*Lagopus muta*)

Rock Sandpiper (*Calidris ptilocnemis*)

Ross's Gull (*Rhodostethia rosea*)

Rough-legged Hawk (*Buteo lagopus*)

Ruddy Turnstone (*Arenaria interpres*)

Ruff (*Philomachus pugnax*)

Rufous-tailed Jacamar
(*Galbula ruficauda*)

Rufous-tailed Hummingbird
(*Amazilia tzacatl*)

Rustic Bunting (*Emberiza rustica*)

Sabine's Gull (*Xema sabini*)

Sandhill Crane (*Grus canadensis*)

Savannah Sparrow
(*Passerculus sandwichensis*)

Scaly-breasted Munia
(*Lonchura punctulata*)

Scarlet Macaw (*Ara macao*)

Short-eared Owl (*Asio flammeus*)

Smew (*Mergellus albellus*)

Smith's Longspur (*Calcarius pictus*)

Snow Bunting (*Plectrophenax nivalis*)

Snow Goose (*Chen caerulescens*)

Snowy Owl (*Bubo scandiacus*)

Song Sparrow (*Melospiza melodia*)

Spotted Dove (*Streptopelia chinensis*)

Spruce Grouse (*Falcipennis canadensis*)

Steller's Eider (*Polysticta stelleri*)

Stilt Sandpiper (*Calidris himantopus*)

Stonechat (*Saxicola torquatus*)

Stripe-throated Hermit
(*Phaethornis striigularis*)

Surfbird (*Aphriza virgata*)

Swainson's Thrush (*Catharus ustulatus*)

Thick-billed Murre (*Uria lomvia*)

Townsend's Warbler
(*Setophaga townsendi*)

Tree Swallow (*Tachycineta bicolor*)

Tree Pipit (*Anthus trivialis*)

Tufted Duck (*Aythya fuligula*)

Tufted Puffin (*Fratercula cirrhata*)

Tundra Swan (*Cygnus columbianus*)

Violet-green Swallow
(*Tachycineta thalassina*)

Wandering Tattler (*Tringa brevipes*)

Wedge-billed Woodcreeper
(*Glyphorynchus spirurus*)

Whimbrel (*Numenius phaeopus*)

Whiskered Auklet (*Aethia pygmaea*)

White-breasted Wood-Wren
(*Henicorhina leucosticta*)

White-collared Manakin
(*Manacus candei*)

White-necked Jacobin
(*Florisuga mellivora*)

White-tailed Ptarmigan (*Lagopus leucura*)

White-throated Sparrow
(*Zonotrichia albicollis*)

Willow Ptarmigan (*Lagopus lagopus*)

Wood Sandpiper (*Tringa glareola*)

Wood Thrush (*Hylocichla mustelina*)

Worm-eating Warbler
(*Helmitheros vermivorum*)

Yellow-winged Cacique
(*Cacicus melanicterus*)

Birds—Systematic Order

Greater White-fronted Goose
(*Anser albifrons*)

Emperor Goose (*Chen canagica*)

Snow Goose (*Chen caerulescens*)

Brant (*Branta bernicla*)

Cackling Goose (*Branta hutchinsii*)

Canada Goose (*Branta canadensis*)

Tundra Swan (*Cygnus columbianus*)

Mallard (*Anas platyrhynchos*)

Northern Pintail (*Anas acuta*)

Green-winged Teal (*Anas crecca*)

Common Pochard (*Aythya ferina*)

Tufted Duck (*Aythya fuligula*)

Steller's Eider (*Polysticta stelleri*)

Smew (*Mergellus albellus*)

Red-breasted Merganser
(*Mergus serrator*)

Plain Chachalaca (*Ortalis vetula*)

Horned Guan (*Oreophasis derbianus*)

Great Curassow (*Crax rubra*)

Spruce Grouse (*Falcipennis canadensis*)

Willow Ptarmigan (*Lagopus lagopus*)

Rock Ptarmigan (*Lagopus muta*)

White-tailed Ptarmigan (*Lagopus leucura*)

Dusky Grouse (*Dendragapus fuliginosus*)

Ocellated Turkey (*Meleagris ocellata*)

Pelagic Cormorant
(*Phalacrocorax pelagicus*)

Great White Pelican
(*Pelecanus onocrotalus*)

American Bittern (*Botaurus lentiginosus*)

Eurasian Bittern (*Botaurus stellaris*)

King Vulture (*Sarcoramphus papa*)

Bald Eagle (*Haliaeetus leucocephalus*)

Northern Goshawk (*Accipiter gentilis*)

Rough-legged Hawk (*Buteo lagopus*)

Crested Caracara (*Caracara cheriway*)

Gyrfalcon (*Falco rusticolus*)

Peregrine Falcon (*Falco peregrinus*)

Sandhill Crane (*Grus canadensis*)

Northern Lapwing (*Vanellus vanellus*)

Black-bellied Plover (*Pluvialis squatarola*)

American Golden-Plover
(*Pluvialis dominica*)

Pacific Golden-Plover (*Pluvialis fulva*)

Black Oystercatcher
(*Haematopus bachmani*)

Gray-tailed Tattler (*Tringa incana*)

Wandering Tattler (*Tringa brevipes*)

Wood Sandpiper (*Tringa glareola*)

Whimbrel (*Numenius phaeopus*)

Bristle-thighed Curlew
(*Numenius tahitiensis*)

Black-tailed Godwit (*Limosa limosa*)

Bar-tailed Godwit (*Limosa lapponica*)

Marbled Godwit (*Limosa fedoa*)

Ruddy Turnstone (*Arenaria interpres*)

Surfbird (*Aphriza virgata*)

Red Knot (*Calidris canutus*)

Long-toed Stint (*Calidris subminuta*)

Rock Sandpiper (*Calidris ptilocnemis*)

Stilt Sandpiper (*Calidris himantopus*)

Ruff (*Philomachus pugnax*)

Pin-tailed Snipe (*Gallinago stenurus*)

Red-necked Phalarope
(*Phalaropus lobatus*)

Sabine's Gull (*Xema sabini*)

Bonaparte's Gull
(*Chroicocephalus philadelphia*)

Black-headed Gull
(*Chroicocephalus ridibundus*)

Ross's Gull (*Rhodostethia rosea*)

Mew Gull (*Larus canus*)

Herring Gull (*Larus argentatus*)

Glaucous-winged Gull (*Larus glaucescens*)

Glaucous Gull (*Larus hyperboreus*)

Little Gull (*Hydrocoloeus minutus*)

Aleutian Tern (*Onychoprion aleuticus*)

Arctic Tern (*Sterna paradisaea*)

Long-tailed Jaeger
(*Stercorarius longicaudus*)

Common Murre (*Uria aalge*)

Thick-billed Murre (*Uria lomvia*)

Pigeon Guillemot (*Cepphus columba*)

Ancient Murrelet
(*Synthliboramphus antiquus*)

Whiskered Auklet (*Aethia pygmaea*)

Tufted Puffin (*Fratercula cirrhata*)

Spotted Dove (*Streptopelia chinensis*)

Scarlet Macaw (*Ara macao*)

Snowy Owl (*Bubo scandiacus*)

Short-eared Owl (*Asio flammeus*)

Long-billed Hermit
(*Phaethornis longirostris*)

Stripe-throated Hermit
(*Phaethornis striigularis*)

White-necked Jacobin
(*Florisuga mellivora*)

Rufous-tailed Hummingbird
(*Amazilia tzacatl*)

APPENDIX-SCIENTIFIC NAMES

Resplendent Quetzal
(*Pharomachrus mocinno*)

American Pygmy Kingfisher
(*Chloroceryle aenea*)

Rufous-tailed Jacamar (*Galbula ruficauda*)

Black Woodpecker (*Dryocopus martius*)

Pale-billed Woodpecker
(*Campephilus guatemalensis*)

Bare-faced Antthrush
(*Gymnocichla nudiceps*)

Black-faced Antthrush
(*Formicarius analis*)

Wedge-billed Woodcreeper
(*Glyphorynchus spirurus*)

Ivory-billed Woodcreeper
(*Xiphorhynchus flavigaster*)

Ochre-bellied Flycatcher
(*Mionectes oleagineus*)

Hammond's Flycatcher
(*Empidonax hammondii*)

Red-capped Manakin (*Pipra mentalis*)

White-collared Manakin
(*Manacus candei*)

Golden Vireo (*Vireo hypochryseus*)

Gray Jay (*Perisoreus canadensis*)

Common Raven (*Corvus corax*)

Carrion Crow (*Corvus corone*)

House Crow (*Corvus splendens*)

Tree Swallow (*Tachycineta bicolor*)

Violet-green Swallow
(*Tachycineta thalassina*)

Bank Swallow (*Riparia riparia*)

chickadees (*Poecile* spp.)

Pacific Wren (*Troglodytes pacificus*)

White-breasted Wood-Wren
(*Henicorhina leucosticta*)

American Dipper
(*Cinclus mexicanus*)

Icterine Warbler (*Hippolais icterina*)

Arctic Warbler (*Phylloscopus borealis*)

Bluethroat (*Luscinia svecica*)

Northern Wheatear (*Oenanthe oenanthe*)

Stonechat (*Saxicola torquatus*)

Gray-cheeked Thrush (*Catharus minimus*)

Swainson's Thrush (*Catharus ustulatus*)

Hermit Thrush (*Catharus guttatus*)

Wood Thrush (*Hylocichla mustelina*)

American Robin (*Turdus migratorius*)

Gray Catbird (*Dumetella carolinensis*)

Eastern Yellow Wagtail
(*Motacilla tschutschensis*)

Gray Wagtail (*Motacilla cinerea*)

Tree Pipit (*Anthus trivialis*)

Olive-backed Pipit (*Anthus hodgsoni*)

Pechora Pipit (*Anthus gustavi*)

Red-throated Pipit (*Anthus cervinus*)

Black-backed Wagtail
(*Motacilla alba lugens*)

Smith's Longspur (*Calcarius pictus*)

Lapland Longspur (*Calcarius lapponicus*)

Snow Bunting (*Plectrophenax nivalis*)

Worm-eating Warbler
(*Helmitheros vermivorum*)

Northern Waterthrush
(*Parkesia noveboracensis*)

Kentucky Warbler (*Geothlypis formosa*)

Hooded Warbler (*Setophaga citrina*)

Townsend's Warbler
(*Setophaga townsendi*)

Savannah Sparrow
(*Passerculus sandwichensis*)

Fox Sparrow (*Passerella iliaca*)

Song Sparrow (*Melospiza melodia*)

White-throated Sparrow
(*Zonotrichia albicollis*)

Golden-crowned Sparrow
(*Zonotrichia atricapilla*)

Rustic Bunting (*Emberiza rustica*)

Red-breasted Chat (*Granatellus venustus*)

Orange-breasted Bunting
(*Passerina leclancherii*)

Orchard Oriole (*Icterus spurius*)

Yellow-winged Cacique
(*Cacicus melanicterus*)

Olive-backed Sunbird (*Cinnyris jugularis*)

Brambling (*Fringilla montifringilla*)

Olive-backed Euphonia
(*Euphonia gouldi*)

Gray-crowned Rosy Finch's
(*Leucosticte tephrocotis*)

Red Crossbill (*Loxia curvirostra*)

Common Redpoll (*Acanthis flammea*)

Hoary Redpoll (*Acanthis hornemanni*)

Eurasian Bullfinch (*Pyrrhula pyrrhula*)

Hawfinch (*Coccothraustes coccothraustes*)

Scaly-breasted Munia
(*Lonchura punctulata*)

About the Author

Kevin Winker, PhD, is curator of Birds at the University of Alaska Museum of the North, and a professor in the Department of Biology and Wildlife at the University of Alaska Fairbanks. He has traveled extensively, studying birds. He lives with his wife, Rose Meier, in Fairbanks, Alaska.